SAN DIEGO
HORTICULTURAL SOCIETY

Seeds page 20

Trees and Shrubs for Dry California Landscapes

Plants for water conservation

An introduction to more than 360 California native and introduced plants which survive with limited water.

By
Bob Perry, Professor
Department of Landscape Architecture
California State Polytechnic University, Pomona

Published by:

||| Land Design Publishing
||| P.O. Box 857 San Dimas, CA 91773

September 1981

All rights reserved.

Copyright© 1981 by Robert C. Perry
ISBN 0-9605988-0-4 Hardcover Trade
ISBN 0-9605988-1-2 Hardcover Text
Library of Congress Catalog Number 81-81013

Contents

	Page
Foreword	IV
Introduction	1

I Regional Plant Environments ... 2
  California plant environment map ... 4
  Plant selection guide ... 7

II Planting Guidelines ... 16
  Landscaping with California natives ... 16
  Planting from containers ... 17
  Planting from seed ... 19
  Planting on slopes ... 22
  Planting for fire safety ... 24

III Plant Lists ... 27
  Evergreen plants ... 28
  Drought deciduous plants ... 29
  Moisture seeking plants ... 30
  Water needy plants ... 30
  Invasive plants ... 31
  Plants resistant to oak root fungus ... 31
  Plants tolerant of alkaline and alkali soils ... 32
  Plants tolerant of saline soils ... 33
  Plants tolerant of fine textured soils ... 33
  Plants tolerant of salt spray ... 33

IV Plant Compendium ... 34-180

Index ... 182

Foreword.

The first steps of this book began while teaching a series of classes at Cal Poly University, Pomona. What started in 1973 as simple investigations of native plant communities, has led to a long term study of the opportunities and limitations of the native flora of California. These efforts have coincided with a renewed interest in developing an "appropriate" form of landscape design; one which respects the full balance of resources in our state. The drought years of 1974-75 brought particular attention to our water resources, its availability, and our use of it.

To supplement academic research and investigation, I have been fortunate to participate in a number of professional projects, ranging from regional parks to residential design. These projects provided the chance to make decisions, solve real problems, and obtain direct field experience.

During the process of developing and assembling information for this book, I have been suppported in a number of ways, and encouraged by many people. Through Cal Poly University, I was able to take a sabbatical leave from instruction to take photographs and complete my writing. Additional time was provided to carry this book to the publishing stages. The faculty of the Department of Landscape Architecture have continuously expressed an interest in this work. Professor D. Rodney Tapp, provided assistance throughout. My students have always been a key source of help and encouragement. Hetty Mitchell, Harry Mestyanek, and Gary Austin are to be recognized for their contributions. Heidi Clendenin and Gill Ellis provided valuable proofreading services. Karen Shaw was of unlimited assistance for organization, proofreading and energy.

Two other people deserve mention. Robert Clapper, Landscape Architect for Orange County, provided photographs, data, and a constant push. In addition, no one has offered more support and encouragement than my wife, Charlotte. Her interest and comments have sustained this work and deserves my highest respect and appreciation. This book has also provided other types of learning experiences, as I have assumed the responsibility for getting it published. In this effort I have relied upon many people at the Ink Spot for technical assistance. Allan James, Tom James, and Bill Horton provided many professional ideas and advice for obtaining high print quality. Jody Sabine was of continuous help while doing the typesetting.

Photographic credits:

The following persons contributed to this book with a variety of photographs. I wish to thank them for their help.

Robert A. Clapper, Landscape Architect, Orange County Environmental Protection Agency. Plates 1, 161, 264

Kenneth S. Nakaba, Associate Professor, California State Polytechnic University, Pomona. Plate 34

John Olaf Nelson, General Manager, North Marin County Water District. Photograph of slope planting in oak forest, page 23.

All other photographs were taken by the author.

Introduction.

The goal of this book is to provide information and illustrations that will help Californians achieve successful landscapes within the limits of water conservation. This material is oriented to the major population areas which experience dry summers, and use significant amounts of supplemental water to support their domestic landscapes. A wide range of plants are discussed, from California natives, to introduced plants from similar mediterranean climate regions. These plants are reviewed in light of their suitability to fit specific plant environments, for both domestic and natural uses. The plant data is supported by more than 500 color photographs, check lists, and recommendations for developing various project situations.
Due to the specialized nature of this work, it should be used in combination with other sources to make it most effective. In addition, the goal of determining drought tolerance, should be approached with an ample amount of judgement and field study. Many efforts are being made to develop specific measurements and to quantify the water needs of the plants we use. This is still an emerging field. At present, the best basis for many of our landscape decisions still rests in understanding plants in terms of their natural adaptations and tolerances. From this basis, we can select and match plants with our landscape needs, without requiring excessive use of our resources. The information in this book recognizes the relative nature of drought tolerance, and stresses the use of plants in areas they are best adapted to.

Landscape opportunity.

Adjusting our landscaping habits can be an exciting process. There are many challenges, from developing design concepts and selecting plant materials, to changing planting, irrigation and management practices. The opportunity exists to develop landscapes which are appropriate to our needs and resources. In this effort, it will be a combination of many people, and numerous decisions, that will bring about change. Water conservation is a goal well within our reach, something that professional and layperson alike can contribute to and derive satisfaction from.

Resource concern:

Water has always been a key issue within California. The development and distribution of this resource has sustained all types of activities, from agriculture and industry, to recreation and urban development throughout the state. We know that water is the single most influential element affecting the pattern and quality of our lives. We also know that regardless of how we use this resource, that certain limitations are always present and must be taken into account. Periodic drought cycles and overdrafting of ground-water basins show us that we do not have unlimited water supplies. As well, we are experiencing increased energy costs and are constructing more complex piping and canal systems whenever we relocate water to meet increased demands. The net result is a vast water collection and distribution system that periodically faces a shortage of supply, and one which always costs more to operate.

Professional responsibility:

Both the landscape design and construction industry are very much a part of the California water situation. Many of the decisions which these professions deal with involve the use of water. The effects of such decisions reaches everyone, from the average homeowner to cities and counties, and concerns projects from small yards to highway and regional park plantings. There is an increasing concern that we have made many decisions leading to the over investment of both water and energy resources within our landscapes. Continuing efforts are needed to reassess our knowledge of plant materials, irrigation, design and management techniques. To supplement this, there is also a real need for a change in attitudes and policies if we are to see a shift in our current water use habits.

This publication represents one area by investigating selected plant groups and species which perform well in various dry landscape situations. The intent is to present a visual aid, along with descriptive information, on a wide range of trees and shrubs. A second, and more important objective, is to help identify a palette of plants which are more fitting to the basic resources and environmental conditions of California. The emphasis is on plant species which do not need continued use of supplemental water in order to perform well in our landscapes.

Citizen participation:

Regardless of the many professions and agencies involved in planning and designing our landscapes, the final impact is felt most significantly by the individual person who lives in California. We are all affected by the tax dollars, which pay for the state water projects, to our individual water bills which supports our community and home landscapes. As well, we are the users of our homes, schools, parks, and highways, and have a good sense of the value such landscapes provide to us. Our concern for water conservation and appropriate landscaping will probably increase proportionally to the rising costs and availability of water. We can anticipate greater interest and demand for plant materials and design ideas as the water situation continues to emerge.

This publication illustrates various plant choices which can reduce our landscape demand for water. It is intended to help us visualize and look at the possible options when we participate in individual or community planting decisions. In all likelihood it will be the cumulative effect of many separate and individual decisions that will have the largest impact on water use and appropriate landscaping in our state in the near future.

I. Regional Plant Environments.

An impressive variety of plants, which survive with limited water, can be grown in dry California landscapes. However, from the start it is important to understand that all dry landscape situations are not alike. There are many critical differences which occur among coastal, inland, and desert environments. If our goal is to select plants which closely fit our basic landscape conditions, then we need to start with an understanding of the regional plant environments before moving on to a study of specific plant types.

A general profile is developed for eight regional plant environments in California. These are environments which experience periods of heat and drought, and have various types of urban development in them. The regional plant environments as discussed, stress climatic factors the most. Plant survival, and successful growth, is primarily regulated by the occurrence of low temperatures and frost conditions. For this reason, it is necessary to particularly look at the average low temperatures for the winter months. The range of maximum summer temperatures, and conditions of fog, wind, and air moisture also contribute to plant survival. This data is also given on a regional basis.

To complement our efforts to regulate water use, we must recognize the potential evapotranspiration stress of an environment. This is a measure of the amount of water that plants will normally consume during a year in order to grow, and to cool themselves. The estimates provided in the various plant environment descriptions indicates the amount of water that turfgrass needs in order to survive in full sun. It should be expected that established trees and shrubs will require less supplemental water as they can tap larger volumes of soil moisture. Keep in mind that these water need measurements are only a rough approximation for plants. We must consider the influence caused by the rainfall cycle, daylight period, and sun exposure. A lot of judgement and checking of plants is necessary to determine the appropriate amounts of supplemental water to supply to a landscape.

Even after we have a feeling for the basic conditions in our particular landscape region, we have a lot of refinements to make. The combination of micro-climates and soil characteristics create many other planting opportunities and limitations. In addition to obtaining more accurate site information, it is always helpful to study existing gardens to observe both plant types and growth habit.

Profile of plant environments.

California has a rich and varied landscape profile. The interaction of marine and continental climate forces, in combination with diverse topographic features, has produced many types of landscape conditions. Illustrated below is a generalized section through California with the basic sequence of plant environments.

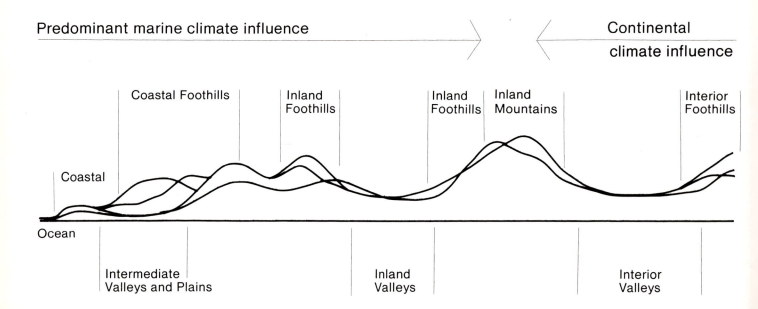

Coastal.

The coastal plant environment in California inlcudes the immediate coastal edge and closely adjacent valley areas. This landscape is dominated by the marine climate conditions of fog, humidity, and persistent wind. Frost, as well as freezing temperatures are rare, with periodic occurrences found in canyon channels where cold air will collect. Soils are highly variable and can consist of sands which contain soluble salts, to uplifted sedimentary marine deposits, of even heavy clays.

This environment experiences low evapotranspiration stress. Summer temperatures are mild and often do not reach levels to support heat loving plants well. Planting along the immediate coastline must contend with salt spray, inland locations experience salt air. This is a very temperate plant zone which supports a rich and diverse range of plant species under low to moderate levels of drought stress.

Northern Coastal:

Winter, average minimum temperature range 22-36° F.
Summer, average maximum temperature range 70-80° F.
Mean annual rainfall 20-40 inches.
Potential evapotranspiration stress 32-40 inches/year
High humidity, persistent winds, mild temperatures.

Southern Coastal:

Winter, average minimum temperature range 24-45° F.
Summer, average maximum temperature range 73-82° F.
Mean annual rainfall 12-20 inches.
Potential evapotranspiration stress 40-48 inches/year.
High humidity, persistent winds, mild temperatures.

Intermediate Valleys and Plains.

This plant environment occurs inland from the immediate ocean edge and consists of low elevation valleys and plains which have climates predominantly regulated by marine conditions. The primary distinction between this environment and the Coastal Edge is the lack of direct salt spray, and a wider range in seasonal temperatures as the landscape moves inland towards foothill locations. Summers are warm, winters are mild. Periodic frost can occur in low basin and canyon locations where cold air drains and concentrates. Heavier soils are often encountered and micro-climates created by landforms must be taken into account. High morning fog creates moderate temperatures and humidity during the summer, which is burned off by the sun, and replaced by cooling afternoon winds. The majority of this landscape is found throughout southern California, from San Diego to Santa Barbara. Similar conditions exist in confined locations all along the northern coastline; the largest occurrences are found in the Monterey and San Francisco Bay regions. This plant environment offers some of the finest conditions for diverse and intensive domestic landscape plantings in our state.

Northern Intermediate Valleys and Plains:

Winter, average minimum temperature range 20-32° F.
Summer, average maximum temperature range 88-94° F.
Mean annual rainfall 20-40 inches.
Potential evapotranspiration stress 40-80 inches/year.
Daily fog and onshore wind in summer, infrequent occurrences of winter frost or prolonged night temperatures below 32° F.

Southern Intermediate Valleys and Plains:

Winter, average minimum temperature range 24-40° F.
Summer, average maximum temperature range 90-95° F.
Mean annual rainfall 12-20 inches.
Potential evapotranspiration stress 48-52 inches/year.
High fog and onshore winds occur in summer, periodic frost in canyons and valley basins in winter.

Coastal Foothills.

Many areas close to the coastline consist of foothill and low mountain ranges. These foothills have climates formed by the marine conditions of fog, humidity, and wind. Such conditions can be periodically interrupted by interior climate forces which develop a few weeks of warming and drying periods each year. Coastal foothills also experience heavier rainfall than adjacent lowland areas. The south and west facing slopes have more intense sun exposure and higher summer temperatures, along with increased evapotranspiration stress. The rise in elevation in these foothills also creates thermal belt conditions during the winter season. Warm air will stabilize above the lower basin and valley floors and protect this environment from frequent experiences of frost.

The many topographic variations associated with coastal foothills create numerous micro-climates and soil conditions, which provide diverse landscaping opportunites. Throughout the northern coastal foothills, there are many instances where fog and increased rainfall conditions support very lush vegetation, which is not stressed by drought. Southern areas experience longer seasons of drought and increased summer temperatures. In addition to housing development, these locations are prime agricultural areas for citrus and avocado orchards.

Northern Coastal Foothills:

Winter, average minimum temperature range 20-32° F.
Summer, average maximum temperature range 78-85° F.
Mean annual rainfall 30-55 inches.
Potential evapotranspiration stress 40-52 inches/year.
Morning fog and afternoon winds occur in summer.

Southern Coastal Foothills:

Winter, average minimum temperature range 24-28° F.
Summer, average maximum temperature range 82-86° F.
Mean annual rainfall 12-30 inches.
Potential evapotranspiration stress 50-60 inches/year.
High morning fog, summer afternoon wind.

Northern California Plant Environments.

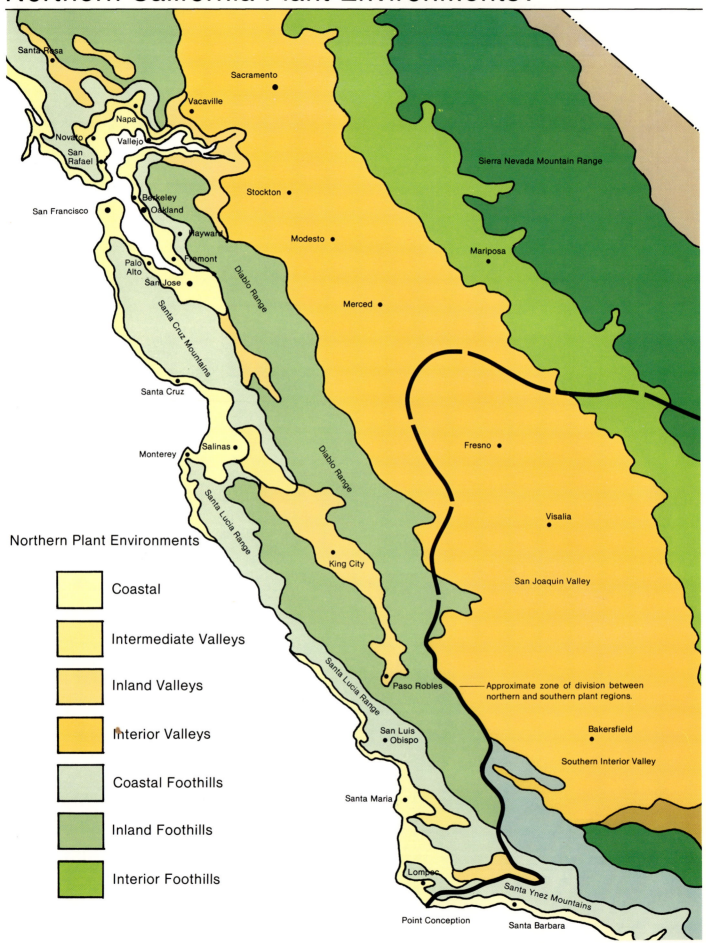

Southern California Plant Environments.

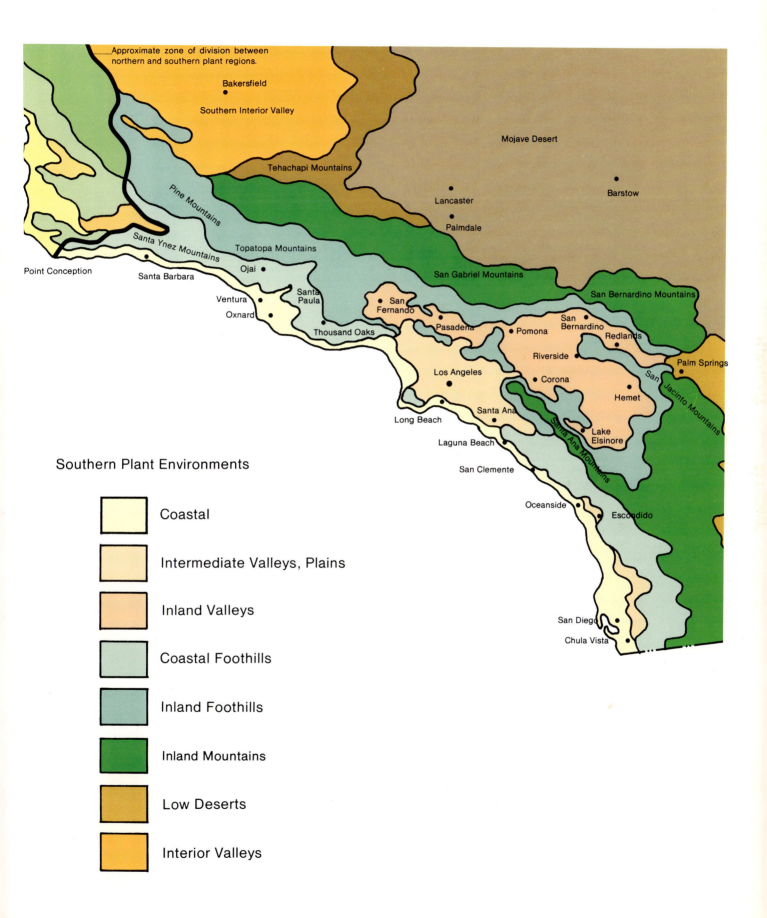

Inland Valleys.

Many populated areas occur several miles away from the coast within inland valley locations. These landscapes are usually separated from Intermediate Valley and Plains by foothill ranges. As a result, winters are moister and cooler, frost is periodic. Summers become warm enough to support heat loving plants. Many areas have richer soils and excellent growing conditions for both agriculture and domestic plantings. High morning fog will cool these valleys in the summer; afternoon breezes from the coast are common. Urban smog becomes a significant problem around densely populated areas.

The Inland Valley plant environments in southern California offer some of the best climate and soil conditions for growing any type of garden. It has been discovered that many species of plants can be grown as long as supplemental water is provided. Areas around San Bernardino, Redlands, and Riverside experience the warmest and driest inland valley conditions, and greater evapotranspiration stress. Similar valley conditions exist in the northern inland valleys and around the San Francisco Bay region. In this part of the state, urban development tends to be less concentrated and several valleys are primarily used for specialty agricultural crops.

Northern Inland Valleys:

Winter, average minimum temperature range 18-28° F.
Summer, averge maximum temperature range 88-94° F.
Mean annual rainfall 15-24 inches.
Potential evapotranspiration stress 48-52 inches/year.
Higher relative humidity and more winter frost conditions than southern inland valley areas.

Southern Inland Valleys:

Winter, average minimum temperature range 24-30° F.
Summer, average maximum temperature range 88-96° F.
Mean annual rainfall 14-20 inches.
Potential evapotranspiration stress 48-56 inches/year.
Periodic high desert winds occur late fall to early winter resulting in weeks of low humidity and high drought stress.

Inland Foothills.

A vast network of foothills occur throughout California. Inland foothills are usually separated from the coast by several miles of valleys or coastal foothills which absorb much of the marine influence. The climate of this landscape is quite warm and dry, which reflects the dominance of the interior climate forces caused by the continental land mass. Rainfall is higher than coastal landscapes, but so are the temperatures. Less fog and humidity occurs; soils tend to be thin and undeveloped. The harshness of this environment is evidenced by the extensive natural growth of chaparral vegetation and high potential evapotranspiration stress.

Southern inland foothills are covered with dense stands of of chaparral vegetation and occur on the fringes of major urban areas. These landscapes are experiencing increased housing development which usually involves extensive grading, slope planting, and high demands for supplemental water. Drought stress and fire hazard conditions are increased in the fall season when periodic high desert winds, known as Santa Anas, cause temperatures to rise and humidity to drop for several days at a time. Northern inland foothills occur within mixed evergreen and Digger Pine forests. This is a picturesque landscape that supports agriculture, cattle grazing, and urban use.

Northern Inland Foothills:

Winter, average minimum temperature range 16-28° F.
Summer, average maximum temperature range 86-93° F.
Mean annual rainfall 18-30 inches.
Potential evapotranspiration stress 48-56 inches/year.
Low humidity, long growing season, intense sunlight and heat.

Southern Inland Foothills:

Winter, average minimum temperature range 22-30° F.
Summer, average maximum temperature range 88-95° F.
Mean annual rainfall 15-28 inches.
Potential evapotranspiration stress 50-58 inches/year.
Low humidity, intense sunlight and heat, seasonal Santa Ana wind conditions.

Interior Foothills.

Many sections of the foothills along the western edge of the Sierra Nevada mountain range experience dry summer conditions. This is a richly diverse strip of land which has cool and moist winters. Temperatures can drop below 10° F., with a normal range between 15-23° F. Rainfall varies 10-20 inches; some of this comes in the form of snow, which can last from several days to weeks. Summer temperatures can reach into the high 80's, but the average maximum range occurs around 74-78° F. Soil textures vary from fine clays to coarse and rocky. The air is clean and crisp, sunlight intense, and humidity is relatively low.

Much of this landscape occurs in mixed evergreen and pine forests. Small towns, along the recreation related housing, is found in scattered locations. Cattle grazing, logging, and national parks are among the primary uses of this land.

Interior Foothills:

Winter, average minimum temperature range 15-23° F.
Summer, average maximum temperature range 74-78° F.
Mean annual rainfall 20-30 inches.
Potential evapotranspiration stress 40-48 inches/year.

Interior Valleys.

Much of the San Joaquin Valley represents an interior regional plant environment which is regulated by continental climate conditions. This landscape experiences a wide range in seasonal weather. Low elevations become cold air basins where freezing temperatures, frost and dense ground fog settle. Summers have long periods of intense sunlight and high daily temperatures. Humidity is often high with all of the agricultural irrigation.

As the elevation begins to rise around the perimeter of this valley region, a thermal temperature belt begins to appear. These slightly higher landscapes have less extreme cold, frost and fog, as air masses tend to flow over them into lower basin locations. In addition, when we travel north toward Stockton and Sacramento, there is more marine influence which comes inland from the San Francisco Bay area. This moderates temperatures through wind, fog and humidity. A significant difference in mean annual rainfall can also be noted. The southern end of the Central Valley is quite dry with high evapotranspiration stress and thinner soils. Rainfall increases toward the northern section of the valley along with deeper, richer soil profiles.

Northern Interior Valley, Sacramento:

Winter, average minimum temperature range 18-28° F.
Summer, average maximum temperature range 90-102° F.
Mean annual rainfall 16-20 inches.
Potential evapotranspiration stress 48-52 inches/year.
Periodic marine influence provides fog and humidity, cold temperatures and frost occur in basin locations.

Southern Interior Valley, Fresno, Bakersfield:

Winter, average minimum temperature range 14-28° F.
Summer, average maximum temperature range 100-106° F.
Mean annual rainfall 6-10 inches.
Potential evapotranspiration stress 52-56 inches/year.
Frequent occurrences of winter ground fog, low temperatures and frost in basin locations, thermal belt conditions towards outlying foothill areas.

Low deserts.

Most of the landscape from Palm Springs to the Salton Sea, and south to El Centro is part of the Colorado Desert. This region varies in elevation from below sea level to 1,000 feet, and has a climate largely determined by the continental air mass. Winter temperatures are consistently warm, but short periods of frost can occur between December and February. Summer temperatures are high. By June the mean daily maximum temperatures reach 100-102° F.; by July 106-108° F. heat is common, with relative humidity ranging between 10 to 20 percent. The average winter rainfall varies between 3 to 6 inches, much of this coming in only two to three storms. The potential evapotranspiration stress is quite high, 56-80 inches per year.

Other conditions exist in low deserts which produce stress on landscape plants. Wind and sand storms are quite common. Soils vary in texture from wind blown sand to sandy loams and clays. Soils in low basin areas, such as the Coachella Valley, are saline in nature and need to be flushed clean before many plants will survive. The best landscape conditions occur in areas which are sheltered by mountain ranges, windbreaks, or in micro-climates created by buildings.

Low Deserts:

Winter, minimum temperature range 28-34° F.
Summer, maximum temperature range 100-108°
Mean annual rainfall 3-6 inches.
Potential evapotranspiration stress 56-80 inches/year.
Summer humidity is quite low, 10-20%, periodic subtropical rainstorms can provide up to one-half inch of water, wind and sand storms are common.

Plant selection guide.

Most plants impress us with their adaptability and capacity to survive in many plant environments and under a diverse range of site conditions. However, their ability to survive with limited water is significantly influenced by how well they are matched to the landscapes they are placed within. To further refine our efforts to select and grow plants with limited amounts of water, a series of charts have been assembled. These charts reflect the variations in California plant environment and identify plants which are adapted to them. These charts should be used as a basic guide, as many exceptions can always be found. An effort has been made to recognize the degree of compatibility between plants and environments, as it should be understood that all plants cannot survive with limited water equally, or in all parts of California.

Plant selection guide.

- Indicates high degree of suitability between plant and environment.
- + Plants can be used in these environments, but need careful matching with exposure and soil conditions for best performance.

Ground Covers.

Plant	Common Name	Northern Environments							Southern Environments					
		Coastal	Intermediate Valleys, Plains	Coastal Foothills	Inland Valleys	Inland Foothills	Interior Valleys	Interior Foothills	Coastal	Intermediate Valleys, Plains	Coastal Foothills	Inland Valleys	Inland Foothills	Interior Valleys	Low Deserts
Acacia redolens		•	•	•	+	•	+	+	•	•	•	•	+		
Achillea species	Yarrow	•	•	•	•	•	+		•	•	•	•	•	•	+
Arctostaphylos densiflora 'James West'		•	+	•	+	•			•	+	•	•	+		
Arctostaphylos edmundsii	Little Sur Manzanita	•	+	•	+	•			•	+	•	•	+		
Arctostaphylos edmundsii 'Carmel Sur'		•	+	•	+	+			•	+	•	•	+		
Arctostaphylos edmundsii 'Danville'		•	+	•	+	•			•	+	•	•	+		
Arctostaphylos edmundsii 'Little Sur'		•	+	•	+	•			•	+	•	•	+		
Arctostaphylos hookeri 'Monterey Carpet'		•	+	•	+	•			•	+	•	•	+		
Arctostaphylos hookeri 'Wayside'		•	+	•	+	•			•	+	•	•	+		
Arctostaphylos uva-ursi	Bearberry	•	•	•	+	•			•	+	•	•	+		
Arctostaphylos uva-ursi 'Point Reyes'		•	•	•	+	•			•	+	•	•	+		
Arctostaphylos uva-ursi 'Radiant'		•	•	•	+	•			•	+	•	•	+		
Arctostaphylos 'Emerald Carpet'		•	•	•	+	•			•	+	•	•	+		
Arctostaphylos 'Indian Hill'		•	•	•	+	+			•	+	•	•	+		
Arctostaphylos 'Sea Spray'		•	•	•	•	+			•	+	•	•	+		
Arctostaphylos 'Winterglow'		•	•	•	•	+			•	+	•	•	+		
Artemisia caucasica	Silver Spreader	•	•	•	•	•	•		•	•	•	•	•	•	
Artemisia pycnocephala	Coast Sagebrush	•	•	•	•	•	+		•	•	•	•	+	+	
Atriplex glauca		+	+	•	+	•			•	•	•	•	•	•	•
Atriplex semibaccata	Australian Saltbush	•	•	•	•	•	•		•	•	•	•	•	•	•
Baccharis pilularis	Prostrate Coyote Brush	•	•	•	•	•	+		•	•	•	•	•	+	
Ceanothus gloriosus	Point Reyes Ceanothus	•	•	•	+	+			•	•	•	+	+		
Ceanothus gloriosus porrectus		•	•	•	+	+			•	•	•	+	+		
Ceanothus gloriosus exaltatus 'Emily Brown'		•	•	•	+	+			•	•	•	+	+		
Ceanothus griseus horizontalis	Carmel Creeper	•	•	•	+	+			•	•	•	+	+		
Ceanothus griseus horizontalis 'Yankee Point'		•	•	•	+	+			•	•	•	+	+		
Ceanothus maritimus	Maritime Ceanothus	•	+	•	•				•	•	•				
Centaurea cineraria	Dusty Miller	•	•	•	•	•	+		•	•	•	•	•	•	+
Cistus salviifolius	Sageleaf Rockrose	•	+	•	•	•			•	+	•	•	•		
Coprosma kirkii	Creeping Coprosma	•	•	•	•	+			•	•	•	+	+	+	
Cotoneaster buxifolius	Bright Bead Cotoneaster	•	•	•	•	•	•		•	•	•	•	•	•	
Cotoneaster congestus		•	•	•	•	•	•		•	•	•	•	•	•	
Eriogonum crocatum	Saffron Buckwheat	•	+	•	•	•			•	+	•	+	•		
Eriogonum fasciculatum	Common Buckwheat	•	•	•	•	•	•		•	•	•	•	•	•	
Gazania species	Gazania	+	•	•	•	+			•	•	•	•	•	+	+
Grevillea lanigera	Woolly Grevillea	•	•	•	•	+			•	•	•	•	+		
Grevillea 'Noellii'		•	•	•	•	+			•	•	•	•	+	+	+
Grevillea rosmarinifolia	Rosemary Grevillea	•	•	•	•	+			•	•	•	•	+	+	+
Helianthemum species	Sunrose	•	•	•	•	•			•	•	•	•	•	•	
Hypericum calycinum	Aaron's Beard	•	•	•	•	•			•	•	•	+	•		
Juniperus species	Juniper	•	•	•	•	•			•	•	•	•	•	•	•
Lantana montevidensis	Trailing Lantana	•	•	•	•	+	+	+	•	•	•	•	+	+	+
Lippia canescens	Lippia	•	•	•	•	+	+		•	•	•	•	+		+
Lobularia maritima	Sweet Alyssum	•	•	•	•	•	•		•	•	•	•	•	•	
Lupinus nanus	Annual Lupine	•	•	•	•	•	•		•	•	•	•	•	•	
Mahonia repens	Creeping Mahonia	•	•	•	•	•	+		•	•	+	+	+		
Myoporum debile		•	•	•	•	•	+		•	•	•	+	+		
Myoporum parvifolium		•	•	•	•	•	+		•	•	•	+	+		
Osteospermum species	African Daisy	•	•	•	•	•	+		•	•	•	•	•	+	+
Pyracantha species	Firethorn	•	•	•	•	•	•		•	•	•	•	•	•	
Ribes viburnifolium	Evergreen Currant	•	•	•	+	+			•	•	•	+	+		
Rosmarinus officinalis 'Prostratus'	Prostrate Rosemary	•	•	•	+	•			•	•	•	+	•	+	+
Salvia sonomensis	Creeping Sage	•	+	•	•	•			•	+	•	•	•		
Santolina chamaecyparissus	Lavender Cotton	•	•	•	•	•	•		•	•	•	•	•	+	+
Santolina virens		•	•	•	•	•	•		•	•	•	•	•	+	+
Trifolium frageriferum O'Connor's	O'Connor's Legume	•	•	•	•	•	+		•	•	•	•	+		
Zauschneria californica	California Fuchsia	•	•	•	•	•	•		•	•	•	•	•		

Plant selection guide.

- ● Indicates high degree of suitability between plant and environment.
- + Plants can be used in these environments, but need careful matching with exposure and soil conditions for best performance.

Small Shrubs. 3-5 feet

Plant	Common Name	Northern: Coastal	N: Intermediate Valleys, Plains	N: Coastal Foothills	N: Inland Valleys	N: Inland Foothills	N: Interior Valleys	N: Interior Foothills	Southern: Coastal	S: Intermediate Valleys, Plains	S: Coastal Foothills	S: Inland Valleys	S: Inland Foothills	S: Interior Valleys	S: Low Deserts
Achillea species	Yarrow	●	●	●	●	●	●	●	●	●	●	●	●	●	●
Arctostaphylos densiflora 'James West'		●	+	●	+	●	●		●	●	+	+	●		
Arctostaphylos hookeri	Monterey Manzanita	●	+	●	●	●	●			●	●	+	+		
Arctostaphylos pumila	Sandmat Manzanita	●	●	●	+	+	●		●	●	●	+	+		
Arctostaphylos 'Green Sphere'		●	●	●	●					●	●	+	+		
Argemone species	Prickly Poppy		+	+	●	●				+	●	●	●		
Artemisia californica	California Sagebrush	●	●	●	●		+		●	●	●	●	●		
Calliandra californica									●	●	●	●	●	●	●
Calliandra eriophylla	False Mesquite								●	●	●	●	●	●	●
Cassia species	Senna	●	●	●	●	+	+		●	●	●	●	●	+	+
Ceanothus purpureus	Hollyleaf Ceanothus	●	●	●	+	+	●		●	●	●	+			
Ceanothus rigidus 'Snowball'		●	●	●	+	+	●		●	●	●	+			
Ceanothus 'Blue Cushion'		●	●	●	●	●	●		●	●	●	+	+		
Cistus species	Rockrose	●	●	●	+	●	+		●	●	●	+	+	+	
Convolvulus cneorum	Bush Morning Glory	●	●	●	●	+	+	+	●	●	●	+	●		
Cotoneaster buxifolius	Bright Bead Cotoneaster	●	●	●	●	+			●	●	●	●	●	+	+
Cotoneaster congestus		●	●	●	●				●	●	●	●	●		+
Encelia californica	California Encelia	●	●	●	●	●			●	●	●	●	●		
Encelia farinosa	Desert Encelia				●	●	●					●	●	+	●
Eriogonum arborescens	Santa Cruz Buckwheat	●	●	●	●	●	●		●	●	●	+	+		
Eriogonum cinerium	Ashyleaf Buckwheat	●	●	●	●	●	●		●	●	●	+	+		
Eriogonum crocatum	Saffron Buckwheat	●	●	●	+	●	●		●	●	●	●	●		
Eriogonum fasciculatum	Common Buckwheat	●	●	●	●	●	●		●	●	●	●	●		
Eriogonum giganteum	St. Catherine's Lace	●	●	●	+	●			●	●	●	●	●		
Eriogonum latifolium rubescens	Red Buckwheat	●	●	●	●	●			●	●	●	●	+		
Eriogonum parvifolium	Seacliff Buckwheat	●	●	●	+	●			●	+	●	+	+		
Eriophyllum confertiflorum	Golden Yarrow	●	●	●	+	+			●	●	●	●	●		
Eriophyllum staechadifolium	Lizzard Tail	●	●	●	●				●	●	●	●	●		
Hypericum beanii		●	●	●	●	●	+		●	●	●	●	+	+	
Juniperus species	Juniper	●	●	●	●	●	●	●	●	●	●	●	●	●	●
Lavandula species	Lavender	●	●	●	●	●	●	●	●	●	●	●	●	●	+
Leptodactylon californicum	Prickly Phylox	●	●	●	●	●	●		●	●	●	●	●		
Leucophyllum frutescens 'Compactum'	Texas Ranger	+	●	●	●	●	●		+	●	●	●	●	●	●
Limonium perezii	Sea Lavender	●	●	●	+	+	.		●	●	●	+			
Lotus scoparius	Deerweed		+	●	●	●	●		+	●	●	●	●		
Lupinus albifrons	Silver Lupine	●	●	●	+	+	●		●	●	●	+	●		
Lupinus arboreus	Tree Lupine	●	●	●	●	●			●	●	●	●	●		
Lupinus chamissonis	Dune Lupine	●	●	●	+	+			●	●	●	●	●		
Mahonia repens	Creeping Mahonia	●	●	●	●	+			●	●	●	●	●		
Mimulus species	Monkey Flower	●	●	●	●	●	●	●	●	●	●	●	●		
Osteospermum species	African Daisy	●	●	●	●	●	+	●	●	●	●	●	●	+	
Pennisetum setaceum	Fountain Grass	●	●	●	●	●	●		●	●	●	●	●	●	●
Penstemon centranthifolius	Scarlet Bugler	+	●	●	●	●	●		+	●	●	●	●		
Penstemon heterophyllus	Blue Penstemon	+	●	●	●	●	●		+	●	●	●	●		
Penstemon spectabilis	Showy Penstemon	+	●	●	●	●	●		+	●	●	●	●		
Pittosporum tobira 'Wheeleri'	Wheeler's Dwarf	●	●	●	●	●	+		●	●	●	●	●	+	
Pyracantha species	Firethorn	●	●	●	●	●	●		●	●	●	●	●	●	●
Ribes speciosum	Fuchsia-Flowering Gooseberry	●	●	●	●	+	+		●	●	●	●	●		
Ribes viburnifolium	Evergreen Currant	●	●	●	+	●	●		●	+	●	●	●		
Rosmarinus officinalis 'Prostratus'	Prostrate Rosemary	●	●	●	●	●	●	●	●	●	●	●	●	+	+
Salvia clevelandii	Cleveland Sage		●	●	●	+	●			●	●	●	●		
Salvia leucantha	Mexican Bush Sage	●	●	●	●	●	●		●	●	●	●	●		
Salvia leucophylla	Purple Sage	●	●	●	●	●	●		●	●	●	●	●		
Salvia mellifera	Black Sage	●	●	●	●	●	●		●	●	●	●	●		
Santolina species		●	●	●	●	●	●	●	●	●	●	●	●	●	●
Trichostema lanatum	Woolly Blue Curls	●	●	●	●	+	●		●	+	●	●	●		

Plant selection guide.

- • Indicates high degree of suitability between plant and environment.
- \+ Plants can be used in these environments, but need careful matching with exposure and soil conditions for best performance.

Medium Shrubs. 5-10 feet

Plant	Common Name	Northern: Coastal	Intermediate Valleys	Coastal Foothills	Inland Valleys	Inland Foothills	Interior Valleys	Interior Foothills	Southern: Coastal	Intermediate Valleys	Coastal Foothills	Inland Valleys	Inland Foothills	Interior Valleys	Low Deserts
Acacia cultriformis	Knife Acacia	•	•	•	•	+	+	•	•	•	•	•	•		
Acacia redolens		•	•	•	•	+			•	•	•	•	•		
Acacia verticillata	Star Acacia	•	•	•	•	•			•	•	•	•	+		
Arbutus unedo 'Compacta'	Dwarf Strawberry Tree	•	•	•	•	+	•	•	•	•	•	•	•	+	+
Arctostaphylos densiflora 'Harmony'		•	•	•	•	+	•	•	•	+	•	+	+		
Arctostaphylos densiflora 'Howard McMinn'		•	•	•	•	+	•	•	•	+	+	+	+		
Arctostaphylos densiflora 'Sentinel'		•	•	•	•	+	+	•	•	+	•	+	+		
Arctostaphylos franciscana		•	•	•	•				•	•		+	+		
Arctostaphylos glandulosa	Eastwood Manzanita	•	•	•	•	•	•	•	•	•	•	•			
Arctostaphylos stanfordiana	Standford Manzanita	•	•	•	•	•	•	•	•	•	•	•			
Artemisia tridentata	Big Basin Sagebrush			•	•	•	•	•						•	
Atriplex canescens	Four-Wing Saltbush	•	•	•	•	•	•	•	•	•	•	•	•	•	•
Atriplex lentiformis	Quail Bush	•	•	•				•	•	•	•	•		•	•
Atriplex lentiformis breweri	Brewer Lenscale							•	•	•					
Atriplex nummularia		•	•	•					•	•	•			•	•
Baccharis pilularis consanguinea	Coyote Brush	•	•	•	•	•	•	•	•	•	•	•			
Baccharis viminea	Mulefat	•	•	•	•	•	•	•	•	•	•	•			
Bougainvillea species	Bougainvillea		+	+	•	+		+	•	•	+	•	+	+	+
Caesalpinia species	Bird of Paradise Bush								•	•	•	•	•	•	•
Calliandra tweedii	Trinidad Flame Bush								•	•	•	•	•	+	+
Callistemon citrinus	Lemon Bottlebrush	•	•	•	•	•			•	•	•	•	•	•	•
Callistemon pallidus		+	•	•	•	+			•	•	•	•	•		
Callistemon rigidus	Stiff Bottlebrush	+	•	•	•	•			•	•	•	•	•	+	+
Cassia species	Senna								•	•	•	•	•	+	+
Ceanothus griseus	Carmel Ceanothus	•	•	•	+	+	+	•	•	•	•	+	•		
Ceanothus griseus horizontalis 'Santa Ana'		•	•	•	+	+	+	•	•	•	•	+	•		
Ceanothus griseus 'Louis Edmunds'		•	•	•	+	+	+	•	•	•	•	+	•		
Ceanothus 'Concha'		•	•	•	+	+	+	•	•	•	•	+	+		
Ceanothus 'Joyce Coulter'		•	•	•	+	+	+	•	•	•	•	+	+		
Ceanothus 'Julia Phelps'		•	•	•	+	+	+	•	•	•	•	+	+		
Ceanothus 'Mountain Haze'		•	•	•	+	+	+	•	•	•	•	+	+		
Ceanothus 'Sierra Blue'		•	•	•	+	+	+	•	•	•	•	+	+		
Cercocarpus ledifolius	Curl-leaf Mountain Mahogany			•	•	•	•	•							
Chamelaucium uncinatum	Geraldton Waxflower	•	•						•	•	•		+		+
Cistus corbariensis	White Rockrose	•	+	•	+	+			•	+	•	•	+		
Cistus purpureus	Orchid Rockrose	•	+	•	+	+			•	+	•	•	+		
Cotoneaster lacteus	Red Clusterberry	•	•	•	•	•	•		•	•	•	•	+	+	+
Cytisus species	Broom	•	•	•	•	•			•	•	•	•	•		
Dendromecon harfordii	Island Bush Poppy	•	+	•	+	+	+		•	•	•	•	•		
Dendromecon rigida	Bush Poppy						•	•				•	•		
Dodonaea viscosa	Hopseed Bush								•	•	•	•	•	+	+
Echium fastuosum	Pride of Madeira	•	•	•	+	+			•	•	+	+	+		
Elaeagnus pungens	Silverberry	•	•	•	•	•			•	•	•	•	•		
Escallonia exoniensis		•	•	•	•				•	•	•	•	+		
Eucalyptus macrocarpa	Desert Malee	+	+						•	•	•	•	•		
Eucalyptus rhodantha		+	+						•	•	•	•	•		
Feijoa sellowiana	Pineapple Guava	+	•	•	•	•			•	•	•	•	•	•	+
Garrya species	Silktassel			•	•	•	•	•							
Grevillea 'Aromas'		•	+	•	•	+			•	•	•	•	•		
Grevillea lanigera	Woolly Grevillea	•	+	•	•	+			•	•	•	•	+		
Grevillea 'Noellii'		•	•	•	•	•			•	•	•	•	•	+	+
Grevillea rosmarinifolia	Rosemary Grevillea	•	•	•	•	+			•	•	•	•	•	+	+
Grevillea thelemanniana	Hummingbird Bush	•	•	•	•	+			•	•	•	•	•	+	+
Isomeris arborea	Bladderpod								•	•	•	•	•		
Jasminum humile	Italian Jasmine	•	•	•	•	+			•	•	•	•	+	+	+
Juniperus species	Juniper	•	•	•	•	•	•	•	•	•	•	•	•	•	•
Lantana camara	Bush Lantana				•	+	+		•	•	•	•	•	+	+
Laurus nobilis	Sweet Bay	+	•	•	•	•	•	•	+	•	•	•	•		
Leptospermum scoparium	New Zealand Tea Tree	•	•	•	•	•			•	•	•	•	•	+	+
Leucophyllum frutescens	Texas Ranger	+	•	•	•				•	•	•	•	•	•	•

Plant selection guide.

● Indicates high degree of suitability between plant and environment.

+ Plants can be used in these environments, but need careful matching with exposure and soil conditions for best performance.

Medium Shrubs. (Cont.)

Botanical Name	Common Name	Northern Environments							Southern Environments					
		Coastal	Intermediate Valleys	Coastal Foothills	Inland Valleys	Inland Foothills	Interior Valleys	Interior Foothills	Coastal	Intermediate Valleys	Coastal Foothills	Inland Valleys	Inland Foothills	Interior Valleys	Low Deserts
Lupinus albifrons	Silver Lupine	●	●	●	+	+	+		●	●	●	●	+		
Lupinus arboreus	Tree Lupine	●	●	●	●				●	●	●	●			
Mahonia amplectans			●	●	●	●	+					+	+		
Mahonia aquifolium	Oregon Grape		●	●	●	+	+	●				+	+		
Mahonia 'Golden Abundance'			●	●	●	+	+	●				+	+		
Mahonia nevinii	Nevin Mahonia				●	●	+					●	●		
Mahonia pinnata	California Holly Grape	●	●	●	+	+	+		●	●	●	+	+		
Nerium oleander	Oleander	+	●	+	●	●	●		+	●	●	●	●	●	●
Penstemon antirrhinoides	Yellow Penstemon	●	●	●	●	●	●		●	●	●	●	●		
Photinia fraseri			+	●	●	●	+				●	+	+	+	+
Pittosporum tobira	Tobira	●	●	●	●	●	+		●	●	●	●	●		+
Pyracantha species	Firethorn	●	●	●	●	●	●		●	●	●	●	●		
Rhamnus californica	California Coffeeberry	●	●	●	●	●	●		●	●	●	●	●		
Rhamnus crocea	Redberry	●	●	●	●	●	●	●	●	●	●	●	●		
Ribes aureum	Golden Currant				●	●	+					●	+		
Ribes sanguineum	Red Flowering Gooseberry	●	●	●	+	+	+		●	●	●	+	+		
Ribes sanguineum 'Glutinosum'		●	●	●	+	+			●	●	●	+	+		
Romneya coulteri	Matilija Poppy		●	●	●	●	●			●	●	●	●		
Rosmarinus officinalis	Rosemary	●	●	●	●	●	●		●	●	●	●	●	●	●
Salvia apiana	White Sage	●	●	●	●	●	●		●	●	●	●	●		
Simmondsia chinensis	Jojoba				●	●	●				+	●	●	●	●
Spartium junceum	Spanish Broom	+	●	●	●	●	●			●	●	●	●		
Tecomaria capensis	Cape Honeysuckle	●	●	●	+	●	+		●	●	●	●	+	+	+
Viguiera species										●	●	●	●	+	+
Xylosma congestum 'Compacta'	Shiny Xylosma	●	●	●	●	●	●		●	●	●	●	●	+	+

Large Shrubs. 10-18 feet

Botanical Name	Common Name	Coastal	Intermediate Valleys	Coastal Foothills	Inland Valleys	Inland Foothills	Interior Valleys	Interior Foothills	Coastal	Intermediate Valleys	Coastal Foothills	Inland Valleys	Inland Foothills	Interior Valleys	Low Deserts
Acacia baileyana	Bailey Acacia	+	●	●	●	●	●	●	●	●	●	●	●		
Acacia b. 'Purpurea'	Purple-Leaf Acacia	●	●	●	●	●	●	●	●	●	●	●	●		
Acacia cultriformis	Knife Acacia	●	●	●	+				●	●	●	●	●		
Acacia cyclopis		●	●	●	+				●	●	●	●			
Acacia decurrens	Green Wattle	●	●	●	●	●			●	●	●	●	●		+
Acacia d. dealbata	Silver Wattle	●	●	●	●	●			●	●	●	●	●		+
Acacia farnesiana	Sweet Acacia				●	●	●					●	●	●	●
Acacia greggii	Catclaw Acacia					●	●					●	●	●	●
Acacia longifolia	Sydney Golden Wattle	●	●	●	●	+			●	●	●	●	+		
Acacia pendula	Weeping Acacia	●	●	●	●	●			●	●	●	+	+		+
Acacia podalyriifolia	Pearl Acacia	●	●	●	●	+			●	●	●	●	+		
Acacia pycnantha	Golden Wattle	●	●	●	●				●	●	●	+	+		
Acacia saligna	Willow Acacia	●	●	●	+				●	●	●	+	+		
Adenostoma sparsifolium	Red Shanks					●	●						●		
Aesculus californica	California Buckeye		●	●	●	●	●	●				●	+		
Agonis flexuosa	Peppermint Tree	●	●	●	+				●	●	●	●	●		
Arbutus menziesii	Madrone		+	●	●	●	●	●			●	+	+		
Arbutus unedo	Strawberry Tree	+	●	●	●	●	●		●	●	●	●	+		
Arctostaphylos glauca	Bigberry Manzanita			●	●	●	●				●	●	●		
Arctostaphylos manzanita	Common Manzanita		●	●	●	●	●				+	●	●		
Baccharis viminea	Mulefat		●	●	●	+	●			●	●	●	+	+	
Bougainvillea species	Bougainvillea	●	+	+	+	+	+		●	●	●	●	+	+	+
Calliandra tweedii	Trinidad Flame Bush		●	●	●					●	●	●	●	+	+
Callistemon citrinus	Lemon Bottlebrush	●	●	●	●	●			●	●	●	●	●	+	
Callistemon viminalis	Weeping Bottlebrush	●	●	+	+	+			●	●	●	●	●	+	+
Ceanothus arboreus	Feltleaf Ceanothus	●	+	●	+	●			●	+	●	+	+		
Ceanothus crassifolius	Hoary-Leaf Ceanothus					●	●					+	●		
Ceanothus cyaneus	San Diego Ceanothus	+	+	+					●	+	+				
Ceanothus griseus	Carmel Ceanothus	●	+	●	+	+	●		●	+	●	+			
Ceanothus impressus	Santa Barbara Ceanothus	●	+	●	+	+	●		●	+	●	+	+		

Plant selection guide.

- ● Indicates high degree of suitability between plant and environment.
- + Plants can be used in these environments, but need careful matching with exposure and soil conditions for best performance.

Large Shrubs. (Cont.)

Plant	Common Name	Northern Environments							Southern Environments					
		Coastal	Intermediate Valleys	Coastal Foothills	Inland Valleys	Inland Foothills	Interior Valleys	Interior Foothills	Coastal	Intermediate Valleys	Coastal Foothills	Inland Valleys	Inland Foothills	Interior Valleys	Low Deserts
Ceanothus 'Frosty Blue'		●	+	●	+	●	+	●	●	+	●	+	+		
Ceanothus 'Ray Hartman'		●	+	●	+	●	+	●	●	+	●	+	+		
Ceanothus 'Sierra Blue'		●	+	●	+	●	+	●	●	+	●	+	+		
Ceratonia siliqua	Carob Tree	+		●		●	+			+	●	●	●	●	●
Cercidium species	Palo Verde				+		+	+		+	●	+	●	●	●
Cercis occidentalis	Western Redbud	●	●	●	●	●	+		+	●	+	●	+		
Cercocarpus species	Mountain Mahogany					●	●	●					●		
Comarostaphylis diversifolia	Summer Holly	●	+	●					●	+	●	+	+		
Cotoneaster lacteus	Red Clusterberry	+	●	●	●	●	+			●	●	●	●	+	+
Dalea spinosa	Smoke Tree						●	●					●		●
Dendromecon harfordii	Island Bush Poppy	●	+	●	●		+	+	●	+	●	+	+		
Dodonaea viscosa	Hopseed Bush	●	●	●	●	●	●	●	●	●	●	●	●	+	+
Elaeagnus pungens	Silverberry	●	●	●	●	●	●	●	●	●	●	●	●	+	+
Eriobotrya deflexa	Bronze Loquat	+	●	●	●	●	●		+	●	●	●	●	+	+
Eriobotrya japonica	Loquat	+	●	●	●	●	●		+	●	●	●	●	+	+
Escallonia bifida	White Escallonia	●	●	●	+	●			●	●	●	+	+		
Eucalyptus erythrocorys	Red Cap Gum	●	●	●	●	●			●	●	●	●	+		
Eucalyptus lehmannii	Bushy Yate	●	●	●	●	+			●	●	●	●			
Eucalyptus macrocarpa	Desert Mallee	+	+			●	●		+	●	●	●	●	+	●
Eucalyptus niphophila	Snow Gum	●	●	●	●	●	+		●	●	●	●	●	+	+
Feijoa sellowiana	Pineapple Guava	+	●	●	●	●	●		+	●	●	●	●	●	+
Fremontodendron species	Flannel Bush	+	●	+	●	+	●		+	●	●	●	●		
Grevillea banksii	Crimson Coneflower	●	●	+	●	●			●	●	●	●	●		
Hakea laurina	Sea Urchin	●	●	●	●	+			●	●	●	●	+		
Hakea suaveolens	Sweet Hakea	●	●	●	+	+			●	●	●	+	+		
Heteromeles arbutifolia	Toyon	+	●	●	●	●	+		+	●	●	●	●		
Jasminum humile	Italian Jasmine	●	●	●	●	●	+		●	●	●	●	●	+	+
Juniperus species	Juniper	●	●	●	●	●	●	●	●	●	●	●	●	●	●
Laurus nobilis	Sweet Bay	+	●	●	●	●	●		+	●	●	●	●		+
Lavatera assurgentiflora	Tree Mallow	●	+	●					●	+	●				
Leptospermum laevigatum	Australian Tea Tree	●	●	●	●				●	●	●	+	+		
Leptospermum scoparium	New Zealand Tea Tree	●	●	●	●	+	+		●	●	●	+	+		
Lithocarpus densiflorus	Tanbark Oak	+	+	●	●	●					+	●	+		
Lyonothamnus species	Catalina Ironwood	●	+	●	●				●	+	●	+	+		
Mahonia higginsae											●	●	●		
Melaleuca armillaris	Drooping Melaleuca	●	●	●	●	+			●	●	●	●	+		
Melaleuca elliptica		●	●	●	●	+			●	●	●	●	+		
Melaleuca nesophila	Pink Melaleuca	●	●	●	●	+	+		●	●	●	●	+		
Metrosideros excelsus	New Zealand Christmas Tree	●	+	●					●	●	●	+			
Myoporum laetum		●	●	●	+	+	+		●	●	●	+	+		
Nerium oleander	Oleander	+	●	+	●	●	●		+	●	●	●	●	●	●
Photinia fraseri		●	●	●	●	●	+	+	●	●	●	●	+	+	+
Photinia serrulata	Chinese Photinia	●	●	●	●	●	+		●	●	●	●	+	+	+
Pistacia vera	Pistachio Nut				●	●	●				●	●	●	+	
Pittosporum crassifolium		●	●	●	+	+			●	●	●	+	+		
Pittosporum phillyraeoides	Willow Pittosporum	●	●	●	●	+	●		●	●	●	●	+		
Pittosporum rhombifolium	Queensland Pittosporum	●	●	●	●	+			●	●	●	●	+		
Pittosporum undulatum	Victorian Box	●	●	●	●	+			●	●	●	●	+		
Pittosporum viridiflorum	Cape Pittosporum	●	●	●	●	+			●	●	●	●	+		
Plumbago auriculata	Cape Plumbago	●	●	●	●	●	●		●	●	●	●	●		
Prunus species	Prunus	●	●	●	●	●	●	●	●	●	●	●	●	+	
Psidium guajava	Guava				●	●	●				●	●	●		
Psidium littorale	Strawberry Guava	●	●	●	●	●	●		●	●	●	●	●		
Punica granatum	Pomegranate	+	●	+	●	●	●		+	●	●	●	●	●	+
Pyracantha species	Firethorn	●	●	●	●	●	●	●	●	●	●	●	●	●	●
Quercus chrysolepis	Canyon Live Oak			+	●	●	●	●			+	●	●		
Quercus dumosa	Scrub Oak	●	●	●	●	●	●		●	●	●	●	●		
Rhamnus alaternus	Italian Buckthorn	●	●	●	●	●	●		●	●	●	●	●		+
Rhamnus californica	California Coffeeberry	●	●	●	●	●	●		●	●	●	●	●		
Rhus integrifolia	Lemonade Berry	●	●	●	+				●	●	●	+	+		

Plant selection guide.

- Indicates high degree of suitability between plant and environment.
- + Plants can be used in these environments, but need careful matching with exposure and soil conditions for best performance.

Large Shrubs. (Cont.)

Scientific Name	Common Name	Northern Environments							Southern Environments					
		Coastal	Intermediate Valleys	Coastal Foothills	Inland Valleys	Inland Foothills	Interior Valleys	Interior Foothills	Coastal	Intermediate Valleys	Coastal Foothills	Inland Valleys	Inland Foothills	Interior Valleys	Low Deserts
Rhus laurina	Laurel Sumac	•	•	•	+				•	•	•	+			
Rhus ovata	Sugar Bush	•	•	•	+	•		+	•	•	•	•	+		
Sambucus species	Elderberry	•	•	•	•	•	+	•	•	•	•	•	+		
Schinus molle	California Pepper	•	•	•	•	•	•	•	•	•	•	•	•		
Schinus terebinthifolius	Brazilian Pepper Tree	•	•	•	•	•	•		•	•	•	•	•	+	+
Tecomaria capensis	Cape Honeysuckle	•	•	•	+	•	+		•	•	•	+	+	+	+
Xylosma congestum	Shiny Xylosma	•	•	•	•	•	+		•	•	•	•	+		+

Small Trees. 15-25 feet

Scientific Name	Common Name	Coastal	Intermediate Valleys	Coastal Foothills	Inland Valleys	Inland Foothills	Interior Valleys	Interior Foothills	Coastal	Intermediate Valleys	Coastal Foothills	Inland Valleys	Inland Foothills	Interior Valleys	Low Deserts
Acacia cyanophylla	Blue-Leaf Wattle	•	•	•	+				•	•	•	+	+		
Acacia greggii	Catclaw Acacia					+						+	+	+	•
Acacia longifolia	Sydney Golden Wattle	•	•	•	•	+	+		•	•	•	•	+	+	•
Acacia pendula	Weeping Acacia	•	•	•	•				•	•	•	+	+		
Acacia podalyriifolia	Pearl Acacia	•	•	•	•	+			•	•	•	•	+		
Aesculus californica	California Buckeye	•	•	•	•		•		•	•	+	•	+		
Agonis flexuosa	Peppermint Tree	•	•	•	+				•	•	•	+			
Arbutus unedo	Strawberry Tree	+	•	•	•	•	•	•		•	•	•	+		
Arctostaphylos manzanita	Common Manzanita		•	•	•	•	•				+	•	+		
Callistemon citrinus	Lemon Bottlebrush	•	•	•	•	•	•		•	•	•	•	•		
Callistemon rigidus	Stiff Bottlebrush	•	•	•	•	•	•		•	•	•	•	•	+	+
Callistemon viminalis	Weeping Bottlebrush	•	•	•	•	•	•		•	•	•	•	•	+	+
Ceanothus arboreus	Feltleaf Ceanothus	•	+	+	+	+	•		•	+	+	+	+		
Ceanothus 'Ray Hartman'		•	+	+	+	+	•		•	+	+	+	+		
Cercidium species	Palo Verde		+	+	+	•	•		+	+	+	+	•	•	•
Cercis occidentalis	Western Redbud	•	•	•	•	•	+		•	+	+	+	+	+	+
Cercocarpus betuloides	Mountain Mahogany		•	•	•	•	+					•	+	+	+
Comarostaphylis diversifolia	Summer Holly	•	+	•	•	+	•		•	+	•	•	+		
Dalea spinosa	Smoke Tree										•	•	•	•	•
Elaeagnus angustifolia	Russian Olive		•	•	•	•	•			•	•	•	•	•	•
Eriobotrya deflexa	Bronze Loquat	+	•	•	•	•	•		+	•	•	•	•	+	+
Eriobotrya japonica	Loquat	+	•	•	•	•	•		+	•	•	•	•	+	+
Escallonia bifida	White Escallonia	•	•	•	+	+			•	•	•	+	+		
Eucalyptus erythrocorys	Red Cap Gum	•	•	•	+				•	•	•	•	+		
Eucalyptus lehmannii	Bushy Yate	•	•	•	+				•	•	•	•	+		
Eucalyptus niphophila	Snow Gum	•	•	•	•	•	+		•	•	•	•	•	+	
Eucalyptus torquata	Coral Gum	•	+	•	•					•	•	•	•		•
Feijoa sellowiana	Pineapple Guava	+	•	•	•	•			+	•	•	•	•		+
Fremontodendron species	Flannel Bush	+	+	+	+	+	+		+	+	+	+	+		+
Geijera parviflora	Australian Willow	•	•	•	•	+	+		•	•	•	•	+		+
Hakea laurina	Sea Urchin	•	•	•	•	+	+		•	•	•	•	+		
Heteromeles arbutifolia	Toyon	+	•	•	•	+	•		+	•	•	•	•		
Koelreuteria paniculata	Goldenrain Tree	+	•	•	•	•	•			•	•	•	•		
Lagerstroemia indica	Crape Myrtle		+	•	•	•	•			•	•	•	•		•
Laurus nobilis	Sweet Bay	+	•	•	•	•	•		•	•	•	•	•		+
Lavatera assurgentiflora	Tree Mallow	•	+	•	•				•	+	+	+			
Leptospermum laevigatum	Australian Tea Tree	•	+	•	•				•	+	+	+			
Lyonothamnus species	Catalina Ironwood	•	+	•	•	+			•	+	+	+	+		
Melaleuca armillaris	Drooping Melaleuca	•	•	•	•	•	+		•	•	•	•	+		
Melaleuca elliptica		•	•	•	•				•	•	•	•	+		
Melaleuca nesophila	Pink Melaleuca	•	•	•	•	+			•	•	•	•	+		
Metrosideros excelsus	New Zealand Christmas Tree	•	+						•	•		•			
Nerium oleander	Oleander	+	•	+	•	•			+	•	•	•	•		
Parkinsonia aculeata	Jerusalem Thorn				•	•					+	•	+	•	•
Photinia fraseri		•	•	•	•	+	+		•	•	+	+	+	+	+
Photinia serrulata	Chinese Photinia		•	•	•	+				•	•	+	+	+	+
Pistacia vera	Pistachio Nut			•									+		

Plant selection guide.

- ● Indicates high degree of suitability between plant and environment.
- \+ Plants can be used in these environments, but need careful matching with exposure and soil conditions for best performance.

Small Trees. (Cont.)

	Northern Environments							Southern Environments						
	Coastal	Intermediate Valleys	Coastal Foothills	Inland Valleys	Inland Foothills	Interior Foothills	Interior Valleys	Coastal	Intermediate Valleys	Coastal Foothills	Inland Valleys	Inland Foothills	Interior Valleys	Low Deserts
Pittosporum crassifolium	●	●	●	+	+	●	●	●	●	●	+	+	●	●
Pittosporum phillyraeoides .... Willow Pittosporum	●	●	●	●	+	+	●	●	●	●	+	+	●	●
Pittosporum rhombifolium ..... Queensland Pittosporum	●	●	●	+	+	●	●	●	●	●	●	+	●	●
Pittosporum viridiflorum .... Cape Pittosporum	●	●	●	+	+	●	●	●	●	●	●	+	●	●
Prunus species .... Prunus	●	●	●	●	●	+	+	●	●	●	+	+	●	●
Psidium littorale .... Strawberry Guava	●	●	●	●	+	●	●	●	●	●	+	+	●	●
Punica granatum .... Pomegranate	+	●	+	●	●	●	●	+	●	●	●	+	●	+
Quercus dumosa .... Scrub Oak	●	●	●	●	+	●	●	●	●	●	●	●	●	●
Rhamnus alaternus .... Italian Buckthorn	●	●	●	●	●	●	●	●	●	●	●	●	+	+
Rhus integrifolia .... Lemonade Berry	●	●	●	+	●	●	●	●	●	+	●	+	+	+
Rhus lancea .... African Sumac	●	●	●	●	+	●	●	●	●	+	●	+	●	●
Rhus ovata .... Sugar Bush	●	●	●	●	+	●	●	●	●	●	●	+	●	●
Sambucus species .... Elderberry	●	●	●	●	●	+	●	●	●	●	●	●	+	+
Schinus terebinthifolius .... Brazilian Pepper Tree	●	●	●	●	●	●	●	●	●	●	●	+	+	+

Medium Trees. 25-40 feet

	Coastal	Intermediate Valleys	Coastal Foothills	Inland Valleys	Inland Foothills	Interior Foothills	Interior Valleys	Coastal	Intermediate Valleys	Coastal Foothills	Inland Valleys	Inland Foothills	Interior Valleys	Low Deserts
Acacia baileyana .... Bailey Acacia	●	●	●	●	●	●	●	●	●	●	●	●	●	+
Acacia decurrens .... Green Wattle	●	●	●	●	●	●	●	●	●	●	●	●	●	+
Acacia podalyriifolia .... Pearl Acacia	●	●	●	●	+	●	●	●	●	●	●	+	●	+
Agonis flexuosa .... Peppermint Tree	●	●	●	+	●	●	●	●	●	●	+	+	●	●
Ailanthus altissima .... Tree-Of-Heaven	●	●	●	●	●	●	●	●	●	●	●	●	●	●
Albizia julibrissin .... Silk Tree	+	●	●	●	●	●	+	+	●	●	+	●	●	●
Arbutus menziesii .... Madrone	●	+	●	●	●	●	●	●	●	●	+	+	●	●
Arbutus unedo .... Strawberry Tree	+	●	●	●	●	●	●	+	●	●	●	+	●	●
Brachychiton acerifolius .... Flame Tree	+	●	●	+	●	+	●	●	●	●	●	●	●	●
Brachychiton populneus .... Bottle Tree	+	●	●	●	●	+	●	●	●	●	●	●	+	●
Callistemon viminalis .... Weeping Bottlebrush	●	●	●	+	●	+	+	●	●	●	●	+	+	+
Casuarina stricta .... Beefwood	+	+	●	●	●	+	+	●	●	+	+	+	●	●
Ceratonia siliqua .... Carob Tree	+	●	●	●	+	●	●	●	●	●	●	+	●	●
Cercidium floridum .... Blue Palo Verde	●	+	●	+	+	●	●	●	●	●	●	●	●	●
Cupressocyparis leylandii .... Leyland Cypress	●	●	●	●	●	●	●	●	●	●	●	●	●	●
Cupressus species .... Cypress	●	●	●	●	●	●	●	●	●	●	●	●	●	●
Dalea spinosa .... Smoke Tree	●	●	●	●	●	●	●	●	●	●	●	●	●	●
Elaeagnus angustifolia .... Russian Olive		●	●	●	●	●	●		●	●	●	●	+	●
Eucalyptus niphophila .... Snow Gum	●	●	●	●	●	+	●	●	●	●	●	●	+	+
Eucalyptus pulverulenta .... Silver Mountain Gum	+	●	●	●	+	●	●	+	●	●	●	+	●	●
Eucalyptus rudis .... Desert Gum	+	●	●	●	●	●	●	+	●	●	●	●	●	●
Eucalyptus sideroxylon .... Red Ironbark	●	●	●	●	●	●	●	●	●	●	●	●	●	●
Geijera parviflora .... Australian Willow	●	●	●	●	+	+	●	●	●	●	●	●	●	+
Juglans species .... Walnut		●	●	●	●	●	●		●	●	●	●	+	●
Koelreuteria paniculata .... Goldenrain Tree	+	●	●	●	●	●	●	+	●	●	●	●	●	●
Laurus nobilis .... Sweet Bay	+	●	●	●	●	+	+	+	●	●	●	●	●	+
Lithocarpus densiflorus .... Tanbark Oak	+	+	●	●	●	●	●	+	●	●	+	●	●	●
Lyonothamnus species .... Catalina Ironwood	+	+	●	●	●	●	●	+	●	●	●	●	●	●
Melaleuca linariifolia .... Flaxleaf Paperbark	+	●	●	+	●	●	●	+	●	●	●	●	●	●
Melaleuca quinquenervia .... Cajeput Tree	●	●	●	●	●	●	●	●	●	●	●	●	+	●
Melaleuca styphelioides .... Black Tea Tree	●	●	●	+	●	●	●	●	●	●	●	●	●	+
Myoporum laetum	●	●	●	●	+	●	●	●	●	●	●	●	●	●
Olea europaea .... Olive	+	●	+	●	●	●	●	+	●	●	●	●	●	●
Parkinsonia aculeata .... Jerusalem Thorn									+	●	●	●	●	●
Pistacia chinensis .... Chinese Pistache		●	●	●	●	●	●		●	●	●	+	●	●
Pittosporum undulatum .... Victorian Box	●	●	●	+	●	●	●	●	●	●	+	+	●	●
Prunus caroliniana .... Carolina Laurel Cherry	●	●	●	●	+	●	●	●	●	●	+	+	●	●
Prunus lyonii .... Catalina Cherry	●	●	●	+	+	●	●	●	●	●	+	●	●	+
Quercus chrysolepis .... Canyon Live Oak		+	●	+	+	●	●		●	●	+	●	●	●
Quercus ilex .... Holly Oak	●	●	●	●	●	●	●	●	●	●	●	●	●	●
Quercus suber .... Cork Oak		●	●	●	+	●	●		●	●	●	●	●	+

Plant selection guide.

- • Indicates high degree of suitability between plant and environment.
- + Plants can be used in these environments, but need careful matching with exposure and soil conditions for best performance.

Medium Trees. (Cont.)

	Northern Environments							Southern Environments						
	Coastal	Intermediate Valleys	Coastal Foothills	Inland Valleys	Inland Foothills	Interior Valleys	Interior Foothills	Coastal	Intermediate Valleys	Coastal Foothills	Inland Valleys	Inland Foothills	Interior Valleys	Low Deserts
Robinia pseudoacacia............Black Locust	•	•	•	•	•	•	•	•	•	•	•	•	•	•
Sambucus species............Elderberry	•	•	•	•	•	+	•	•	•	•	+	•	•	•
Schinus polygamus............Peruvian Pepper Tree	•	•	•	+	+	+	•	+	•	•	+	•	•	+
Schinus terebinthifolius............Brazilian Pepper Tree	•	•	•	•	+	+	•	•	•	•	+	•	+	+
Tamarix aphylla............Athel Tree	+	•	+	+	•	•	•	•	•	•	•	•	•	•
Tristania conferta............Brisbane Box	•	+	+	•	•	•	•	•	•	+	•	•	•	
Zelkova serrata............Sawleaf Zelkova	+	•	•	•	•	•	•	•	•	•	•	+	+	+
Zizyphus jujuba............Chinese Jujube		•	+	•	•	•	•		+	•	•			

Large Trees. 40 feet and higher

	Coastal	Intermediate Valleys	Coastal Foothills	Inland Valleys	Inland Foothills	Interior Valleys	Interior Foothills	Coastal	Intermediate Valleys	Coastal Foothills	Inland Valleys	Inland Foothills	Interior Valleys	Low Deserts
Acacia decurrens............Green Wattle	•	•	•	•	•	•	•	•	•	•	•	•	•	+
Acacia d. dealbata............Silver Wattle	•	•	•	•	•	•	•	•	•	•	•	•	•	+
Acacia melanoxylon............Blackwood Acacia	•	•	•	•	•	•	•	•	•	•	•	•	•	•
Ailanthus altissima............Tree-of-Heaven	•	•	•	•	•	•	•	•	•	•	•	•	•	•
Arbutus menziesii............Madrone		+	•	•	•	•			+	+	+			
Brachychiton acerifolius............Flame Tree	+	•	+	•	+	•		•	•	•	•	•	•	•
Casuarina cunninghamiana............Australian Pine	•	•	+	•	+	•	•	•	•	+	•	+	•	•
Casuarina equisetifolia............Horsetail Tree	+	•	•	•	•	•	•	+	•	+	•	+	•	•
Cedrus atlantica............Atlas Cedar	+	•	•	+	•	•	•	+	•	•	•	•	•	+
Cedrus deodara............Deodar Cedar	+	•	•	+	•	•	•	+	•	•	•	+	•	•
Ceratonia siliqua............Carob Tree	+	•	•	•	+	•		•	•	•	•	+	•	•
Cupressocyparis laylandii............Leyland Cypress	•	•	•	•	•	•	•	•	•	•	•	•	•	•
Cupressus species............Cypress	•	•	•	•	•	•	•	•	•	•	•	•	•	•
Eucalyptus calophylla.............	+	+		+	•	•	•	+	•		+			
Eucalyptus camaldulensis............Red Gum	•	•	•	•	•	•	•	•	•	•	•	•	•	•
Eucalyptus cladocalyx............Sugar Gum	•	•	•	•	•	•	•	•	•	•	+	+	•	•
Eucalyptus globulus 'Compacta'............Dwarf Blue Gum	+	•	•	•	•	•	•	+	•	•	•	•	+	•
Eucalyptus leucoxylon............White Ironbark	•	•	•	•	•	•	•	•	•	•	•	•	•	•
Eucalyptus polyanthemos............Silver Dollar Gum	•	•	•	•	•	•	•	•	•	•	•	•	•	•
Eucalyptus rudis............Desert Gum	+	•	•	•	+	•	•	+	•	•	+	•	•	•
Eucalyptus sideroxylon............Red Ironbark	•	•	•	•	•	•	•	•	•	•	•	•	•	•
Eucalyptus viminalis............Manna Gum	•	•	•	•	•	•	•	•	•	•	•	•	•	•
Grevillea robusta............Silk Oak	+	•	+	•	•	•			•	•	•	+	•	•
Lithocarpus densiflorus............Tanbark Oak	+	+	•	+	+	•	•		+	•	+			
Lyonothamnus species............Catalina Ironwood	•	+	•	•	•			•	+	•	+	•		
Pinus canariensis............Canary Island Pine	•	•	•	•	•	•	•	•	•	•	•	•	•	+
Pinus coulteri............Coulter Pine		+	•	•	•	•	•			•	•	•	•	
Pinus halepensis............Aleppo Pine	•	•	•	•	•	•	•	•	•	•	•	•	•	•
Pinus pinea............Italian Stone Pine	•	•	•	•	•	•	•	•	•	•	•	•	+	+
Pinus radiata............Monterey Pine	•	+	•	+	+	+		•	+	•	+	+		
Pinus sabiniana............Digger Pine		+	•	+	+	+	•		•	•	+	+	•	
Pinus torreyana............Torrey Pine	+	•	•	•	+	+		•	•	•	+	+	•	
Pistacia chinensis............Chinese Pistache		•	•	•	+	•	•		•	•	+	+	•	
Quercus agrifolia............Coast Live Oak	•	•	•	+	•	•	•		•	•	•	•	•	
Quercus chrysolepis............Canyon Live Oak		+	•	+	•	+	•		+	•	+	+	•	
Quercus douglasii............Blue Oak		+	+	•	•	•	•			•	+	+	•	
Quercus engelmannii............Mesa Oak			+	•	+	+	•	+	•	•	+	+		
Quercus ilex............Holly Oak	•	•	•	•	•	•	•	•	•	•	•	•	•	•
Quercus lobata............Valley Oak		•	•	•	+	•	•		•	+	•	•	•	
Quercus suber............Cork Oak	•	•	•	+	•	•	•	+	•	•	•	•	•	+
Robinia pseudoacacia............Black Locust	•	•	•	•	•	•	•	•	•	•	•	•	•	•
Schinus molle............California Pepper	+	•	•	•	•	•	•	+	•	•	•	•	•	•
Schinus polygamous............Peruvian Pepper Tree	•	•	•	+	•	•	•	•	•	•	+	•	•	+
Tamarix aphylla............Athel Tree	+	•	•	+	•	•	•	+	•	+	+	•	+	•
Zelkova serrata............Sawleaf Zelkova	+	•	•	•	•	•	•	•	•	•	•	+	•	+

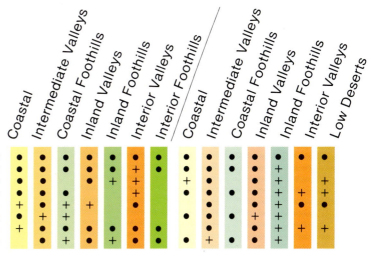

II. Planting Guidelines.

Any landscape project consists of a variety of conditions and needs. Hopefully, we can make the most of the opportunities to establish an appropriate planting concept that is consistent with function, aesthetics, costs, resources and maintenance. Even when we have water conservation first in mind, it is doubtful that we should try to develop landscapes with only low water requiring plants. There is a need to achieve a balance in design. This sense of balance will often involve the use of lawns, as well as tropical and exotic plantings. However, when we do feel the pressure from limited water supplies, or increased costs, then it is time to emphasize our planting for water conservation. To this end, we can look to both California native and introduced plants from similar mediterranean environments. Within these plant groups we can find many species which survive in our landscapes with use of limited supplemental water.

Landscaping with California Natives.

There has been renewed interest in using our own California native plants to solve some of our landscape problems. It is hoped that these plants can be grown with minimum water, require little maintenance, and can be used for natural and domestic situations alike. It is true that some of our natives can perform a number of tasks very well. It is also true that natives have particular requirements and limitations which influence their performance. In any project we should consider the choices and conditions which apply to native plants.

California natives offer us a wealth of choices. Close to 7,000 fern and seed bearing species, coming from some 60 plant communities, occur within our state. Both the size and diversity of our native flora is truly impressive and should cause us to look with care at our own resources. In light of this vast natural diversity, we have come to use only about 150-200 species and varieties in our landscapes. In reality, we rely on only 60-80 native species with any degree of regular use. This situation reflects the many demands which are placed upon our landscape plants. Any plant must be reasonable to propagate, handle, and establish, as well as offer good year-round aesthetics and be able to mix with other plants. To this end, the list of native plants which we are using continues to expand as more research, higher availability and changing attitudes help to make them become a viable part of our landscape situations. When considering the use of these plants, we need to be aware of certain factors.

Types of native plants:

Both natural species and horticultural varieties of California native plants are available to work with. Many natural species serve best for naturalizing, slope stabilization, regional park and open space plantings. Such plants often experience problems when grown in domestic areas that have regular summer water, fertilizers added to the soils, and poor drainage conditions. However, there are many good examples of natural species, such as the Toyon and Western Redbud, that tolerate a wide range of conditions, as well as provide rich aesthetic character. In addition to the natural species, we have the opportunity to work with plants which have been purposefully hybridized or bred for certain traits. These are the horticultural cultivars. In the process of developing such plants, many conditions have been tested for ease of propagation, aesthetics, and tolerance of garden water and fertilizer conditions. These horticultural varieties are often the best choices for use in ornamental landscape settings.

Drought tolerance:

All native plants are not drought tolerant. Many species come from environments with high moisture and rich soils. As a starting point, care should be taken to select plants which naturally grow in areas of limited moisture. These species have developed the adaptations and tolerances which are best suited to dry landscape situations.

In addition, native plant species should be used within reasonable limits of their adaptations. It is difficult to mix plants from northern regions with those of southern regions. Natives also show distinct preferences to coastal, valley, or foothill conditions. Efforts need to be made to recognize different project locations and to use plants from related habitats.

Balanced plant palette:

Usually, it is not recommended that a landscape be planted with only natives. Unless we are attempting to restore a disturbed area back to its natural state, there are many fine introduced plants to consider using. These introduced plants also adapt well to dry conditions and provide excellent visual interest, growth characteristics, and tolerances which fit many project situations. The intent is to find compatible groupings of plants which enable us to develop appropriate landscapes in light of costs, function, and aesthetics.

Native Plants (Continued)

Cultural requirements:

The cultural needs of native plants very often include coarse, well draining soils and restricted summer water. The drought tolerant species, particularly large shrubs and trees, prefer a dry soil layer within their foliage drip line. It is often recommended that natural leaf litter or other mulching materials be placed under these plants. Opportunities for deep root development should be considered, as many plants have adapted to our dry regions by developing extensive root systems in search of water.

Watering should be restricted largely to the winter and spring months to compliment the natural rains and growing cycle. Summer water, particularly from overhead spray systems, causes unseasonal growth and greatly increases the possibility of disease. Soil organisms are most active in moist, warm soils which can lead to root rot and fungus diseases.

Certain natives will tolerate heavier soils, as long as water does not collect and stand, and when good drainage is provided. Raised planters and slope areas work well when natives are to be grown in heavy or clay soils.

We can also take advantage of micro-climates in order to fit our plants into specific sites. Coastal species can adapt to inland locations when given partial shade and limited summer moisture. Heat loving plants, from desert and interior environments, can be used in selected coastal areas when placed next to south facing walls and in areas of full sunlight. Frost sensitive plants do well in protected areas having more winter warmth. By carefully understanding the specialized growing conditions that exist on a small scale, we can select and use many plants with a high degree of success.

Availability:

The availability of native plants has been a source of problems over the years. Fortunately, this is improving. While it is still quite hard to find good sources throughout areas like southern California, more nurseries are supplying plants through shipping and postal services. These conditions will continue to improve as more interest and demand is expressed for natives.

For large projects which anticipate the need for specialized types and large quantities of natives, it is good advice to consider contract growing. A time frame of one to two years is needed to have nurseries grow the necessary plants. While this takes a good deal of coordination and planning, it is becoming a popular way to have reliable plant supplies.

Selected bibliography:

In addition to the guidelines and photographs included in this publication, there are several other important sources which deal with California natives. These include:

California Native Trees and Shrubs, For Garden and Environmental Use in Southern California and Adjacent Areas. Lee W. Lenz, John Dourley. Rancho Santa Ana Botanic Garden, 1981.

Growing California Native Plants. Marjorie G. Schmidt, U.C. Press, 1980.

Native Plants for Use in California Landscapes. Emile L. Labadie, Sierra City Press, 1978.

Selected California Native Plants in Color and **Selected California Native Plants with Commercial Sources.** Saratoga Horticultural Foundation, 1980.

New Sunset Western Garden Book. Lane Publishing Co., 1979.

Planting from containers.

By far the largest volume of planting done in our landscapes today is with container grown species. Traditional practices, where we freely use water, have led to year-round planting, use of large plant sizes, and application of long term irrigation. We seem to always want the landscape to provide the quickest effect possible, at any time our schedules demand it. In an attempt to fit the conditions of limited water and to encourage maximum self-sufficiency of plants, including natives, the following guidelines are proposed:

Planting season:

The optimum time frame for container planting occurs twice a year. The first choice would be in the late fall to early winter. During this period, we still have warm soils and mild temperatures. Plants that are installed at this time can become settled and established prior to the winter cold and will benefit from the seasonal rains. These plants will not produce much foliage growth, but they will be set for spring and will perform strongly. In addition, such plants can be settled enough to survive the first summer with only periodic deep watering.

The second choice for planting occurs in the early spring months. This is after the danger of frost is past and while there is a chance of getting late seasonal rains. The days become warmer and longer, which promotes quick development. The later the planting occurs in the spring, the less time the plants will have to get set for summer, which usually means providing more frequent summer water for the first season.

Plant sizes:

An inherent advantage lies in using small plant sizes for establishing any type of plant. When installed from flats, 2¼ inch pots, and one gallon containers, plants are easier to handle and are more adaptable to new environments. It is found that smaller plants have a high proportion of root development to foliage mass, and can establish themselves more quickly and with greater survival rates. Project costs are also lower and proper irrigation practices can lead to better long term self-sufficiency. It is also important to note that most California native plants are rarely available from nurseries in large sizes. This situation favors plant survival, but does not support the desire for instant visual effects.

Planting from containers (Continued)

Supplemental water:

The application of supplemental water must be determined by judgment and observation. There are no charts which tell us of the exact water needs of specific plants or for individual site conditions. The estimated potential evapotranspiration stress which occurs in any region is a start, but regular checks and adjustments need to be made in any watering program. However, keep in mind, the primary objective of supplemental water is to promote proper root development. Any plant that is not encouraged to develop its optimum root system, and is continually given ample surface moisture, is going to be less drought tolerant throughout its lifespan.

Proper watering from the very beginning does the most to help a plant fit the natural moisture conditions of its new environment. Any watering schedule should take into account several guidelines. (a) Upon installation, all plants should be watered to settle the plant and soil into proper position. (b) Water can then be given once or twice a week for the first two to three months, depending upon the weather conditions. All plants have a need to receive good initial watering in their early establishment stages. (c) When the rain season ends and warmer temperatures occur, the watering schedules should be adjusted to meet the minimum plant needs. We are essentially trying to replace the soil moisture that has been lost through direct evaporation from the soil and from the transpiration loss coming from the plant. An excess of water can lead to greater foliage growth, but when the moisture runs out, the plant can die back. (d) Supplemental water should be applied on an infrequent basis and be heavy enough to achieve deep percolation. This technique, where we let the surface soil dry out inbetween waterings, will cause the plants to search for the deeper moisture. Frequent surface watering will supply all the water a plant needs, so that it will develop more surface roots and not have to reach into lower soil depths. This initial root system will continue to develop and cause plants to have a higher dependence on surface water supplies throughout its life. Of course, when the regular water supply is stopped, these shallow rooted plants will quickly suffer and be ill prepared for any length of drought. Even a "drought tolerant" plant which has been supplied with ample surface moisture will not have the root system to support its foliage mass when grown under these conditions. (e) Most low water requiring plants experience a period of rest and dormancy during the summer and fall. After they are established, it is not desirable to supply too much moisture in an effort to keep everything green and growing. This extended growth causes plants to expend excessive energy, become weak limbed, and die earlier. It is also important to realize that soil fungus diseases are highly active in our soils when there is high moisture content and warm soil temperatures. California natives are quite susceptible to such diseases and have a better chance of surviving if soils are kept dry during the summer. (f) After young plants have survived a full season, it is time to think of letting them survive on their own. It becomes important to encourage the plants to grow and fit within the basic conditions of the landscape. To a large extent, they will regulate their growth, remain healthy, and perform quite well without a lot of assistance. This is not to suggest that all care, such as pruning, checking for pests and diseases, and periodic deep watering is no longer necessary. Even light applications of fertilizer in the early spring is helpful to these plants. The idea is to provide assistance to the plants in a manner that helps them adapt to their environment.

Planting hole preparation:

Healthy plant adjustment begins with good planting hole preparation. Do not underestimate the value of a large, deep plant pit. This effort will always pay off as it supports deep watering practices and full root growth. Plant holes should also allow for good drainage, insuring that water will not stand around the plant roots for extended periods. This is a problem that occurs frequently in clay type soils. In addition, water basins can be constructed, which will assist in catching rainfall and in holding supplemental water for deep percolation.

Fertilizers and amendments:

Light applications of fertilizer and use of organic amendments can often assist in the initial establishment and growth of most plants. Unfortunately, we have cultivated the habit of adding fertilizers and water too frequently throughout the year. Restricted quantities of fertilizer work well in early spring when rains can still come. We should avoid their use during the late summer as a way of stimulating growth and greener appearance. Both soil amending and fertilizing should be done to assist in the plant establishment process and natural growing cycle. We should not attempt to correct a fundamental deficiency or problem with the soils. Plants must be selected to fit the parent soil conditions and not require prolonged fertilizer treatments.

Inspection and installation:

All plants should be checked for coiled roots and health conditions prior to installation. Rootballs can be loosened in order to encourage freedom of development. Plants should be settled in place with water and tamping to set the root crown level at the same grade as the surrounding site. A water basin can be constructed 4-6 inches high, 2-3 feet in diameter, to assist in periodic deep watering. In areas where rabbits and deer browse, it is sometimes helpful to enclose plants with a wire screen that is firmly anchored to the ground.

Mulching:

An effective technique to reduce surface water evaporation and provide weed control can be achieved through the practice of mulching. A 3-6 inch layer of shredded wood or leaf litter will hold in soil moisture, restrict weed growth, and lower soil temperatures. Sometimes a layer of wood bark or natural rock is used for the same purposes. This treatment is quite effective under large shrubs and trees, and can serve as a ground cover while small plants are maturing.

Planting from Seed.

One of the most desirable ways to establish many drought tolerant plant species is through seeding. Planting from seed can work at any scale, from residential gardens to extensive slope areas created by housing projects. It offers many advantages, from low costs, to quick soil coverage, and can be designed to establish natural or domestic landscape character.

A number of California native and introduced plants lend themselves to seed planting techniques with very good success. Outlined below are a number of considerations involved in planting from seed in large scale and commercial projects.

Advantages of seeding:

Perhaps the most important advantage of establishing plants by seed lies in the complete development of the plant in its new environment. Seeds which germinate and survive, indicate that they are basically adapted to the site conditions. A selection process has occurred which tends to eliminate plants that are poorly suited to the conditions of a particular project.

In addition to the natural selection process, we find that young seedlings are quick to establish deep root systems. Many plants that are grown in containers will have confined roots, which can inhibit their adjustment on a site. Seed plants show more continuous root development, produce more vigorous growth, and quickly exceed the size of plants that are installed from containers. Seedlings are also able to develop their roots in small cracks and difficult areas when planted in rocky soils, or on steep slopes.

Other advantages to seed planting pertain to natural competition and adaptation to limited moisture. Seedlings that do establish will be competing for space, nutrients, and moisture. Healthy plants will survive, while weaker species decline and die. A natural level of competition and equilibrium is more likely to occur in landscapes planted from seed than from containers. This equilibrium is also encouraged by regulating the supplemental water that seedlings receive. Seeded plants will develop root systems and foliage mass that are in balance and within the limits of the moisture conditions better than most container grown plants. By developing a program of deep and infrequent watering, we can encourage seedlings to regulate their growth and become more self-sufficient at an earlier age.

Limitations of seed planting:

Not all plants can be established in the field from seed. Some species produce seeds that need carefully controlled temperature and moisture conditions in order to germinate. This low rate of germination success often discourages this method of planting for such plant species. Other types of plants, such as horticultural selections and hybrids, must be grown from cuttings in order to maintain their true characteristics. These plants will have to be propagated, grown in containers and installed by hand if they are to be used in a project.

Above: Small scale residential seeding can be done on an annual basis for mixed wildflower effects.

Right: Commercial seeding can cover large scale areas to install a balanced planting of annuals, shrubs and trees, for fast coverage and low cost.

Planting from seed. (Continued)

Seeding techniques:

The most commonly used technique for large scale seed planting is by hydroseeding. This is a method by which different seeds are mixed into a slurry, consisting of water, wood fiber, and fertilizer. This mixture is then sprayed onto a planting area with the use of pumping equipment. It is an effective technique for covering large or small areas, with any combination of seeds. The specific types of seed, amount of wood fiber and fertilizer, can be designed to meet the conditons of each project to insure maximum success.

A second technique involves direct seeding. This is a method by which small numbers of seed are hand planted in the ground. This approach is useful when we want to locate plants more carefully and when we are dealing with special types of seed. Large seeds, such as acorns or walnuts, and seeds that need to be specially treated before they will germinate, are often planted by this technique. In most instances, these seeds are placed in a small planting capsule which contains an improved growing medium and fertilizer. During the planting stages, we also have the opportunity to place these seeds in favorable areas which offer deeper soils, more moisture, or any necessary shade.

Seed mixture:

The choice of seeds to be used for any landscape planting will vary with the specific project situation. However, in these projects, this mixture of seeds should be designed with several thoughts in mind, including: nurse crop species, primary and secondary plant species, and quality of seed material.

Nurse crop species are plants that germinate quickly and provide fast soil coverage. Their role is to stabilize the soil and minimize erosion that can be caused by winter rains or heavy irrigation. Often, these are annual plants, which provide a lot of color and survive long enough for slower growing species to germinate. A second group of seeds includes the primary and secondary plants that will provide the long term landscape character. This is a more complex seed mixture. We want to incorporate a range of shrub and tree species which will establish a balanced planting scheme. In this process we can emphasize certain plant types which will create the dominant plant groups. This might include the longer lived species, as well as the larger tree elements. Secondary species can be added to provide diversity and accent character, which enriches the total planting effect.

Designing a seed mixture which incorporates nurse crops and long-term species offers several advantages. On one hand, since it is hard to predict the success of any one species, it is better to provide a range of plant types so that we can be assured of some plants surviving. On the other hand, this approach of using a variety of plant seeds, reflects plant groupings found in natural landscapes. Very seldom do we find just one or two types of plants inhabiting a natural area. Plant diversity is a response to the many types of conditions that can be found on a project site. This diversity will also provide visual variety and can lead to plants becoming established in areas that they are best adapted to.

Seed quality also plays an important role in the success of a project. Many seeds germinate best if they are fresh, or have been stored and protected from heat and moisture. Also, California native plant seed should be collected from the region which surrounds a project site. This seed will come from plants which are more likely to be adapted to the climate and soil conditions of the project. It can be expected that the same native plant which is growing in northern California, will have different adaptations and tolerances than a plant that has evolved in southern California environments. Listed below are plant species and seed techniques which are commonly used in commercial landscape projects.

Plants suitable for hydroseeding:

Nurse Crops, Ground covers, Wildflowers

Abronia species	Sand Verbena
Achillea species	Yarrow
Atriplex semibaccata	Creeping Saltbush
Coreopsis species	Coreopsis
Dimorphotheca species	African Daisy
Eschscholzia californica	California Poppy
Gazania species	Gazania
Leptodactylon californicum	Prickly Phlox
Lobularia maritima	Sweet Alyssum
Lotus scoparius	Deerweed
Lupinus species	Lupine
Pennisetum species	Fountain Grass
Penstemon species	Penstemon
Salvia columbariae	Chia
Salvia sonomensis	Creeping Sage
Trifolium fragiferum O'Connor's	O'Connor's Legume
Zauschneria species	California Fuchsia

Trees and Shrubs:

Acacia species	Acacia
Artemisia species	Sagebrush
Atriplex species	Saltbush
Baccharis pilularis ssp. consanguinea	Coyote Brush
Cercocarpus species	Mountain Mahogany
Cistus species	Rockrose
Encelia species	Encelia
Eriogonum species	Buckwheat
Eriophyllum confertiflorum	Golden Yarrow
Eucalyptus species	Eucalyptus
Fremontodendron species	Flannel Bush
Isomeris arborea	Bladderpod
Rhus species	Sumac
Salvia species	Sage
Trichostema lanatum	Woolly Blue Curls
Viguiera species	Sunflower

Plants suitable for direct seeding techniques:

Aesculus californica	California Buckeye
Arbutus menziesii	Madrone
Arctostaphylos species	Manzanita
Ceanothus species	Wild Lilac
Cercis occidentalis	Western Redbud
Comarostaphylis diversifolia	Summer Holly
Heteromeles arbutifolia	Toyon
Juglans species	Walnut
Lithocarpus densiflorus	Tanbark Oak
Lupinus species	Tree Lupine
Pinus species	Pine
Prunus species	Evergreen Cherry
Quercus species	Oak
Rhamnus species	Buckthorn
Rhus species	Sumac
Simmondsia chinensis	Jojoba

Planting from seed. (Continued)

When to seed:

Seed planting can be conducted during several times of the year. The fall season is usually preferred as many seeds will be planted in conjunction with their natural cycle of germination and development. Such plantings will also benefit from the seasonal rains, which provide much of the moisture that is needed. Projects which are planted in the fall are usually done early enough to get a nurse crop established for soil stabilization. This is a critical step, as it is not possible to predict the intensity of the first rains.

A second season for seed planting occurs during early spring. Longer days, warmer temperatures and late season rainfall, combine to make conditions good for rapid plant growth and development. This planting period does not provide as much time for advanced plant establishment and usually results in needing to provide more supplemental water into the summer.

It has also been possible to plant seeds during the summer months in many areas. Seeds can be planted and supplemental water provided for germination. Planting at this time of year can produce good soil coverage for the next winter rain cycle. It has also been observed that many plants respond quite well to the warmer conditions and produce very rapid growth.

Supplemental irrigation:

The use of supplemental water plays an important role in establishing plants from seed. Several options are available to consider for different project situations and intended landscape effects. In certain cases, there might be little need to provide supplemental water; we then rely upon the seasonal rainfall. In other situations, we should plan for permanent irrigation systems, which can provide water to contend with high fire hazard areas or periods of drought.

Landscape projects often deal with remote sites, such as highway plantings, regional parks, and outlying natural areas. Under these circumstances, it is possible to plant from seed and not to provide supplemental water. This planting approach works when we are developing a natural landscape character and are not attempting to achieve an instant effect. In these situations, it becomes important to select and match plant species with the site conditions. Direct seeding, or hydroseeding operations, should be done at the beginning of the winter rain cycle to take advantage of natural moisture and cool temperatures. Since seasonal rains are unpredictable, we can expect variable plant development, and should allow 2-4 years before an established planting effect is produced. While this approach does not offer quick results, the plants which survive will be adjusted to the project conditions and require little or no additional assistance.

A second approach which provides supplemental water to seed plantings, involves the design of a temporary irrigation system. This system would be set up to apply water during the initial seed germination and plant development stages. The first two to three weeks after seed planting is the most critical to the germination of seeds. If the seeds can be kept moist during this period, maximum potential germination is possible. In this process, it is better to provide light treatments of water, several times a day, than to apply one heavy treatment every other day. The surface soil should be moist at all times for seeds to germinate. Once the initial germination period is complete, then the application of water should be adjusted. It becomes preferable to provide moisture on a periodic basis which is spaced far enough apart to allow the surface soil to become dry. Water will percolate into lower soil levels and the young plant roots will follow after it. If the surface layer of soil is kept consistently moist after the two to four week plant establishment period, then the plant roots will remain shallow and can develop a long term dependency upon regular water. The temporary irrigation system can remain in use for one to two years and can be operated on a periodic basis during the warm seasons to help the young plants to survive. The intent is to use the supplemental water to increase the rate of seed germination and plant survival, with the assistance of minimum amounts of moisture. Each project situation should be considered independently to determine the appropriate quantity of water that is needed, and to gradually withdraw it as plants become self-sustaining.

In some project situations it is desirable to install a permanent irrigation system. This system would be operated in the same manner as a temporary system during the seed germination and plant establishment stages. The additional advantage it provides is to be able to provide water to meet special circumstances. Landscapes in fire hazard locations can be given sufficient moisture to keep plants viable and fire retardant. We also experience drought cycles, which are very stressful on many plants. Permanent irrigation systems can be regulated to help reduce this stress. Even with these uses in mind, it is necessary to properly assess the water needs of our landscapes and to develop an appropriate watering schedule. We should not simply plan to apply water without considering the seasonal variations and techniques needed to develop deep root systems in our plants.

Planting on slopes.

As development continues to expand into foothill locations, we are experiencing a large amount of slope planting situations. These slope areas have special needs and conditions which can be treated with landscape planting. However, from the start, it is important to understand that slopes must be engineered and constructed in a manner where they are fundamentally stable and durable. Planting can provide effective surface erosion control and add aesthetic character, but it cannot be relied upon to remedy basic structural problems caused by difficult soil types, or weaknesses in subgrade materials. Summarized below are several guidelines and considerations which help to establish an effective planting program for slope planting projects.

Cut and fill conditions:

The process of designing a successful landscape solution for slope areas begins with the physical slope surface itself. Wherever possible, slopes should be constructed with contoured shapes and have rough, irregular finish surfaces. By contouring the face of a slope, we will create differences in sun exposure and influence the drainage of moisture, which will support different types of plant growth. This approach can also soften the visual impact of slopes by creating shapes that fit into the surrounding land character. Rough and irregular surfaces provide niches which collect soil and moisture. On cut slopes in particular, we are often dealing with the subgrade soil conditions. When we cut into bedrock or consolidated subsoils, the cut slopes should consist of many small terraces to improve the conditions which support more vigorous plant growth. Fill slopes normally have a smooth finish surface and have been compacted to a uniform soil density. While fill slopes provide better conditions for planting, it is still recommended that the finish surface be rough enough to trap small amounts of water and nutrients to support plant growth.

Planting guidelines:

The planting program which is designed for slope areas should incorporate a variety of plants, be installed by seed and container, and be planned for both short and long-term effects. Quick growing plants, which offer good soil coverage, are necessary in any slope project. If effective plant coverage is not achieved, surface erosion can be caused by winter rains or heavy irrigation practices. However, in our effort to provide fast soil coverage, we should remember that these slopes are going to last for many years. We need to balance our plant palette to include slower growing, longer-lived plants, which will develop the landscape character in the years to come. From the standpoint of water consumption, we can select tree and shrub species which have deep rooting habits. Wide, spreading shrubs and mounding trees will eventually provide good surface coverage, stablize lower soil levels, and be less demanding of supplemental water. This approach to expand our plant choices provides other advantages. Different plants tolerate different site conditions and provide resistance to pests and diseases. When only one or two plant types are used, they are likely to

Above: Cut slopes which reveal subgrade soil conditions will support more vigorous plant growth if many small terraces are constructed.

Below: Plant diversity, as well as combined seed and container planting assures the best chances for soil coverage, short and long term landscape character.

Right: Slope planting achieved in a northern oak woodland landscape with California natives. Manzanita and Prostrate Coyote brush are the primary plant types.

Planting on slopes. (Continued)

perform poorly in some areas, or suffer greatly if they experience disease problems.

In addition to providing for plant diversity, it is also advisable to install slope plantings with both seed and container plant materials. Seed planting is most effective in establishing plants on difficult sites, as seedlings get their roots started in small cracks and can produce very quick growth. Most of the cover crops and ground cover plants are suited to seed planting techniques. To support the plants grown directly from seed, we should also consider planting small plants from containers. Since many plant types cannot be established by seed, the use of container grown plants insures that other desirable plants are used. These can be located in a manner which takes advantage of good site conditions and provides more control over the design character.

Supplemental irrigation:

The use of supplemental irrigation for slope plantings should be done with the intent of encouraging deep root development. For both seed and container plants it is necessary to establish a program of deep and infrequent watering as soon as possible. We have often achieved high levels of plant growth and quick soil coverage by applying ample amounts of water. However, in this process of providing a regular supply of moisture, we tend to encourage plants to become shallow rooted and more water needy. While this is an area of judgment, we should manage the application of water in a manner which encourages plants to send roots downward into the soil to seek moisture that collects in the lower soil levels.

Two guidelines can be recommended which lead to deep rooting habits in plants on slopes. The first consideration deals with the use of overhead spray systems. Water should be provided in many light applications instead of during one continuous time period. Water that is applied for 8 to 10 minute periods, with 30 to 60 minute intervals in between, increases percolation and reduces runoff. This schedule can be repeated many times in one day until the desired amount of water has been applied. After this process is completed, water should be withheld for enough days to allow the surface soil to become dry. By allowing the surface soils to become dry, we discourage surface root growth and cause plants to depend upon deep soil moisture. A second consideration to plant for, is the gravitational flow of water, from the tops of the slopes to the lower portions. Irrigation systems should be designed to provide separate coverage of the top and bottom areas. More water should be applied to the upper slope location, as these will dry more quickly when moisture percolates downhill. Lower slope sections can become oversaturated and weakened if the concentration of water is too great. The best method for achieving the appropriate balance and distribution of water is through field testing and observation. The time schedule can be adjusted to the seasonal weather conditions and to fit the needs of the plants.

Planting for fire safety.

California landscapes experience anywhere from 9,000 to 12,000 wildland fires each year. Fire has been an ever present force for many decades in our state and has played an important role in the evolution and adaptation of most native plants. It can be stated that fire provides a beneficial role in our natural landscapes, by cleaning and revitalizing aging vegetation. However, it is of much greater concern that we are losing property and lives as we push our developments further into high fire hazard areas. More and more we are faced with the need to make our communites fire safe while anticipating the recurrence of fires around us.

The most frequent fire safety problem we are experiencing today, occurs in our residential developments which are located in foothill plant environments. In both new and existing housing projects, we often encounter homes which are located in areas of dense natural vegetation. Much of this vegetation is highly valued, and sometimes retained close to our buildings, which has resulted in many devastating fires. These fires not only cost property and lives, but lead to potential flood and erosion problems. From various studies and documentation of such occurrences, several observations and guidelines have been derived which help to provide reasonable fire safety. It is generally concluded that this goal is difficult to achieve, as many other issues are involved, ranging from slope stabilization, water use, and aesthetics, to costs and maintenance. Based upon these considerations, a set of recommendations can be suggested.

Design:

Fire safety begins with total project design. While landscaping plays a major role in this situation, it is clear to see that architectural design and site planning provide keys to our success. Landscaping alone cannot solve our problems if we continue to construct buildings with wood roofs and projecting overhangs, or when we nestle buildings into canyons and slopes within dense plantings of natural vegetation.

Vegetation management zones:

The basic prerequisite in providing fire safety begins with isolating our structures from fire hazard conditions. This is largely achieved through modifying and managing a landscape buffer around our buildings. It is recognized that a minimum distance of 100-150 feet around structures should receive a comprehensive landscaping program. However, there are many environments and site conditions where even more modification is necessary and each situation must be evaluated individually. Within this buffer distance, at least four management zones and planting treatments can be established. These include: Zone 1 –Selective thinning of native vegetation; Zone 2 – Low volume, slow burning planting; Zone 3 – Fire retardant planting; Zone 4 – Domestic planting. It is the combination of these planting treatments which can produce the most successful solution from the standpoint of safety, cost, maintenance, and aesthetics. These zones are discussed on the following pages.

Above: Many developments occur in areas which are surrounded by attractive natural vegetation, but are highly susceptible to damage by wildland fire.

Above, below: Wildland fires of all scales lead to the destruction of property and loss of lives. Fires pose a direct threat, but winter rains and flooding can be as extensive in damage.

Planting for fire safety. (Continued)

Zone 1 – Selective thinning of native vegetation.

Starting with the undisturbed natural vegetation which surrounds a development, we begin the process of fire safety with the selective removal of any highly flammable plant species. This also includes removing large shrubby plants and dense groupings as a way to limit the overall foliage mass. We are attempting to reduce the fuel volume and lower the intensity of any fire that should approach our buildings. At the same time we do not want to expose too much soil area as to cause erosion problems. Hopefully, this thinning process will be done in a manner to create a natural appearance and not be done in a simple straight line technique. It will be necessary to keep abreast of returning plant growth every 3-5 years and to perform follow-up removal of high vegetation concentrations. The following lists of plants can provide us with suggestions for possible species to retain or remove.

High fire hazard species:

Adenostoma fasciculatum	Chamise
Adenostoma sparsifolium	Red Shanks
Artemisia californica	California Sagebrush
Eriogonum fasciculatum	Common Buckwheat
Salvia species	Sage

*Valuable watershed species:

Arctostphylos species	Manzanita
Ceanothus species	Wild Lilac
Comarostaphylis diversifolia	Summer Holly
Garrya species	Silk Tassel
Heteromeles arbutifolia	Toyon
Juglans species	Walnut
Rhamnus species	Buckthorn
Rhus species	Sumac
Quercus species	Oak

*These plants provide good slope and soil stabilization, wildlife habitat, and are not as flammable as the high fire hazard species. However, all of these plants should be thinned to reduce their foliage mass, and be retained in limited numbers to prevent high intensity fires.

Zone 2 – Low volume, slow burning planting.

Within an intermediate zone, between the native landscape and a housing project, we intensify our efforts to reduce the volume of vegetation and to replace it with low growing, slow burning plant species. This is the first area in which we actually provide planting and it frequently occurs on slope and disturbed areas, which resulted from grading practices. We are attempting to achieve a planting which consists of selected native and introduced plants which offer some natural character. Their low profile and limited foliage mass can diminish the rate and intensity of fires, as well as provide reasonable soil coverage.

This zone can be established by direct seeding or by installing plants from containers. Some supplemental water is needed to start this planting, but the proper species will be able to survive on their own after one to two seasons. Periodic maintenance is needed to remove invasive grasses and plants that become too large or crowded together. While several plants can be used in this landscape zone, it has been found that most will burn when exposed to intense fires. Any plant that is surviving without supplemental water will have very low moisture content in their leaves during the dry summer months. The effectiveness of this planting is achieved by slowing fires with plants that have little to burn. A mixture of plant types is a good idea, as site conditions vary and different species will survive better in different locations. Plants which are considered of value in low volume, slow burning landscape zone include:

Low fuel volume native plants:

Eriophyllum species	Yarrow
Eschscholzia californica	California Poppy
Lotus scoparius	Deerweed
Lupinus species	Annual Lupines
Mimulus species	Monkey Flower
Penstemon species	Penstemon
Salvia columbariae	Chia
Salvia sonomensis	Creeping Sage
Trichostema lanatum	Woolly Blue Curls
Zauschneria species	California Fuchsia

Low fuel volume introduced plants:

Artemisia caucasica	Silver
Atriplex glauca	Saltbush
Atriplex semibaccata	Creeping Saltbush
Cistus crispus	Rockrose
Cistus salviifolius	Sageleaf Rockrose
Santolina chamaecyparissus	Lavender Cotton
Santolina virens	Green Santolina

Planting for fire safety. (Continued)

Right: Foothill housing development in high fire hazard location.

Domestic planting buffer. Fully irrigated, low growing ground covers.

Avoid dense vegetation next to houses, particularly highly flammable plants.

Avoid using wood roofs and projecting overhangs.

Right: After a chaparral fire. Complete burning of native vegetation, minimal damage to structures and domestic plantings.

Domestic landscape buffer. Irrigated groundcover, no shrubs or trees.

Areas of native vegetation, burned. Will regrow and return to natural state in 3-5 years.

Planting for fire safety. (Continued)

Zone 3 – Fire retardant planting.

The third planting zone establishes the maximum fire prevention edge. The use of low groundcover plants which receive regular irrigation will be the best suited to stop any ground fire that could reach this area. The low foliage level, in combination with high moisture content, is the key to this planting. Nothing in this zone should be over 18 inches high and a regular program of watering and weed control is necessary. This planting is much more domestic in appearance, provides high soil stabilization, and can be developed to mix into parts of the natural vegetation. Depending upon the degree of fire risk, this planting can vary from 25-50 feet in width in order to achieve the appropriate level of safety. While there are some drought tolerant plants which can provide good fire safety in this zone, we should invest a little more water and maintenance to achieve the maximum fire barrier well away from our homes.

Low growing, high fire retarding plants:

Carpobrotus species	Sea Fig
Delosperma 'Alba'	White Trailing Ice Plant
Drosanthemum floribundum	Rosea Ice Plant
Lampranthus spectabilis	Trailing Ice Plant
Malephora crocea	Croceum Ice Plant

Low growing, moderate fire retarding plants:

Arctotheca calendula	Cape Weed
Baccharis pilularis	Prostrate Coyote Bush
Coprosma kirkii	Creeping Coprosma
Gazania rigens leucolaena	Trailing Gazania
Lippia canescens	Lippia
Myoporum parvifolium	Myoporum
Osteospermum fruticosum	African Daisy
Santolina species	Lavender Cotton
Trifolium fragiferum var. O'Connor's	O'Connor's Legume
Vinca species	Periwinkle

Zone 4 – Domestic planting.

The final planting zone occurs within the immediate property area of our residential yards. Wildland fires become very intense and often occur in conjunction with high seasonal winds. Sparks and burning debris can be blown over large distances and will catch new areas on fire. There have been several instances where houses located deep within a development, and away from the perimeter housing edge, have burned because their wood roofs or domestic plantings have caught fire from burning embers.

The planting which is located around buildings should be carefully placed and consist of species which do not readily catch fire. We often compromise our buffer treatment by creating heavily planted landscapes in our yards which are susceptible to fire during the dry season. In addition to avoiding plants that burn easily, we should limit the amount of tall trees and make efforts to thin foliage and dead branches from large plants next to our houses.

*Acceptable domestic plant species:

Arbutus unedo	Strawberry Tree
Arctostaphylos species	Manzanita
Ceratonia siliqua	Carob Tree
Cercis occidentalis	Western Redbud
Convolvulus cneorum	Bush Morning Glory
Feijoa sellowiana	Pineapple Guava
Metrosideros excelsus	New Zealand Christmas Tree
Myoporum species	Myoporum
Nerium oleander	Oleander
Pittosporum species	Pittosporum
Prunus species	Evergreen Cherry
Punica granatum	Pomegranate
Pyracantha species	Oak
Rhamnus alaternus	Italian Buckthorn
Ribes species	Currant, Gooseberry
Schinus terebinthifolius	Brazilian Pepper
Simmondsia chinensis	Jojoba
Tecomaria capensis	Cape Honeysuckle

Undesirable domestic plant species:

Acacia species	Acacia
Cedrus species	Cedar
Cupressus species	Cypress
Dodonaea viscosa	Hopseed Bush
Eucalyptus species	Eucalyptus
Juniperus species	Juniper
Pennisetum	Fountain Grass
Pinus species	Pine

*These plants are able to survive with limited supplemental water, as well as show moderate fire retardance. Other plants are suitable for domestic planting in high fire hazard areas, but require ample amounts of moisture for best performance.

III. Plant lists for landscape situations.

Presented on the following pages are a number of plant lists for landscape situations. A range of plant types which survive with limited moisture exist and provide us with choices of growth characteristics and survival strategies. In addition, when we encounter difficult site conditions, we can find several plant species which can meet our project needs.

Evergreen Plants.

Perhaps the most popular type of plant for dry landscape situations is the evergreen tree or shrub which requires little supplemental water while retaining good foliage character through the dry summer months. Many plants satisfy this demand, but they are in need of proper treatment suited to their lifestyle. These are plants which usually produce moderate levels of growth, primarily in early spring to mid-summer, and often have heavy, leathery leaves which aid in the conservation of moisture. They rely upon well developed root systems to acquire deep ground moisture during dry periods. When natural sources of moisture are low, these evergreen plants enter a period of rest and semi-dormancy and are quite content to survive without producing new foliage and flowers. Many of the plants that are found within our Chaparral plant community are drought enduring with evergreen foliage. There is also a large number of introduced plant species from similar mediterranean climate areas which show the same characteristics.

Drought enduring evergreen plants are best located in areas where good root development is possible. They prefer well draining soils and will achieve good drought resistance when planted as small sizes and given proper supplemental water. Planting should occur in late fall or early spring in conjunction with mild temperatures and seasonal rains. A regulated program of infrequent deep watering for the first 1-3 years will encourage deep root growth that is in balance with the foliage mass. As these plants mature, they should be able to achieve good independence from supplemental water and survive within the natural climate conditions.

This group of evergreen plants is sometimes harmed by traditional maintenance and watering practices. Excessive fertilizing and moisture through the summer and fall creates too much growth that cannot be supported when

Heteromeles arbutifolia, Toyon, is a good example of an evergreen drought enduring plant. It develops an extensive root system, has leathery foliage, and restricts its growth under dry soil conditions.

soil moisture becomes restricted. California native plants, in particular, are highly prone to pests and soil diseases that are associated with warm soils, excessive watering and extensive foliage growth. Supplemental water and fertilizers will help most when provided during the late winter and early spring in an attempt to compliment the winter rains. By early summer, it is not desirable to keep adding water in hopes of stimulating growth in these plants. They need a period of rest and their growth will naturally taper down as soil moisture conditions become restricted.

Acacia species (most)	Acacia
Arbutus species	Arbutus
Arctostaphylos species	Manzanita
Baccharis species	Coyote Brush
Callistemon species	Bottlebrush
Ceanothus species	Wild Lilac
Cedrus species	Cedar
Eucalyptus species	Eucalyptus
Garrya species	Silktassel
Grevillea species	Grevillea
Hakea species	Hakea
Hetermeles arbutifolia	Toyon
Leptospermum laevigatum	Australian Tea Tree
Leptospermum scoparium	New Zealand Tea Tree
Mahonia species	Mahonia
Melaleuca species	Paperbark
Nerium oleander	Oleander
Olea europaea	Olive
Pinus species	Pine
Pittosporum species	Pittosporum
Prunus species	Evergreen Cherry
Psidium species	Guava
Pyracantha species	Firethorn
Quercus species	Evergreen Oaks
Rhamnus species	Buckthorn
Rhus species	Sumac
Santolina species	Santolina
Schinus terebinthifolius	Brazilian Pepper
Simmondsia chinensis	Jojoba

Drought deciduous plants.

Plants that use the survival strategy of losing some of their foliage during periods of high drought stress are said to be "drought deciduous". Such plants use water freely when it is available, and attempt to lessen the pressures of drought by shedding their leaves when soil moisture is low. This adaptation is reflected to varying degrees by many plants, but it is highly distinctive among species which are native to scrub and desert plant communities. The drought deciduous plants coming from scrub plant groups, including species of the California Coastal Sage plant community, provide us with many choices for use in dry landscape situations. They are well adapted to harsh conditions, and offer good naturalizing, accent, and soil stabilization uses. These plants are fast growing, short-lived, and have shallow, fibrous root systems. They respond quickly to seasonal rains, or surface irrigation, and have a natural growing season from early winter to late spring. Planting is quite successful from untreated seed, if done in conjunction with the rain cycle. Supplemental water from temporary irrigation systems can improve plant establishment, particularly if the rains are infrequent or lower than normal. Supplemental water can also prolong the growing season and enable these plants to retain their foliage for longer periods of time. However, it is known that most species are stressed and prone to disease when given continuous watering. They do need a period of rest and dormancy during the dry season, and should not be encouraged into year-round growth.

The visual character of drought deciduous plants becomes an area of concern in many landscape situations. It is often found that these plants look most attractive from mid-winter to spring, and when in flower. By late summer, many of these species are sparse looking, and are not suited to highly visible areas in domestic gardens.

In addition to the visual considerations, we note that fire hazard becomes another area of concern. During the dry season, in conjunction with cycles of drought stress, the moisture content in most drought deciduous plants is quite low. These species will burn readily, producing a low intensity, fast moving fire. It is for this reason that they should not be massed around structures where damage could result. When planted on slopes and in natural areas, a fire will remove the older plants and enable new seedlings to germinate and revitalize the planting during the next two to three seasons. Listed below are various shrub types of drought deciduous plants which provide landscape uses.

Artemisia californica	California Sagebrush
Baccharis viminea	Mulefat
Cassia species	Senna
Cistus species	Rockrose
Eriogonum species	Buckwheat
Eriophyllum species	Yarrow
Isomeris arborea	Bladderpod
Lotus scoparius	Deerweed
Salvia species	Sage
Sambucus species	Elderberry

In addition to the drought deciduous scrub plants, other useful species are naturally adapted to desert environments, and also survive water stress by loosing their foliage. These plants are often found in desert washes and rely upon far reaching root systems to collect seasonal moisture. They have shown high adaptability to domestic landscapes, and respond to periodic deep applications of supplemental water. Plant types coming from desert environments include species listed below.

Acacia farnesiana	Sweet Acacia
Acacia greggi	Catclaw Acacia
Caesalpinia species	Bird-of-Paradise Bush
Calliandra californica	
Calliandra eriophylla	False Mesquite
Cercidium species	Palo Verde
Dalea spinosa	Smoke Tree
Encelia farinosa	Desert Encelia
Fouquieria splendens	Ocotillo
Parkinsonia aculeata	Jerusalem Thorn

Below: Salvia leucophylla, Purple Sage, is a good example of a drought deciduous plant. During the summer months, it sheds leaves and becomes noticeably sparse in appearance while it survives with limited moisture.

Summer drought deciduous stage.

Winter and spring foliage and flower character.

Moisture seeking plants.

All plants attempt to develop an optimum root system to acquire soil moisture and nutrients to sustain themselves. Some plants do this better than others and are sometimes not truly drought resistant. Listed below are several plant groups and species which frequently develop aggressive root systems from which they draw moisture from large volumes of soil area. The ability of aggressive plants to survive and take advantage of remote moisture sources often makes them quite useful in our landscapes, as they do become independent from supplemental water after they are established. The drought tolerance of such plants can be improved if infrequent deep watering is applied when they are young. Shallow watering is to be avoided as much as possible as it often draws roots up to the soil surface and causes these plants to become dependent upon regular surface irrigation. It should also be noted that many of these plants, particularly when they develop shallow spreading roots, can rob the upper soil of moisture and nutrients at the expense of other smaller plants located around them. Other problems occur when the root systems invade drain and sewer lines in search of moisture.

Plants with shallow or invasive roots:

Acacia baileyana	Bailey Acacia
Acacia longifolia	Sydney Golden Wattle
Acacia melanoxylon	Blackwood Acacia
Acacia saligna	Willow Acacia
Ailanthus altissima	Tree-of-Heaven
Alibzia species	Silk Tree
Casuarina species	Beefwood
Eucalyptus species	Eucalyptus
Grevillea robusta	Silk Oak
Myoporum laetum	Myoporum
Pittosporum undulatum	Victorian Box
Tamarix species	Tamarisk

A second listing of plants recognizes species which rely upon deep and far reaching root systems to survive in dry landscapes. These plants are not quite as troublesome as some of the aggressive plants identified above, but they do need optimum root development before they are considered to be drought tolerant. In most cases, these plants prefer deep soils and good drainage. They should be given deep and infrequent water in order to establish their roots.

Several California native plants are identified on this list. In natural environments, these plants rely on deep ground moisture and subsurface drainage areas as a source of supplemental water. These plants are often found in seemingly dry landscape areas, but are near underground moisture supplies and have developed root systems to obtain it.

Plants with deep root systems:

Bougainvillea species	Bougainvillea
Brachychiton species	
Cedrus species	Cedar
Ceratonia siliqua	Carob Tree
Cupressus glabra	Arizona Cypress
Eriobotrya species	Loquat
Feijoa sellowiana	Pineapple Guava
Olea europaea	Olive
Pistacia species	Pistachio
Pittosporum species	Pittosporum
Prunus species	Evergreen Cherry
Psidium species	Guava
Quercus species	Oak
Zelkova serrata	Sawleaf Zelkova
Zizyphus jujuba	Chinese Jujuba

Water needy plants.

If we look at water conserving landscapes from another standpoint, it is possible to identify many species of plants which are high water consumers. These plants are often appreciated for their quick growth and foliage and flower character. The idea is not to eliminate these plants altogether, but to more carefully group them to control their use. Every landscape can enjoy such water intensive plants, particularly around entries, patios and in shady locations. When these plants are concentrated together, it then becomes possible to provide the water, care, and soil amendments they require with more efficiency. Listed below are plant groups and species which rely on ample water for best performance.

Abutilon species	Flowering Maple
Acer species	Maple
Agrostis species	Bent Grass
Alnus species	Alder
Asparagus species	Ornamental Asparagus
Asplenium species	Ferns
Azara species	
Begonia species	Begonia
Betula species	Birch
Campanula species	Bellflower
Chamaedorea species	Palms
Dichondra micrantha	Dichondra
Ensente	
Equisetum hyemale	Horsetail
Erica	Heath
Festuca rubra	Creeping Red Fascue
Fraxinus species	Ash
Fuchsia species	Fuchsia
Gardenia species	Gardenia
Hydrangea species	Hydrangea
Liriope species	Lily Turf
Lolium species	Ryegrass
Musa species	Banana
Parthenocissus species	
Petunia hybrida	Common Garden Petunia
Pieris species	
Polystichum species	Ferns
Populus species	Popular, Cottonwood
Primula species	Primrose
Salix species	Willow
Skimmia species	
Soleirolia soleirolii	Baby's Tear
Syzygium species	
Veronica species	Speedwell
Zantedeschia species	Calla

Invasive plants.

Over the years we have made many efforts to solve difficult landscape problems through the use of a large variety of plants. In this process, we have had our successes, as well as our failures. While much can be credited to the use of introduced plants which are adapted to California landscapes, there is always the potential that some of these species will naturalize and escape into areas where they are not wanted. Even our own natives can be used without caution, and can become undesirable if they establish beyond our control and in areas not intended. Identified below are plants which have been used in dry landscape situations and have adapted so well that they not only survive, but grow beyond our liking.

Acacia baileyana	Bailey Acacia
Acacia decurrens	
Acacia melanoxylon	Blackwood Acacia
Achillea millefolium	Common Yarrow
Ailanthus altissima	Tree-of-Heaven
Albizia distachya	Plume Albizia
Atriplex semibaccata	Creeping Saltbush
Centranthus ruber	Red Valerian
Cortaderia jubata	
Cotoneaster lactea	Red Clusterberry
Cytisus monospessulanus	French Broom
Cutisus racemosus	Easter Broom
Cytisus scoparius	Scotch Broom
Lathyrus latifolius	Wild Sweet Pea
Lobularia maritima	Sweet Alyssum
Pennisetum setaceum	Fountain Grass
Robinia pseudoacacia	Black Honeylocust
Schinus terebinthifolius	Brazilian Pepper
Spartium junceum	Spanish Broom
Tamarix aphylla	Athel Tree
Ulex europaeus	Gorse

Spartium junceum, Spanish Broom, has naturalized extensively in the foothills of southern California.

Plants resistant to oak root fungus.

Oak root fungus *(Armilaria mellea)* is one of the most widespread plant diseases in California. It is native to areas throughout the state, where it survives in the soils of many plant environments. The popular name comes from the heavy damage it causes among our native oaks, but it also attacks many other woody plant species, native and introduced.

This fungus initially grows on the surfaces of plant roots, then moves into the bark. It will spread among plants which have their roots in contact, resulting in whole stands of plants becoming afflicted. In addition, this fungus remains alive in dead roots, which can be spread if dug up and scattered around. Diseased plants will become less vigorous in health and sometimes loose leaves or wilt in the process of dying.

Oak root fungus is most active in warm, wet soils. It can be controlled by maintianing dry conditions, particularly by limiting frequent summer watering. Under natural conditions, there is usually a lengthy dry season between seasonal rains which keeps this fungus in check. Plants which are attacked by this disease can be saved, if certain measures are taken in the early stages of development. Treating the afflicted parts with disinfectants, and exposing the soil around plant trunks for drying, are successful techniques. However, it is recommended that a plant specialist be called upon to diagnose the extent of the problem and prescribe the best corrective measures.

Listed below are plants which show good resistance to oak root fungus. Since these plants survive with limited water, they also help to restrict the activity of this disease by not needing frequent summer irrigation.

Acacia longifolia	Sydney Golden Wattle
Acacia verticillata	Star Acacia
Ailanthus altissima	Treee-of-Heaven
Brachychiton populneus	Bottle Tree
Ceratonia siliqua	Carob Tree
Cercis occidentalis	Western Redbud
Elaegnus angustifolia	Russian Olive
Juglans hindsii	California Black Walnut
Mahonia aquifolium	Oregon Grape
Mahonia nevinii	Nevin Mahonia
Melaleuca styphelioides	Black Tea Tree
Pinus canariensis	Canary Island Pine
Pinus radiata	Monterey Pine
Pinus torreyana	Torrey Pine
Pistacia chinensis	Chinese Pistache
Pittosporum rhomifolium	Queensland Pittosporum
Prunus caroliniana	Carolina Laurel Cherry
Prunus ilicifolia	Hollyleaf Cherry
Prunus lyonii	Catalina Cherry
Psidium littorale	Lemon Guava

Plants tolerant of alkaline and alkali soils.

Alkaline soils reflect conditions where the hydrogen-ion activity (pH rating) in a soil is greater than 6.5. These conditions are associated with soils that have been derived from materials such as limestone or calcium, and commonly occur in areas having poor drainage. A pH rating of 6.5. to 8.5 is generally classified as being alkaline. If the pH rating is higher, 8.5 to 14, then the soils are classified as alkali. Alkali soils result from an excess of exchangeable sodium, which makes soils impervious to water and harmful to most plant growth.

The only effective method for improving alkaline or alkali soils is by adding gypsum, or sulphur, and by improving the drainage conditions. These substances replace the exchangeable sodium, and lower the pH, while improved drainage enables the excess salts to be flushed away.

Plants tolerant of alkaline soils:

Agonis flexuosa	Peppermint Tree
Artemisia californica	California Sagebrush
Baccharis species	Coyote Brush
Callistemon species	Bottlebrush
Cassia artemisioides	Feathery Cassia
Cercidium floridum	Blue Palo Verde
Cistus corbariensis	White Rockrose
Cistus ladanifer	Crimson-Spot Rockrose
Cistus purpureus	Orchid Rockrose
Coprosma kirkii	Creeping Coprosma
Cupressus species	Cypress
Echium fastuosum	Pride of Madeira
Encelia species	Encelia
Eriobotrya species	Loquat
Eriogonum fasciculatum	Common Buckwheat
Eucalyptus camaldulensis	Red Gum
Eucalyptus cladocalyx	Sugar Gum
Eucalyptus globulus	Blue Gum
Eucalyptus leucoxylon	White Ironbark
Eucalyptus polyanthemos	Silver Dollar Gum
Eucalyptus rudis	Desert Gum
Eucalyptus torquata	Coral Gum
Feijoa sellowiana	Pineapple Guava
Hypericum species	St. Johnswort
Juniperus species	Juniper
Lantana species	Lantana
Laurus nobilis	Sweet Bay
Lavandula angustifolia	English Lavender
Leptospermum laevigatum	Australian Tea Tree
Lobularia species	Sweet Alyssum
Mahonia aquifolium	Oregon Grape
Melaleuca species	Paperbark
Nerium oleander	Oleander
Olea europaea	Olive
Parkinsonia aculeata	Jerusalem Thorn
Pennisetum species	Fountain Grass
Pinus halepensis	Aleppo Pine
Pittosporum species	Pittosporum
Plumbago capensis	Cape Plumbago
Prunus ilicifolia	Hollyleaf Cherry
Punica granatum	Pomegranate
Rhus integrifolia	Lemonade Berry
Salvia greggii	Autumn Sage
Salvia leucantha	Mexican Bush Sage
Schinus species	Pepper
Zizyphus jujuba	Chinese Jujube

Plants tolerant of alkali soils:

Acacia longifolia	Sydney Golden Wattle
Acacia melanoxylon	Blackwood Acacia
Atriplex species	Saltbush
Brachychiton populneus	Bottle Tree
Casuarina species	Beefwood
Dodonaea viscosa	Hopseed
Elaeagnus species	Elaeagnus
Leucophyllum frutescens	Texas Ranger
Melaleuca nesophila	Pink melaleuca
Myoporum laetum	Myoporum
Pittosprum crassifolium	Pottosporum
Pittosporum phillyraeoides	Willow Pittosporum
Tamarix aphylla	Tamarisk Tree

Plants tolerant of saline soils.

Saline soils contain soluable salts which can lead to chlorosis and reduced vigor in plant growth. One type of salinity occurs in coastal areas where the collection of salts has come from the ocean. Another type of saline soil is found in arid areas where water has carried dissolved salts and deposited them in valley and basin locations. This second soil condition often occurs in combination with alkalinity, which creates a very harmful situation for plants to grow in.

The only effective method to reduce the concentration of soluable salts in soil is to develop good drainage conditions. By improving drainage, water can be applied which flush the salts downward.

Atriplex species	Saltbush
Artemisia pycnocephala	Sandhill Sage
Callistemon rigidus	Stiff Bottlebrush
Casuarina species	Beefwood
Elaeagnus angustifolia	Russian Olive
Eucalyptus camaldulensis	Red Gum
Eucalyptus rudis	Desert Gum
Eucalyptus torquata	Coral Gum
Gazania species	Gazania
Lavatera assurgentiflora	Tree Mallow
Melaleuca nesophila	Pink Melaleuca
Metrosideros tomentosus	New Zealand Christmas Tree
Myoporum laetum	Myoporum
Myoporum parvifolium	Myoporum
Nerium oleander	Oleander
Pinus halepensis	Aleppo Pine
Pittosporum crassifolium	Pittosporum
Pittosporum phillyraeoides	Willow Pittosporum
Schinus terebinthifolius	Brazilian Pepper
Tamarix species	Tamarisk
Zizyphus jujuba	Chinese Jujube

Plants tolerant of fine textured (clay) soils.

Various areas in California have deposits of fine textured or clay type soils. These soils have ample amounts of nutrients, but have a tight particle structure which restricts the infiltration and percolation of water. They are difficult to wet, but once saturated, they hold water for long periods of time.

Many California native and introduced plants which tolerate drought, do not grow well in fine textured soils. They have adapted to more porous soil types which contain generous air space, and which loose their excess water quickly. These plants suffer from root rot and fungus diseases during the summer months when soils are both warm and wet. The addition of organic matter, and sometimes gypsum, will improve the aeration and drainage of clay soils. While the following plant list identified species which tolerate fine textured soils, it is always recommended that they be given the best possible drainage conditions.

Botanical Name	Common Name
Adenostoma sparsifolium	Red Shanks
Arbutus unedo	Strawberry Tree
Arctostaphylos edmundsii	Little Sur Manzanita
Arctostaphylos franciscana	
Arctostaphylos hookeri	Monterey Manzanita
Ceanothus gloriosus	Point Reyes Ceanothus
Ceanothus griseus	Carmel Ceanothus
Ceanothus griseus var. horizontalis	Carmel Creeper
Ceanothus 'Concha'	
Cedrus atlantica	Atlas Cedar
Comarostaphylis diversifolia	Summer Holly
Cotoneaster species	Cotoneaster
Cupressocyparis leylandii	Leyland Cypress
Cupressus forbesii	Tecate Cypress
Dendromecon ridida	Bush Poppy
Encelia californica	California Encelia
Eriobotrya japonica	Loquat
Eriogonum species	Buckwheat
Escallonia species	
Eucalyptus polyanthemos	Silver Dollar Gum
Eucalyptus sideroxylon	Red Ironbark
Garrya elliptica	Coast Silktassel
Heteromeles arbutifolia	Toyon
Hypericum species	St. Johnswort
Isomeris arborea	Bladderpod
Juniperus californica	California Juniper
Lagerstroemia indica	Crape Myrtle
Lavandula angustifolia	English Lavender
Lavatera assurgentiflora	Tree Mallow
Lithocarpus densiflorus	Tanbark Oak
Lupinus species	Lupine
Mahonia species	Mahonia
Melaleuca quinquenervia	Cajeput Tree
Mimulus species	Monkey Flower
Photinia serrulata	Coulter Pine
Pinus coulteri	Chinese Photinia
Pinus radiata	Monterey Pine
Pinus sabiniana	Digger Pine
Pinus torreyana	Torrey Pine
Prunus caroliniana	Carolina Laurel Cherry
Prunus ilicifolia	Hollyleaf Cherry
Prunus lusitanica	Portugal Laurel
Psidium littorale	Lemon Guava
Punica granatum	Pomegranate
Pyracantha species	Firethorn
Quercus chrysolepis	Canyon Live Oak
Quercus lobata	Valley Oak
Rhus species	Summac
Ribes viburnifolium	Evergreen Currant
Salvia clevelandii	Cleveland Sage
Salvia leucophylla	Purple Sage
Viguiera laciniata	San Diego Sunflower

Plants tolerant of salt spray.

A variety of conditions exist in coastal areas which place special demands upon plants. Soils vary widely and consist of wind-blown sand, to heavy soils comprised of sedimentary deposits. Soils which occur immediately adjacent to the shoreline are often saline in nature and lacking in organic matter. Drainage is good, but sandy soils are usually low in essential plant nutrients and have low water holding capacity. Plant species which grow along coastline areas also have to contend with frequent fog, high humidity, low sunlight intensity, and cooler temperatures. In addition, plants that are close to the ocean edge will experience periodic salt spray that can damage the foliage of most plants. The list below identifies plant species which tolerate salt spray, as well as other coastal conditions.

Botanical Name	Common Name
Acacia longifolia	Sydney Golden Wattle
Acacia melanoxylon	Blackwood Acacia
Acacia pycnantha	
Albizia lophantha	Plume Albizia
Arctostaphylos edmundsii	Little Sur Manzanita
Arctostaphylos uva-ursi	Bearberry
Artemisia pycnocephala	Sandhill Sage
Atriplex species	Saltbush
Baccharis pilularis	Dwarf Chaparral Broom
Caesalpinia gilliesii	Bird of Paradise Bush
Callistemon species	Bottlebrush
Cupressus goveniana	Gowen Cypress
Cupressus macrocarpa	Monterey Cypress
Elaeagnus pungens	Silverberry
Encelia californica	California Encelia
Eriogonum giganteum	St. Catherine's Lace
Escallonia species	
Eucalyptus lehmanni	Bushy Yate
Eucalyptus torquata	Coral Gum
Gazania species	Gazania
Grevillea banksii	
Grevillea thelemaniana	Hummingbird Bush
Hakea suaveolens	Sweet Hakea
Isomeris arborea	Bladderpod
Jasminum humile	Italian Jasmine
Juniperus conferta	Shore Juniper
Lavatera assurgentiflora	Tree Mallow
Leptospermum laevigatum	Australian Tea Tree
Melaleuca nesophila	Pink Melaleuca
Melaleuca styphelioides	Black Tea Tree
Metrosideros tomentosus	New Zealand Christmas Tree
Pinus pinea	Italian Stone Pine
Pinus radiata	Monterey Pine
Pinus torreyana	Torrey Pine
Pittosporum species	Pittosporum
Prunus lyonii	Catalina Cherry
Rhus integrifolia	Lemonade Berry
Schinus terebinthifolius	Brazilian Pepper
Tamarix species	Tamarisk

IV Plant Compendium.

Presented on the following pages are more than 360 plants. The majority of these are illustrated by color photographs and have been discussed with text. The intent is to enable the reader to identify and visualize a range of plant species which can survive with limited water. It is necessary to mention again that the successful growth of these plants is largely dependent upon their use in landscape situations to which they are adapted. Efforts should be made to associate such plants with specific regions or zones where they can perform under conditions of limited moisture. To this end, the Plant Selection Charts in Section I, as well as local sources, should be consulted for selection and use of these plants.

Botanical plant names.

A number of labels are used to identify the botanical names of plants. Several examples are developed below, which show the typical variations encountered in this book. Efforts have been made to identify and describe all plants with their current scientific names, as well as to include any other names by which they are recognized.

Full botanical name

Genus   Species

Arctostaphylos densiflora 'Howard McMinn'

Cultivar: Indicating a horticultural or cultivated variety which is propagated for desirable characteristics.

Genus   Species

Ceanothus griseus var. *horizontalis*

Variety: A variation in plant form or habit, foliage or flower characteristics.

Genus   Species   Common Name

Caesalpinia gilliesii.   Bird-of-Paradise Bush

(*Poinciana gilliesii*)

Synonym: Previous botanical name.

Acacia.

Australia, California

A diverse group of evergreen and deciduous shrubs and trees with many form and foliage variations. Most species are native to warm regions throughout the world, mainly Australia, and adapt well to temperate plant environments in California. Two dozen or so species are in common landscape use, with at least half of these showing good performance in dry and difficult landscapes. In addition to these, many other varieties are being experimented with and show a lot of promise for use with limited water.

Acacias are well known for their bright yellow flowers and are appreciated for their rapid growth and tolerance of many landscape conditions. They have been used with very good success throughout mild coastal and inland areas across California, from San Diego to Marin counties. The more cold tolerant species also adapt to interior valley and low desert regions. They prefer full sun, good drainage, restricted watering and protection from the prolonged cold. They accept heat, aridity, smog and most soils, with some plants becoming chlorotic under alkaline conditions. These plants are easily established from seed or containers and typically develop shallow spreading root systems.

Most Acacias are relatively short-lived, anywhere from 10-40 years. Lots of water given to young plants will produce amazing growth, but will often result in earlier deaths. Infrequent deep watering is advised in order to achieve deeper roots, increase drought tolerance and to moderate growth. Older plants tend to be brittle wooded, produce lots of litter and can become disfigured as branches of any size will periodically die. In addition, several species have naturalized in certain locations and pose difficult problems in native plant communities.

Despite the many considerations pertaining to Acacias, they are a very valuable and frequently used group of plants. They are members of the Leguminosae plant family and most species are valued for their contribution to soil improvement by fixing nitrogen with their root systems. Their size and aggressiveness makes them well suited for large spaces and quick effects. They can serve in both domestic and natural landscapes for screens, windbreaks, soil stabilizers and in mass background plantings. Most species respond well to pruning and can become striking accent and patio plants.

Name	Character	Remarks
A. baileyana Bailey Acacia	Medium sized tree, 20-30 ft. tall, developing a rounded crown 15-35 ft. wide. Finely divided grey-green foliage creates soft texture; very showy yellow flower balls occur Jan.-Mar. Variety A. b. 'Purpurea' offers striking blue-purple foliage and is quite popular. Both varieties also grow into many branched shrubs if not pruned.	Attractive shrub or tree well suited for accent, slope and background plantings. Good qualities when young, but can create much litter and build up dead branchlets as it ages. Pruning controls shape, reduces problems caused by brittle wood. A widely used species which has naturalized along the coast from Monterey to Marin counties. Plates 1, 2
A. cultriformis Knife Acacia	Rounded shrub to small tree with a height and width of 10-15 ft. Distinctive knife-like grey leaves are set closely on upright branches. Showy yellow flowers Jan.-Mar.	A good foliage and flowering accent plant useful for screens, slopes and background contrast plantings. Can be treated as a formal hedge; tolerates wind, aridity and most soils. Plates 3, 4
A. cyanophylla Blue-Leaf Wattle	Large shrub to small tree to 30 ft. high, 15-20 ft. wide. Long light blue leaves, 6-10 in. long, with heavy clusters of orange flower balls Mar.-April.	A graceful plant, usually having several trunks low to the ground, and long branches which droop with flowers. Good for screens, erosion control, banks, and individual specimens in small spaces.
A. cyclopis	Dense shrub, 10-15 ft. high, 15-20 ft. spread, with narrow dark green leaves to 3 in. long. Small clusters of yellow flower balls are not showy, occur in early spring and intermittently through summer.	Handsome shrub with rich billowy foliage and soft texture. Commonly used for slopes and highway plantings where it resists drought without supplemental water. Planted from container or untreated seed with a low germination rate between 10-15%. Plates 5, 6
A. decora Graceful Wattle	Small rounded shrub, 6-8 ft. high, with thin pointed leaves to 2 in. long, bluish-green. Groups of yellow flower balls are showy in spring.	A good drought tolerant species with light texture and well suited for smaller garden areas. Can be used for banks, background and foliage accent plantings. Plates 7, 18
A. decurrens Green Wattle	Open airy tree, 30-50 ft. high, with broad crown and spread to 50 ft. Finely divided leaves are dark green; showy clusters of yellow flowers occur mainly Feb.-Mar. and late summer.	A species which is longer lived and more cold tolerant than most other Acacias. Accepts low desert conditions, heat, aridity, drought and alkaline soils. Protect from wind and expect much litter. Good for large parks, background and slope plantings.
A. d. dealbata Silver Wattle	A. d. dealbata, Silver Wattle, is a variety with larger leaves, still finely divided, but are silvery green in appearance.	This variety offers a more intensive display of flowers in early spring and is more often used due to its rich foliage. Tolerates saline or alkaline soils, drought, heat, salt spray and coastal conditions. Protect from wind, expect inconsistent growing habits and litter. Plates 8, 9

Acacia. (Cont.)

Name	Character	Remarks
A. farnesiana Sweet Acacia	Deciduous large shrub to small tree, 15-20 ft. tall, with upward growing branches that are covered with 1 in. long thorns. Very finely divided leaves are dark green. Fragrant yellow flower balls are noticeable Jan.-June.	A shrubby species which works best as a background, barrier or slope plant unless lower branches are removed. Tolerates heat, drought and cold. Has naturalized throughout canyons of San Diego County and survives well in desert regions of the Southwest. Plates 10, 11
A. greggi Catclaw Acacia	Deciduous shrub to small open tree to 10 ft. high, with finely divided leaves and thorns on the branches. Rounded yellow flower balls occur late fall through winter.	This species is native to dry riparian areas of the Southwest which finds limited use in most domestic landscapes. A good accent plant in desert and rock gardens. Otherwise, can be used as a barrier and in background areas on slopes. Plate 12
A. longifolia (A. latifolia) Sydney Golden Wattle	Large dense shrub or tree to 20 ft. high and as wide. Medium green leaves ½ in. wide, 3-6 in. long create a coarse textured appearance. Very showy yellow flowers occur on long spikes from Feb.-Mar.	A very common slope shrub for erosion control. Fast growing, needs infrequent deep watering for best rooting. Easily planted from containers or seed, with 50-60% germination success. Tolerates all soils, including alkaline and sandy. Accepts wind, salt spray, heat and sun. Often used along highways, to stabilize beach soils, and for large screen plantings. Resistant to oak root fungus. Plates 13, 14
A. melanoxylon Blackwood Acacia	Tall upright tree, 30-50 ft. high, 20-30 ft. spread. Mature trunks have dark brown bark; leaves are deep green, 2-5 in. long. Pale white flowers are noticeable from Mar.-May.	Largest of the Acacias in use. Needs generous room and is best situated in parks, greenbelts and background areas. Very drought tolerant, but is messy and develops aggressive suckers from the base and shallow roots. Can be used for street trees with caution. Tolerates smog, coastal to interior conditions. Plate 15
A. pendula Weeping Myall	Slender tree to 20 ft. high, drooping branches and narrow grey-green leaves 3-4 in. long. Has an interesting weeping effect, develops fissured bark on the trunk and usually does not flower. One of the most attractive species for domestic gardens, but often quite hard to find in nurseries.	A slow growing plant which is naturally found in areas of ample moisture. However, it can survive with limited water and accepts many soil conditions, including clays and alkalinity. Grows well in coastal or inland environments and is often used as a small garden specimen or espalier. Soft texture, hanging branches and light foliage color make it a very good accent plant. Plate 16
A. podalyriifolia Pearl Acacia	Rounded tree to 25 ft. high and as broad, with open branching habit, and soft pointed grey leaves. Light yellow flower clusters are fragrant and showy from early November to March.	Good small tree which needs pruning. Use for lawn and patio specimens, and background groupings. Fast growing, but short lived. Prone to wind damage. Tolerates heat, aridity, drought and prefers inland conditions. Plates 17, 18
A. pycnantha Golden Wattle	Dense, mounding to upright shrub, 15-20 ft. high, with large curved yellow-green leaves to 4 in. long. Very heavy displays of bright yellow flower balls cover the plant Feb.-March.	A fast growing species which performs very well under coastal conditions, including salt air. Naturalizes in poor and shallow soils and is mainly used for windbreaks, screens and on slopes. Can be pruned into a tree form with age and is a striking accent when in bloom. Plate 19
A. redolens (A. ongerup)	Fast growing spreading shrub with light greyish green leaves. Showy sulphur yellow flowers cover some plants from Feb.-April. Grows 2-4 ft. high and spreads 12-15 ft. in 3-4 years.	A very prostrate Acacia which is becoming a favorite for dry highway plantings and exposed slope areas which receive very little water. Tolerates both coastal and inland conditions including heat, wind, smog and most soils. Provide plenty of room and periodically remove taller branches for best appearance. Plates 20, 21
A. saligna Willow Acacia	Broadly mounding shrub to small tree 15-20 ft. tall, 15-25 ft. spread. Rich, dark green leaves grow 6-8 in. long and hang from branches. Showy yellow flower balls occur from Feb.-May.	A fine textured graceful species which is suited for slopes, mass and background plantings. Needs lots of space. Grows fast from seed or containers, develops a weeping quality with age. Plates 22, 23
A. verticillata Star Acacia	Rounded shrub to 15 ft. high. Needle-like leaves are light to medium green and give the plant a fine textured and airy quality. Pale yellow flower spikes are noticeable Apr.-May.	A lightly scaled species which can be used for informal hedges, on banks, and in mixed plantings. Tolerates poor soils, including heavy and alkaline conditions, aridity and heat. Resistant to oak root fungus. Plates 24, 25

1 Acacia baileyana

2 Acacia baileyana 'Purpurea'

4 Acacia cultriformis
6 Acacia cyclopis

3 Acacia cultriformis
5 Acacia cyclopis

7 *Acacia decora* (See also Plate 18)

8 *Acacia decurrens dealbata*

10 *Acacia farnesiana*
11 *Acacia farnesiana*

9 *Acacia decurrens dealbata*
12 *Acacia greggi*

13 Acacia longifolia

14 Acacia longifolia

15 Acacia melanoxylon
17 Acacia podalyriifolia

16 Acacia pendula
18 Acacia podalyriifolia (Acacia decora, Lower left)

19 Acacia pycnantha

20 Acacia redolens

21 Acacia redolens

22 Acacia saligna

23 Acacia saligna

24 *Acacia verticillata*

25 *Acacia verticillata*

26 *Achillea filipendulina*

27 *Achillea clavennae*

28 *Achillea millefolium*

Achillea . Yarrow

Europe, Asia

Introduced perennial plants which grow well in full sun in all plant environments, from the coastal edge to interior valleys throughout California. Yarrows range in size from 6 inches to over 3 ft. tall, have divided grey or green leaves and usually produce large clusters of white or yellow flowers from spring to fall. White flowering species include: *A. clavennae*, Silver Yarrow; *A. millefolium*, Common Yarrow; and *A. ptarmica*. Yellow flowering species include: *A. filipendulina*, Fernleaf Yarrow; *A. tomentosa*, Woolly Yarrow; and *A. taygetea*. Several hybrids have now been produced from these species which also provide flower colors of gold, pink and red.

Yarrows are easily established from seed or rooted cuttings and show good drought tolerance once established. In warm inland and interior areas these plants need periodic water, but overwatering produces excessive foliage growth. They accept any type of soil and easily spread where additional moisture is provided. While the flowers are showy, they become quite unattractive as they die and will persist on the plants through winter. Cutting of old flower stalks prolongs the blooming period and reduces visual problems.

Yarrows work in domestic gardens for borders, mixed plantings and for cut flowers. Several species have become popular in seed mixes for soil stabilization, where germination rates of 60-80% are possible. Plates 26, 27, 28

Adenostoma sparsifolium . Red Shanks

Southern California

Large evergreen shrub or small tree, 6-20 ft. high, with soft linear leaves. Noticeable plumes of white flowers occur July-Aug. and turn to rust and brown colors as the seeds mature. Young bark is greenish, becoming red-brown and shredded on older branches.

Red Shanks is a California native which is found in intermittent locations in the chaparral foothills from Santa Barbara to San Diego counties. It has several pleasing characteristics, including fine texture, sculptural branching and interesting flowers and bark. It performs well in warm coastal and inland mountain areas within its natural range. It has proven to be good for slope stabilization when planted from small containers. Domestic landscape applications are mostly limited to background and accent uses in dry gardens. This plant is highly flammable during the summer season and mass plantings around structures should be avoided. Plate 29

Aesculus californica . California Buckeye

California

Deciduous shrub to mounding tree, 15-30 ft. high, with smooth white to grey bark on trunks and branches. Deep green leaves are palmately divided into 5-7 leaflets that have serrated edges. Flowers are fragrant and grouped into very showy cylindrical clusters, vary in color from white to pink, occur Apr.-June. Large pear shaped seed capsules mature in late summer and are noticeable after the leaves have dropped.

A highly attractive plant providing spectacular flowering and rich foliage and branch character. This species grows on dry foothills and canyon slopes of the Sierra Nevada and Coast Ranges, in the Chaparral and Foothill Woodland plant communities. It has a wide range of adaptability throughout California and prefers well draining sites and limited summer water. Easily grown from fresh seed or small containers. Leaves start to drop by mid-summer as moisture runs out. During this period it can look as if it is dying and is not too attractive.

California Buckeye is useful for slopes, naturalizing and accent plantings. It performs well in domestic landscapes and will retain its leaves longer if given some supplemental water. The seeds are sometimes used in dry arrangements, but should be treated with care as they are quite poisonous. Plates 30, 31

Agonis flexuosa . Peppermint Tree

Australia

Evergreen tree to 40 ft. high, 25 ft. wide, with rough red-brown bark on the trunks. Narrow leaves reach 6 in. long, are dull green with reddish cast, smell like peppermint when crushed, and droop from the branches. Noticeable, small white flowers occur in May and June.

Peppermint Tree is a good choice for fine texture and weeping effects within coastal and valley regions from San Diego to the San Francisco bay area. It prefers good drainage and soils on the dry side, but is very adaptable to clays and additional moisture. Accepts heat, wind, and aridity. It is sensitive to temperatures below 25° F. and is not highly drought tolerant until mature. Responds well to pruning and makes a good yard specimen, background plant, espalier and street tree. Plate 32

Ailanthus altissima . Tree-of-Heaven

North China

Deciduous tree developing quickly into a dome shape, 30-50 ft. high. Very long, medium green leaves, 12-30 in., are divided into 13-25 leaflets. Inconspicuous flowers in spring are followed by attractive clusters of red-bronze winged fruits through summer.

A very aggressive tree that grows well in all plant environments of California. Tolerant of heat, wind, smog and drought. Also grows in poor, saline or boggy soils. Often suckers from shallow roots, as well as reseeds. Should be used with caution, as extensive naturalization has produced many unwanted plants in both domestic and natural landscapes where it is virtually indestructable. However, it is a plant for very difficult urban areas and provides a rich and almost tropical appearance. Plate 33

29 Adenostoma sparsifolium

32 Agonis flexuosa

30 Aesculus californica
31 Aesculus californica

33 Ailanthus altissima

Albizia julibrissin . Silk Tree

Asia

Broadly spreading deciduous tree, with a low branching habit, 20-35 ft. high, 25-40 ft. spread. Light to medium green leaves are finely divided and feathery in appearance. Flowers are showy, pink to white, and look like round puff balls, occur late summer to fall. Many seed pods are developed and persist on these trees and are often unsightly.

A popular shade and accent tree which grows well in many environments, from coastal valleys to high and low deserts of California. Its best performance is achieved in inland and interior valleys where it responds well to heat, but it adapts to many climate and site extremes. Likes good drainage and full sun. Accepts cold, poor and alkaline soils. Naturally develops with several trunks, but can be shaped into a single trunk depending upon use. Has shallow roots, creates lots of litter and is well situated in ground cover and shrub areas. Plates 34, 35

A less commonly used species, *A. distachya* (also *A. lophantha*), Plume Albizia, is a semi-deciduous species from Australia, which has softer foliage that is dark green. Produces pale yellow flowers. Best used in mild coastal areas where it grows in sand, withstands drought and often naturalizes. It grows quickly to 25 ft. for fast screening effect, but loses good character at an early age.

34 Albizia julibrissin

Arbutus menziesii . Madrone

California Mixed Evergreen Woodland

Dense evergreen tree, 30-50 ft. high, developing from a rounded shrub into a tall dome with age. Trunks have distinctive red-brown bark that peels each year. Large leaves are dark glossy green above, lighter green below. Fragrant and showy white to pale pink flowers, occur Jan.-March.

Madrone is considered to be the most beautiful broadleaf evergreen native tree in California. It inhabits the Coast Ranges and Sierra Nevada foothills in well draining soils and on sites receiving over 24 inches minimum rainfall. It is often difficult to establish from containers, gets rootbound, and will not tolerate surface water or alkaline soils. Small container sizes are mostly available and provide the best chance for successful establishment. Recommended for coastal and inland mid-elevation areas from central to northern California, but it can be used in southern regions with protection from extreme heat and sun exposure and if given periodic deep water.

Madrone is well suited as a background accent or park tree, where long periods of time can enable it to reach good size. Natural leaf litter or shredded wood mulches can protect the tree within the dripline from soil compaction and to prevent the need for surface spray irrigation. In domestic landscapes it provides rich specimen character, with the flowers and fruit being of particular interest. Establishes best in areas of partial shade. Plates 36, 37, 38

Arbutus unedo . Strawberry Tree

Europe, Mediterranean Region

Evergreen shrub or tree, 10-25 ft. high, with equal spread. Dark green leathery leaves have red stems and serrated edges. Red-brown bark develops on trunks that twist and gnarl with age. Conspicuous, small white urn shaped flowers occur in groups from Oct.-Jan. Noticeable red to yellow round fruit matures from late fall to winter. Another variety, *A. u.* 'Compacta', grows slowly to 6 ft., and produces large amounts of flowers and fruit for rich ornamental character.

The Strawberry Tree is a good all around performer in dry regions of California. It prefers deep watering in the summer and withstands heat, aridity and smog. Accepts most soils, including clays and is resistant to oak root fungus. A plant for small patios, on slopes and for specimen uses where pruning can reveal bark and form characteristics. It is relatively slow growing and will take a number of years to grow to large sizes. A very handsome plant for many landscape situations. Plates 39, 40

35 Albizia julibrissin

36 Arbutus menziesii

37, 38 Arbutus menziesii (Above, Below)

39 Arbutus unedo

40 Arbutus unedo

Arctostaphylos . Manzanita

Western U.S.A.

The manzanitas have been a popular evergreen plant group for many years, in both natural and domestic landscapes. Some 50 species occur from North to Central America, with at least 38 varieties and forms native to California. They are particularly well known for their reddish-brown bark, interesting branch structure, and urn shaped flowers, which occur in late winter to early spring. Several species also produce interesting berries which persist for many months.

A lot of people have come to know this plant group to be hard to establish and difficult to grow as consistently as they would like. Achieving proper growing conditions of loose, well draining soils is critical, as is avoiding surface watering in the summer. Warm moist soils create fungus problems for most species, as do heavy and poorly draining soils.

Many domestic and cultivated varieties of manzanita have now been developed which have greater tolerance of garden conditions, including fertilizing, summer water and slightly heavy soils. Most of these varieties have been derived from natural plants that usually occur in central to northern plant communities. Such plants prefer the milder coastal conditions, but will perform well when given partial shade and periodic deep summer water if planted in inland areas. Other species are found throughout the drier and warmer foothills of California and offer only limited domestic use. These inland plants are best used in natural areas where they can survive on their own with little care.

Manzanitas are primarily propagated by cuttings and are most easily established from small container sizes to assure proper root development. Mulching around plants is very desirable to control weeds, retain soil moisture and to reduce the tendency to use spray irrigation. Planting in the later fall or early spring will usually result in good growth, as most species show relatively slow growing habits if not properly planted. Efforts to develop new and hardier varieties have resulted in many new flower and foliage characteristics which can be used in many landscape situations. However, the availability and information on the newer plant types is somewhat incomplete and untested. Several species work well as large scale ground covers or in mass plantings, but it is much easier to work with manzanitas on a more limited scale where time and care can be given to them. Shrub forms can be pruned as they mature to form small trees and to reveal interesting branch structure and bark color. Regardless of the many considerations surrounding these plants, they do provide us with some of the most hardy and picturesque plants for low water requiring gardens. The chart below organizes the major species and varieties which have landscape applications.

Name	Character	Remarks
A. densiflora Sonoma Manzanita Vine Hill Manzanita	Native to only one location in Sonoma County. Plants are rounded, 3-5 ft. high and have distinctive red-brown bark on crooked stems. Medium green leaves to 1 in. long are densely grouped and positioned at stiff upright angles from the stems. A. densiflora and its related varieties offer the largest number of flower clusters of almost all manzanitas, which makes them highly ornamental in character. Flowers are rosy-pink and cover the plant from Feb.-Mar.	This species is seldom used as it has become a very good parent to more improved and garden tolerant selections and hybrids. These selections have proven to be some of the best shrub plants for domestic landscapes, providing extensive flowering and handsome foliage characteristics.
A. d. 'Harmony'	A spreading shrub, 6-9 ft. high and 8-10 ft. wide. Dark green leaves to 1 inch; many pink flowers occur Mar.-Apr. The overall foliage character is dull green which contrasts nicely with dark red-brown bark. Becomes open with age.	This plant offers good form, flowers and wide tolerances for coastal and protected inland gardens. A good background, screen and seasonal accent plant.
A. d. 'Howard McMinn'	A densely mounding shrub, 5-7 ft. high, spreading 6-10 ft. across. Rich dark green leaves, ¾-1 in. produce a fine textured appearance. Plants are covered with many clusters of pale pink flowers from late winter into spring. Interesting branch structure and bark color can be revealed with pruning as these plants age.	A highly garden tolerant species which offers many domestic qualities for foliage, flowers and form. It is the most intensive flowering plant that adapts well to urban and natural gardens. Can be used for screens, specimen and mixed plantings. One of the best for coastal and inland gardens. Plates 42, 43
A. d. 'James West'	A smaller selection growing 3-4 ft. high and as wide, with small dark green leaves to 2 in. Produces a fine textured mat, with pink flowers growing at the tips of the stems during late winter and spring.	This is a less commonly found species which offers very pleasant qualities in small garden areas. Works well among rocks, on banks and as a ground cover in small areas.
A. d. 'Sentinel'	A tall and upright variety which reaches 6-8 ft. high with a 5-7 ft. spread. Medium green leaves are larger than other species, to 1½ in., downy in appearance, and more openly placed on the branches. Large rose-white colored flowers occur in winter.	A handsome specimen plant which provides rich foliage, flower and branch structure qualities. Can become a striking flowering accent as well as a background and slope plant. Plate 44

42 *Arctostaphylos densiflora* 'Howard McMinn'

43 *Arctostaphylos densiflora* 'Howard McMinn'

44 *Arctostaphylos densiflora* 'Sentinel'

45 *Arctostaphylos edmundsii*

46 *Arctostaphylos edmundsii*

Arctostaphylos. (Cont.)

Name	Character	Remarks
A. edmundsii Little Sur Manzanita	Native to Monterey County around Point Sur. Grows 2-3 ft. high, spreads 6-8 ft. across. Light green leaves have bronze cast when young, persistent red edges, pointed apex, and look whorled on the branches. Showy white flowers occur Jan.-Mar., followed by conspicuous light red berries.	Little Sur Manzanita is a very attractive ground cover that has produced several other varieties which appear more heat and drought tolerant than the popular A. uva-ursi species. These low growing plants show good tolerance of garden conditions in coastal regions. They can be planted with good success in inland areas if given partial shade and periodic deep water. As with other manzanitas, it is desirable to locate these plants in well draining soils, or on slopes. Avoid overhead spray irrigation. Plates 45, 46
A. e. 'Carmel Sur'	This is perhaps the fastest growing variety which reaches 9-10 in. high, 4-6 ft. across. Produces limited numbers of light rose flowers. Has attractive grey-green foliage and spreading branching habit.	This selection offers good foliage and soil coverage possibilities for small ground cover and garden areas. Stems will root when in contact with moist soil. Prefers coastal conditions, but does nicely in protected inland landscapes.
A. e. 'Danville'	Low ground cover from 12-15 in. high, spreading 4-5 ft. Branches are covered with many rounded deep green leaves which are tinged with bronze when new.	A subtle variation from the parent species, A. Edmundsii, which is appreciated for its colorful white flowers and many red berries.
A. e. 'Little Sur'	Very low dense mat form which grows moderately fast to 10 in. high and 5 ft. across. Shiny green leaves lie flat on branches; showy white flowers are followed by red berries in summer.	Almost identical to the parent species but lower in overall height and tighter in foliage growth. Will produce a very uniform profile and can be used for banks, rock gardens and in small ground cover areas in coastal or inland landscapes.
A. franciscana	Rounded shrub which grows slowly to 3 ft. high and 4-6 ft. across. Rich green foliage is sharply pointed and produces a medium textured appearance. Possibly an offspring from A. hookeri, which is a little larger, and produces similar light pink flowers in late winter.	A good species for more sun and drought in coastal and inland regions. It is valued for its tight foliage habit and evergreen character. Works well on slopes, along borders and in background plantings. Plates 47, 48
A. glandulosa Eastwood Manzanita	A widespread species with numerous subtle variations in its distribution from del Norte County to the inland mountains of southern California. A broad shrub up to 8 ft. high, with smooth, crooked and reddish branches.	This plant is usually identified by its grey-green leaves, 1½ in., which are covered with stiff hairs on both sides. It is not a garden species, but is suitable for naturalizing and planting in chaparral landscapes. It offers good wildlife value and will crownsprout after fires when it is burned.
A. glauca Bigberry Manzanita	A large upright growing shrub usually 8-12 ft. high and as wide. Short main trunks are covered with many branches that have red-brown bark. Leaves are chalky grey-green on both sides and occur on pale green branchlets. Numerous pale pink-white flowers come in early winter and are followed by large ½ in. diameter berries.	A common inland species which inhabits dry Coastal Sage and Chaparral plant communities throughout southern California. It is seldom used in domestic gardens, but can work well in background and slope plantings. Its main value is as a naturalizing and accent plant in rural landscapes. Plates 49, 50
A. hookeri Monterey Manzanita	A tall spreading ground cover or low shrub from Monterey, reaching 2-4 ft. high, spreading 4-6 ft. across. Upright, pointed leaves are bright green, ¾-1 in. long. It has distinct red stems, pale pink flowers from Feb.-Mar., and bright red fruit by summer. Main branches turn very dark red-brown to deep purple and have a twisting habit.	Monterey Manzanita is a fine textured plant which shows high tolerance of sun, wind, salt spray, and sandy soils. In inland areas, it prefers some protection from extreme heat and sun exposure. A reliable species which has produced two varieties for landscape use. Plates 51, 52
A. h. 'Monterey Carpet'	A lower growing and more compact form to 1 ft. high, 12 ft. wide. Produces small dark green leaves and delicate pink flowers.	A variety which prefers sandy soils and partial shade. It is suitable for small ground cover areas, along borders, and on banks.
A. h. 'Wayside'	A vigorous and mounding ground cover, 2-3 ft. high, up to 12 ft. wide. Similar flower, foliage and bark characteristics to the parent species.	A good spreading shrub for rock gardens and on banks. This variety tolerates both coastal and inland conditions, with a preference for well draining sites and periodic summer moisture in warm locations.

47 *Arctostaphylos franciscana*

48 *Arctostaphylos franciscana*

49 *Arctostaphylos glauca*

50 *Arctostaphylos glauca*

51 *Arctostaphylos hookeri*

52 *Arctostaphylos hookeri*

53 Arctostaphylos manzanita

54 Arctostaphylos manzanita

55 Arctostaphylos pumila
56 Arctostaphylos pumila

57 Arctostaphylos stanfordiana

Arctostaphylos. (Cont.)

Name	Character	Remarks
A. manzanita Common Manzanita	A large shrub growing 8-20 ft. high, with heavy branches and dark red-brown bark. Large leathery leaves to 1½ in. long, ¾ in. wide, tend to be pale green. Conspicuous white to pale pink flower clusters occur Feb.-April.	Common Manzanita inhabits the low foothills and outwash slopes of the North Coast Ranges and Sierra Nevadas throughout northern California. Its primary value is within its natural habitat, where it develops extensive stands on well draining soils and with little summer water. However, it has been periodically used in landscapes as far south as San Diego County, and eventually becomes a large specimen with tree-like proportions. In warm areas it prefers periodic deep water and is best maintained with natural leaf litter within its dripline. Another variety, A. m. 'Dr. Hurd', has similar light green leaves and white flowers, but is lower growing, to 15 feet. This plant shows greater tolerance of garden conditions and is more readily available from nurseries. Plates 53, 54
A. pumila Sandmat Manzanita Dune Manzanita	A medium sized mounding shrub, 2-4 ft. high, 3-6 ft. across. Distinctive light grey-green leaves are small, to ¾ in. long and ¼ in. wide; small clusters of white to light pink flowers are conspicuous from Feb.-May.	Sandmat Manzanita naturally inhabits the coastal edge and bluffs around Monterey Bay, and is often mixed with A. hookeri and Ceanothus rigidus. It shows good tolerance of sandy soils, salt spray and wind. It is suitable for rock gardens, bank plantings and its light foliage makes it a good accent and border plant. In warm inland environments, it needs well draining soils, periodic moisture and protection from extreme heat and sun. Plates 55, 56
A. stanfordiana Stanford Manzanita	An upright shrub, growing 4-8 ft. high, with clear deep green foliage and smooth reddish-brown bark. Leaves are large, 1-1¾ in. long and to 1 in. wide, and have a pointed apex. Rich pink flowers come in large clusters from Mar.-April and are followed by a few reddish berries.	Stanford Manzanita grows throughout northern California, in the foothills from the coast into the Sierra Nevadas. It is a very handsome and ornamental native which has been used in many landscapes over the years. It likes light soils, but shows good tolerance to ones that are heavy if planted on a sloping site. A smaller selection, A. s. 'Trinity Ruby', grows into a 4 foot mound and has deep pink-red flowers and smaller pointed leaves. This plant offers even greater ornamental flower qualities, but requires well draining soils and tolerates little disturbance. Both of these species are good slope, accent and naturalizing plants, but they show high sensitivity to improved garden conditions including frequent summer water. Plates 57, 58, 59

58, 59 Arctostaphylos stanfordiana 'Trinity Ruby'

Arctostaphylos. (Cont.)

Name	Character	Remarks
A. uva-ursi Bearberry Kinnikinnick	Low growing ground cover, 6-12 in. high, spreading up to 12 ft. across. Glossy green leaves are rounded at the apex and occur on small red branches. Noticeable white flowers come in early winter and are followed by red to pink berries.	Bearberry is native to the coastal edge from northern California to Alaska, in sandy soils and grassy plant communities. It is a very popular and successful shrub for banks and under trees throughout the Pacific Northwest. In inland environments, it needs protection from intense summer sun and wants periodic watering. It is slow to establish, but will eventually become a dense mat with the stems rooting in moist soils. Improved varieties offer greater drought tolerance in warmer landscapes. Plates 60, 61
A. u. 'Point Reyes'	A low growing shrub to 18 in. high, 3-5 ft. spread. Small leathery leaves are rounded and grow on red stems in a whorled manner. Small clusters of pink flowers are showy during the mid-winter.	This is a very handsome foliage and flowering plant which shows good tolerance for many growing conditions. It survives well in inland areas in full sun and can cover large areas of soil. Periodic summer moisture and well draining soils will help this plant to cover faster and remain healthy. It is good for banks, borders, in partial shade and has a preference for coastal conditions and loose soils. Plates 62, 63
A. u. 'Radiant'	A very low growing mat, 6-8 in. high, creeping 3-5 ft. across. Light to medium green leaves are rounded and more widely spaced on red stems than A. u. 'Point Reyes'. Light pink flowers are followed by showy red berries.	A selection coming from Oregon which offers very rich foliage character. Well suited to coastal gardens, but can be planted in protected inland areas when given some supplemental water. Shows moderate drought resistance and works nicely on small slopes, as an understory plant to tall trees, and in mixed native plantings.

Arctostaphylos selections – Additional horticultural cultivars

Name	Character	Remarks
A. 'Emerald Carpet'	A low growing shrub reaching 10-18 in. high, spreading 2-3 ft. across. Densely grouped leaves are deep glossy green, pointed and grow to ½ in. long. Small displays of pale pink flowers occur in mid-winter.	A hybrid, coming from A. uva-ursi and A. nummularia, which shows very good fungus and heat resistance. Luxuriant foliage and compact growth make this plant very suitable for banks, rock gardens and ground cover areas. Plate 64
A. 'Greensphere'	A tight and rounded ball shaped shrub, to 4 ft. high and as wide. Pointed leaves are medium green, to ¾ in. long, and align in rows along red stems. Whitish flowers are occasionally showy during late winter.	This is a very uniform and compact shrub which offers a pleasant formal appearance. It is a hybrid derived from A. edmundsii and shows good tolerance of garden conditions. Can be used along edges, in mixed plantings and in small groupings. Plate 65
A. 'Indian Hill'	Very low growing ground cover selection which reaches 6-10 in. high, and has medium green foliage. Leaves are oval and small, to ½ in., have a pointed apex which hooks downward. New foliage growth is bronze-red; many small clusters of light pink flowers are followed by ¼ in. dia. berries.	Another new selection which is showing good use for small banks and planting areas. It provides handsome foliage character, accepts conditions in coastal and inland landscapes. In hot locations it should be given protection from intense sun and periodic moisture.
A. 'Sea Spray'	A low growing gound cover having bright green foliage which is tinged bronze when new. Small pointed leaves have distinct mid-vein, light margins, and are arranged on the branches in a whorled manner. Small clusters of light pink flowers occur in spring.	A tight growing plant which reaches 10-15 in. high, spreads nicely over banks and along borders. Shows good tolerance of heat and limited moisture in coastal areas, prefers partial shade in inland locations.
A. 'Winterglow'	Prostrate ground cover, 10-15 in. high, providing good displays of white flowers in spring. Leaves are covered with fine hairs, have red margins, and turn coppery during the winter.	A recent introduction which is showing very good adaptability to warm environments. In inland areas it prefers some protection from full sun, tolerates heat and periodic summer moisture. Another choice for banks, borders and small ground cover areas.

60 *Arctostaphylos uva-ursi*

61 *Arctostaphylos uva-ursi*

62 *Arctostaphylos uva-ursi* 'Point Reyes'
64 *Arctostaphylos* 'Emerald Carpet'

63 *Arctostaphylos uva-ursi* 'Point Reyes'
65 *Arctostaphylos* 'Greensphere'

Artemisia. Sagebrush
Asia, Europe, U.S.A.

A diverse plant group found throughout the world, containing over 200 evergreen, deciduous and woody perennial species. Approximately 20 species are native to California and are commonly known for their grey-green leaves which are often highy aromatic. Three native species are most frequently used in dry landscapes and usually work best for naturalizing and revegetating disturbed areas within range of their natural environments. Other species have been introduced from various regions and are popular for garden use, with some showing good heat and drought tolerance. Such plants prefer loose and well draining soils and little, or no summer water. Due to the wide variety and extensive distribution of this plant group, additional research is needed to identify other useful species for various landscape applications.

Name	Character	Remarks
A. californica California Sagebrush	A bushy grey-green shrub, 3-6 ft. high, with a shallow fibrous root system. Finely divided leaves have a distinct sage-like fragrance, occur on thin, semi-woody stems and will be dropped under periods of high drought stress. Inconspicuous flowers occur July-Oct.	California Sagebrush is one of the most common and widely distributed members of the Coastal Sage plant community. Landscape use is restricted to slope planting, particularly road scars, and nuturalizing disturbed areas. Its foliage contains a high amount of oil and is highly flammable during the summer. Seeds require no treatment to germinate, but a low, 20-30% rate of establishment is usually achieved. Plates 66, 67
A. caucasica Silver Spreader	Low spreading shrub, 2-5 in. high and sometimes reaching 2 ft. across. Evergreen silvery-grey foliage is finely divided and accented in early summer by small yellow flowers.	An introduced species which shows very good sun, heat, and drought resistance. It grows in many plant environments from coastal edges to interior valleys and low deserts. Needs good drainage conditions and is best suited for rock gardens and small banks. With its low foliage profile, it resists fire well. However, it is not suited for large areas as interior portions of the plant will die out and give an overall spotty appearance. Plant from flats, 12-18 in. apart, and expect a relatively short life span ranging from 3-5 years. Plate 68
A. pycnocephala Coast Sagebrush	Low growing perennial shrub, 1-2 ft. high, spreading 3-4 ft. Handsome grey foliage, conspicuous pale yellow flower spikes occur Apr. July.	A member of the Coastal Strand plant community of northern California, where it survives without summer water and tolerates salt spray. This native species is often used in domestic gardens and is valued for its foliage color along borders and in cut arrangements. Requires little water after establishment and should not be pruned except for the removal of dead flower stalks. This plant has shown good success in many coastal and inland landscapes, where it survives on heavy clay, as well as coarse and sandy soils. In warm areas, it needs some protection from intense sun and requires periodic summer water. Becomes leggy with age and should be replaced every 2-3 years. It can also be used in seed mixes for planting coastal slopes for naturalizing effects. Plate 69
A. schmidtiana Angel's Hair	Small perennial shrub, 1-2 ft. high, to 15 in. wide. Silvery grey-green leaves have finely divided lobes. Small spikes with inconspicuous flowers occur in spring.	A good border and rock garden plant with attractive foliage character. Tolerates heat, sun, and drought in all plant environments. A lower growing variety, A. s. 'Silver Mound', reaches 12 in. high, spreads 1-3 ft. Leaves are quite similar to Dusty Miller (Centaurea). Good for small banks, provides fair fire resistance.
A. tridentata Big Basin Sagebrush	A many branched evergreen shrub, 5-15 ft. high and as wide. Trunks become furrowed with age, fragrant light grey-green leaves usually have three lobes on the tips. Inconspicuous flowers in late summer into early winter.	This plant is an extremely widespread shrub throughout the Great Basin area of North America. In California it also inhabits the edges of the Mojave and Colorado deserts on dry slopes and plains. It is most commonly used for naturalizing and slope planting on fill soils within areas of its normal distribution. However, it can become a very striking accent or specimen plant in sunny inland and desert gardens with its grey foliage and interesting branch structure. Should be planted in loose, well draining soils and needs no summer water after establishment. Plates 70, 71

66 Artemisia californica

67 Artemisia californica

68 Artemisia caucasica

69 Artemisia pycnocephala

70 Artemisia tridentata

71 Artemisia tridentata

Atriplex . Saltbush
Australia, California

Herbaceous ground covers and woody shrubs that include over 100 evergreen and deciduous species from many parts of the world. Most types of Saltbush have distinctive grey-green foliage and are valued for their tolerance of alkaline and saline soils, full sun exposure and drought. They have been grown quite successfully from the coastal edge to interior deserts throughout much of central to southern California. They are most frequently used for such utilitarian purposes as slope and soil stabilization, screening and revegetation of disturbed areas. The lower growing species are particularly valuable in foothill locations with high fire hazard conditions, due to their limited foliage volume and moderate fire resistance. Atriplex species can be established from seed or containers and will improve soil conditions by fixing nitrogen with their root systems. However, care should be exercised when using this plant group as they easily naturalize and can become overly invasive.

Name	Character	Remarks
A. canescens Four-Wing Saltbush Wingscale	A many branched evergreen shrub, 2-5 ft. high, 3-6 ft. wide, with narrow grey leaves. Conspicuous pale yellow flowers occur July-Aug. Seed clusters of 4 winglike fruits turn brown with age and are noticeable.	Four-Wing Saltbush is one of several Atriplex species which does very well under a variety of landscape conditions in warm and exposed areas, with poor soils and limited water. Its natural range extends from the Mojave Desert to the Salton Sea, but it is frequently used in many inland and interior areas for slope plantings, naturalizing, and informal or clipped hedges. Provides valuable food and shelter for wildlife and is fire resistant. Large scale plantings can be done with untreated seed, but germination success varies between 15-50%. Plates 72, 73
A. glauca	A low spreading shrub from Australia that reaches 5-10 in. high and spreads 8-12 ft. in dia. Grey-green leaves grow to ½ in., small white flowers on long spikes are inconspicuous. Typically develops deep roots that also spread beyond the foliage area.	A fast growing plant that shows very wide adaptability to coastal and inland plant environments. Accepts such conditions as clay or rocky soils, salt spray, saline water and summer drought. It is established by seed or container with good success. Limited water and pruning can keep plants dense and compact for higher visual appearance.
A. lentiformis Quail Brush	Densely branched shrub, 3-9 ft. high, 6-12 ft. wide with broad grey-green leaves. Conspicuous pale yellow flower balls cover the female plants in mid summer, followed by dense clusters of light brown seed bracts.	Quail Brush is native to alkaline places from Mojave and Colorado deserts to the San Joaquin and Salinas valleys of California. Easily planted from seed, it can be used for slope stabilization, mass plantings and naturalizing. This species is usually planted in interior regions and deserts, while its more attractive relative, A. l. breweri, is used more in southern coastal regions.
A. breweri Brewer Lenscale	Evergreen shrub to 8 ft. high and 10 ft. wide, densely branched with broad grey-green foliage. Large amounts of pale yellow-gold flowers and extensive seed clusters are conspicuous during the summer. This variety is a larger leaved and denser form of the desert species A. lentiformis. It naturally grows in saline and alkaline soils from the coastal edge to inland valleys of southern and central California.	Brewer Lenscale is highly adaptable to many areas and tolerates such conditions as salt spray, heat, aridity, drought, and marine clay soils. It is popular for seed planting, 50-60% germination rate, and provides good wildlife value and fair fire resistance. Recommended uses include screens, windbreaks, soil stabilization and mass plantings, where its lusher foliage makes it more attractive than most other Atriplex species. Plates 74, 75
A. nummularia	An introduced species from Australia which develops into a dense shrub, 6-9 ft. high and as wide. Rounded, grey-green foliage contrasts with conspicuous pale flowers and brown seed clusters in late summer.	Well adapted to southern coastal soils and exposures, this species has naturalized on the coastal bluffs throughout Los Angeles County. Planted either from seed or container, it is used for screening, mass planting and slope stabilization. It is another good performer on marine clay soils. Can be clipped into a hedge in domestic landscapes. Plate 76
A. semibaccata Creeping Saltbush Australian Saltbush	A low evergreen ground cover, reaching 1 ft. high and 1-5 ft. in spread. Small, simple grey-green leaves, insignificant flowers and small red fleshy seed bracts.	Creeping Saltbrush has been introduced from Australia, and has proven to be an easy to establish drought tolerant and fire resistant ground cover for both coastal and inland environments. It is adaptable to rocky, clay type or saline soils and is best used as a secondary species in slope stabilization and naturalization projects. Plants tend to have a short 2-3 year lifespan and will die back under periods of high drought stress. Care should be taken as this species easily naturalizes. Germination from seed can reach 60%. Plate 77

72 Atriplex canescens

73 Atriplex canescens

74 Atriplex lentiformis breweri

75 Atriplex lentiformis breweri

76 Atriplex nummularia

77 Atriplex semibaccata

Baccharis. Coyote Brush

California

A very useful group of evergreen shrubs and herbaceous perennials, with 9 species being found throughout California. Most species are of coastal origin where they inhabit the Coastal Strand, Coastal Sage and Grassland plant communities. They have shown remarkable adaptation to many environments, including inland and interior valleys and foothills, as long as supplemental summer moisture is provided. Such plants are appreciated for their rich green foliage, and tolerance of heat, heavy or light soils, and limited water needs. All species are dioecious, with the female plants usually not being preferred in ornamental landscapes due to their cottony seed clusters.

The prostrate forms of Coyote Brush are the most commonly used in domestic plantings. They are well suited to large ground cover areas and on slopes where their extensive root systems provide good soil stabilization. All varieties become dormant in late fall and will shed some leaves when under high drought stress. However, they will produce bright green foliage during the early spring months after the winter rains.

Name	Character	Remarks
B. pilularis Prostrate Coyote Brush Dwarf Chaparral Broom	Evergreen shrub, 12-30 in. high, with a spread of 6-12 ft. Simple, dark green leaves are rounded with a slightly toothed margin. These plants produce conspicuous yellow-green flowers from Sept.-Oct. which have a pleasant honey-like fragrance.	Prostrate Coyote Brush has proven to be a highly versatile and dependable native plant for ground cover use in both domestic and natural landscapes. Two improved varieties are also commonly grown: B. p. 'Twin Peaks' and B. p. 'Pigeon Point'. The Twin Peaks variety has a more compact appearance, grows lower to the ground, and has distinctly toothed leaves. Pigeon Point Baccharis has slightly larger and lighter green leaves and is considered to grow faster. These plants tolerate a wide range of soil conditions, from clays to rocky slopes, and need little or no summer water in coastal areas. When used in inland and interior valleys with full sun exposure, they should be given regular deep watering. In foothill locations, these low growing ground covers are appreciated for their moderate resistance to fire. Usually planted from flats at least 24-30 inches apart. It will take two full growing seasons for good coverage of the soil. Excellent for slopes, banks, and cascading over walls. A layer of dead stems will build up over time. Extensive mowing or pruning every 3-5 years improves the health and appearance of these plants. Plates 78, 79, 80
B. pilularis ssp. consanguinea Coyote Brush Chaparral Broom	A many branched evergreen shrub 6-10 ft. high. Simple toothed, glossy green leaves, conspicuous cottony white flower plumes on female plants Jan.-Mar.	Coyote Brush has become one of our best native species for slope planting and naturalizing throughout many areas of California. It naturally inhabits the Coastal Sage and Coastal Grassland plant environments from the southern to northern ends of the state. However, it is successfully used in inland areas and requires no summer water after establishment. Easily grown from seed with a 50-60% germination rate, it often develops into dense stands which can be thinned as required. Supplemental water for the first season increases both germination and plant establishment. Periodic summer water for plants in hot inland locations will also keep these plants more lush in appearance. Coyote Brush grows in both shallow and dry soils, as well as heavy, wet areas. Usually not a garden plant, but it can become a medium sized screen as it responds nicely to shearing. Plates 81, 82
B. viminea Mulefat	Erect willow-like shrub, 6-12 ft. high by 4-6 ft. wide. Open branching habit with long linear pale green leaves. Conspicuous white flower clusters occur Apr.-July.	Mulefat is willow-like plant that often gets established in disturbed areas and along intermittent stream courses in the Coastal Sage and Chaparral plant communites. It is very adaptable and airborne seeds have spread this plant throughout the state. There is little opportunity to use this species in domestic landscapes, as its main value lies in stabilizing fill slopes in natural environments. Easily established from seed with a germination rate up to 75%, or from containers or cuttings. Plate 83

78 Baccharis pilularis
79 Baccharis pilularis 'Twin Peaks'

80 Baccharis pilularis 'Twin Peaks'

81 Baccharis pilularis ssp. consanguinea

82 Baccharis Pilularis ssp. consanguinea
83 Baccharis viminea

Bougainvillea.

South America

A popular group of large evergreen shrubs or vines, offering rapid growth and intensive displays of flowers throughout the summer months. Plants are usually densely covered with medium green leaves and stems which have many long sharp thorns. Numerous garden varieties are available, providing a wide choice of flower colors, including scarlet, orange, pink and yellow. Within this range, different species offer either single or double flowers and/or variegated foliage combinations. *B. spectabilis* (also *B. brasiliensis*) is one of the most commonly recognized species, with its magenta-purple flowers. Bougainvilleas should not be considered true drought tolerant plants until well established. Plants respond best to good soil moisture and supplemental fertilizers during the spring growing season, but some drought stress by early summer will intensify the production of flowers. Established plants rely on extensive root systems to acquire available soil moisture. However, all varieties perform best in full sun and in warm locations, with a preference for the mild temperatures of the southern coastal zones of California. Many varieties will do well in inland and interior environments, including deserts, where the primary concern is for periods of prolonged cold spells. Both young and mature plants alike will die back to the ground with frost and from successive nights where temperatures fall below freezing, but regrowth is very rapid. These plants prefer a deep, well draining soil, even sand, and extreme care sould be taken not to disturb the root system when planting from containers or after establishment in the ground. Their fast and aggressive growth often needs support and frequent pruning, but they can be controlled and shaped for almost any purpose, including vines, cascading shrubs, and espaliers. Local sources should be consulted for varieties best suited to various project situations and conditions. Plates 84-88

Bougainvillea 'Rosenka'

Brachychiton.

(Sterculia)

A small group of trees coming from the dry regions of Australia. They provide rich green foliage and achieve good drought tolerance when planted in deep soil areas. Certain species offer striking flower clusters, but large brown seed pods from most varieties can cause maintenance problems. They are very well suited to interior valley and desert conditions, where they are often used for shade, street tree and park plantings. These trees are highly adaptable and have been used in landscapes throughout California for many years.

Name	Character	Remarks
B. acerifolius *(Sterculia acerifolia)* **Flame Tree**	A slow growing tree, eventually to 50 ft. high, with large, light green leaves that are deeply lobed. This species goes briefly deciduous just prior to its July-Aug. blooming season when spectacular clusters of light red to scarlet-red flowers can cover the tree. Large brown seed pods follow the flowers, which can become unsightly and eventually litter the ground. The flowering and fruiting habits tend to be inconsistent from one tree to the next.	The Flame Tree prefers deep soils for proper development of its tap root and for best drought resistance. It performs very well in inland and interior valley areas with extensive heat and full sun and where heavier soils naturally occur. Will tolerate colder areas where temperatures reach 25-30° F. Due to its slow growth, eventual large size and tendency to be messy, recommended uses include park, greenbelt, and open space plantings. However, it can become a striking accent, or street tree. Plates 90, 91
B. populneus *(Sterculia diversifolia)* **Bottle Tree**	An upright ellyptical tree to 40 ft. high, 20-30 ft. spread, with a smooth grey to green trunk that is swollen at the base. Small light green leaves have varying shapes and densely cover the branches. Small, inconspicuous white flowers occur in early summer, followed by clusters of large brown fruit pods.	An excellent tree which tolerates a wide range of environments, from low deserts to the immediate coast. Prefers the exposure conditions and deeper soils of inland and interior valleys, but it is used successfully in all warm areas. Trees are slow to moderate growing, sensitive to cold when young and litter the ground with their dried fruit pods. This species is a very consistent performer and can be used as street trees, yard and park trees. Much of the appreciation of the Bottle Tree is due to the shimmering bright green foliage which adds a pleasant feeling in dry landscapes. Plate 89

84 *Bougainvillea* 'Hawaii'

85 *Bougainvillea* 'Barbara Karst'

88 *Bougainvillea brasiliensis*

86 *Bougainvillea* 'James Walker'

87 *Bougainvillea* 'Orange King'

90 *Brachychiton acerifolius*
91 *Brachychiton acerifolius*

89 *Brachychiton populneus*

Caesalpinia gilliesii . Bird-of-Paradise Bush

(*Poinciana gilliesii*)

South America

A lightly foliaged shrub to small tree, 6-10 ft. high, with finely divided leaves and an open branching habit. Large terminal clusters of yellow and red flowers occur throughout the summer.

An unusual plant that is appreciated for its showy display of flowers and interesting form. It is evergreen in warm coastal and inland areas, partly deciduous after cold winters in other locations. Prefers full sun and well draining slightly acid soils throughout many of the southern areas of California. Tolerates heat and some drought, and likes periodic deep watering. Selective pruning can shape this plant into an interesting accent or specimen element. Plate 92

Caesalpinia pulcherrima (also *Poinciana pulcherrima*), Red Bird of Paradise Bush, has similar form and foliage character. It produces spectacular red flowers at the tips of branches. It is well adapted to inland and desert environments, where it accepts heat and sun. It also prefers some water during the blooming season.

92 Caesapinia gilliesii

Calliandra .

Southwestern U.S.A., Baja California, South America

A large group of plants, including over 200 species, which come mainly from warm parts of Baja California through South America. These plants are recognized by their pink to red flower balls which consist largely of stamen. Several species are used in dry landscapes and show wide tolerance of drought and difficult site conditions. However, the majority of these plants need mild temperatures, ample moisture and enjoy enriched soil conditions.

The low water requiring species are adapted to desert and mesa conditions and work well in inland and interior environments throughout the southern part of California. They prefer rocky or well draining soils, and can survive with limited supplemental water in the hottest areas. Most plants become sparse looking by late fall, but will quickly respond to the winter rains with new growth. Puff-ball flowers provide very showy displays from late winter into spring, then intermittently all year.

Name	Character	Remarks
C. californica	A small shrub, 2-5 ft. high and as wide, with a stiff branching habit. Medium green leaves are divided into 9-11 leaflets and are shed under high drought stress. Showy red flowers accent the plant throughout the late summer to early fall.	A relatively unknown Calliandra which offers good use in rock gardens, on banks and in mixed plantings. It is native to northern Mexico and is quite tolerant of drought conditions within low desert and dry landscapes throughout southern California. Accepts full sun, heat and aridity. Tends to get sparse and leggy by early winter and provides the highest value when in bloom. In overall appearance this species resembles *C. eriophylla*, but has richer foliage and flower characteristics. Plates 93, 94
C. eriophylla False Mesquite Fairy Duster	A semi-deciduous shrub, growing 1-3 ft. high, spreading 2-4 ft. Feathery leaves are twice divided and occur on stiff grey branches. Leaves are shed under high drought stress, but will be kept all year with regular moisture. Showy clusters of light to deep pink flowers last 2-3 weeks during March and May.	A hardy plant, native to hot and arid areas from San Diego and Imperial counties to Texas and south into Mexico. Very tolerant of desert and inland foothill conditions where it thrives on infrequent deep watering. Uses include borders, banks and in small mass plantings as a flowering accent. Plants do become noticeably sparse in foliage when in need of water. Plates 95, 96
C. tweedii (*C. guildingii*) Trinidad Flame Bush	Mounding to upright shrub, 8-12 ft. high, with light textured, finely divided leaves. Showy scarlet-red flower clusters occur mainly in early spring and fall, intermittently inbetween.	A plant from South America that is nicely suited to warm coastal gardens, as it needs protection from cold when young. Tolerates a wide range of soils, and prefers full sun and heat, as well as humidity. Becomes drought tolerant with age, but should receive deep watering in inland locations. Can be easily shaped into a screen next to a wall or fence, or as a specimen or background plant. Very much liked for its showy flowers with fine texture appearance. Plates 97, 98

93 Calliandra californica

94 Calliandra californica

95 Calliandra eriophylla

96 Calliandra eriophylla

97 Calliandra tweedii

98 Calliandra tweedii

Callistemon. Bottlebrush

Australia

A hardy group of evergreen shrubs and trees offering many uses in dry landscape situations. These plants are known mainly for their red flower spikes and long, linear leaves. Most species grow well in full sun and adapt to all plant environments, from coastal bluffs and valleys, to inland and interior valleys and foothills throughout California. Not particular as to soils and accept clay conditions, as well as small amounts of alkalinity and salinity. Tolerate temperatures to 20°F. Drought resistance improves with age as young plants prefer regular moisture and well draining conditions.

They are often used on slopes, along highways and are highly valued as flowering accents. Most plants will naturally develop into mounding shrubs, but several can be pruned into small scale garden and street trees.

A good selection of species and improved varieties of Callistemon, offering plant forms from compact shrubs to small trees, is currently available to work with. New species are also being introduced, which indicates potential for expansion of this plant group.

Name	Character	Remarks
C. citrinus (C. lanceolatus) Lemon Bottlebrush	Evergreen rounded shrub, to 12 ft. tall, or small dome tree, 15-25 ft. high. Long green leaves are tinged with bronze when young. Very showy red flowers in 6 in. brushes occur at intervals all year. Selected varieties provide different plant sizes, flower colors and branching habits.	Lemon Bottlebrush is one of the most versatile performers, tolerating many difficult conditions, ranging from poor soils to cold temperatures. Prefers full sun and periodic deep moisture and is very accepting of heat, smog, wind and aridity. Tolerates alkaline and saline soils, but will show signs of chlorosis. Shrub forms are highly suited for slopes, mass and roadside plantings, or can be espaliered. Tree forms need careful staking to develop trunk caliper and can work well as a small street tree or patio accent specimen. Several varieties have been developed from this species which offer variations in plant forms and flower sizes. Plates 99, 100
C. pallidus	A dense evergreen shrub to 14 ft. tall, 8-12 ft. wide. The foliage and growth habit is very similar to C. citrinus. This species differs as it offers numerous pale yellow flower spikes which cover the plant through the summer.	A relatively unknown bottlebrush which shows the same adaptability and hardiness as the red flowering species. It can be trimmed into a small tree or hedge or can be used in background and slope plantings. It requires only periodic deep watering for best appearance. Plate 103
C. phoeniceus Fiery Bottlebrush	Medium size shrub, 5-8 ft. high, 5-10 ft. wide, with dense foliage character. Linear leaves grow 3-5 in. long, are dull green, stiff and pointed. Intense clusters of bright red flowers reach 4 in. long, occur in spring and intermittently through summer. A lower growing variety, C. p. 'Prostratus' reaches 4-6 ft. high. Branches cascade irregularly along the ground to form plants 6-8 ft. wide.	Fiery Bottlebrush is similar to C. citrinus, but develops stiffer foliage appearance. It is well suited for slopes and background areas where it provides good screening and flowering accent qualities. Accepts full sun, heat and wind. Prefers well draining soils and periodic deep water during the summer. The ground cover form, C. p. 'Prostratus', is useful on banks and along roadsides. Periodic clipping will keep this variety low and more dense.
C. rigidus Stiff Bottlebrush	Sparse evergreen shrub to 10 ft., or small dome tree to 18 ft. tall. Small, grey-green leaves are narrow and pointed, giving the plant an overall stiff appearance. Red flower clusters are showy and occur primarily in spring and summer.	Stiff Bottlebrush accepts the same difficult conditions as C. citrinus, but has a lower visual appearance. This restricts its use to background and slope plantings where it is quite drought tolerant. Plates 101, 102
C. viminalis Weeping Bottlebrush	Large shrub, to small tree, 15-30 ft. tall, 10-15 ft. spread. Narrow leaves to 3 in. long occur on weeping branches. Showy red flower spikes to 6 in. long hang from the ends of the stems from May-July, and intermittently all year.	This species is not as drought tolerant as other bottlebrushes until well established. It accepts ample water when young and produces very fast growth. It does tolerate more cold and grows well in poor or clay type soils. Accepts lots of heat, but is damaged by strong winds and needs periodic pruning to maintain a good visual appearance. Several varieties are available which offer dwarf and compact foliage forms. A good street or lawn tree, as well as a weeping and flowering accent. Plate 104

99 Callistemon citrinus

100 Callistemon citrinus

101 Callistemon rigidus

102 Callistemon rigidus

104 Callistemon viminalis

103 Callistemon pallidus

65

Cassia . Senna

Asia, Australia, South America

A diverse group of evergreen or deciduous shrubs and small trees, native to many tropical areas of the world. Commonly known for their divided leaves and bold yellow flowers which come in spring, as well as occur intermittently all year. These plants will also produce many clusters of brown seed pods which become unsightly and can be removed with light pruning. All species need full sun, good drainage conditions, and some protection from cold.

One shrub species in particular, C. artemisioides, is in common landscape use and shows good resistance to drought. Most other species which are on the market prefer regular deep moisture for best performance. However, there are many lesser known types of Cassia coming from dry regions which show good promise in our landscapes and should be given greater attention.

Name	Character	Remarks
C. artemisioides Feathery Cassia	Airy, evergreen shrub, forming an upright mound 3-5 ft. high. Feathery grey-green leaves are divided into 6-8 needle-like leaflets. Showy sulphur yellow flowers occur Jan.-Apr.	A small scale garden plant for inland, interior and desert gardens which tolerates full sun, heat, aridity, and wind. Prefers coarse soils with periodic deep watering to prevent foliage loss under high drought stress. Feathery Cassia is a delicate plant that works well in small places where it can be valued as a foliage and flowering accent element. Light pruning after flowering increases plant density and removes seed pods which can become unsightly as they turn brown. Under the right conditions, these seeds will germinate and form small masses of plants. While it grows quite rapidly, it often becomes too open and leggy for long use in many landscape situations. Plates 105, 106
C. wislizeni Shrubby Senna	Rounded shrub, 3-5 ft. high, with a stiff and upright branching habit. Foliage is divided and will be shed during times of drought stress.	This species is native to Mexico and the dry mesas of southwest U.S.A. It shows good adaptability to many dry environments in California, but often has a sparse looking character unless given periodic moisture. Profuse displays of yellow flowers occur from June to October. It is a good slope, background and summer accent plant. Plate 107

Casuarina . Beefwood, She-Oak

Australia

Evergreen trees with needle-like branchlets and having a distinct pine-like appearance. Most species come from Australia and are very well suited to extreme environments, from the immediate coastal edge to stressful high and low desert regions. They tolerate wind, salt spray, sandy and alkaline soils, heat and aridity. These plants become very drought resistant, but usually depend upon shallow and aggressive roots to find moisture sources. Periodically shaping and removing dead wood will result in more handsome plants. Flowers are not noticeable. Female plants produce a small woody seed cone.

Name	Character	Remarks
C. cunninghamiana Australian Pine River She-Oak	A large tree, quickly growing 50-70 ft., with a 25 ft. spread. Dark green branchlets produce a pine-like quality that is airy and fine textured.	Australian Pine is the most vigorous and hardiest member of the beefwood group. It is often used for street trees, in regional parks and background plantings. An excellent performer in desert regions, where it survives well with deep and infrequent watering.
C. equisetifolia Horsetail Tree	Large, fine textured tree, growing narrow and upright to 50 ft. high. Long, soft needle-like branchlets produce an open and soft effect. Flowers and fruit are inconspicuous, roots tend to be shallow.	Horsetail Tree is a highly adaptable plant. It tolerates most environments, from the coastal edge to interior valleys and deserts. It is a good performer in both alkaline and saline soils and accepts salt spray. It can be used to stabilize shoreline and desert sand. Provides service as a windbreak or to revegetate disturbed areas. It will develop shallow roots and is best planted in ground cover areas where its large volume of litter can be absorbed. Plate 108
C. stricta She-Oak	An upright tree to 25 ft. high, with long slender branches which are densely covered with dark green branchlets. Tends to be shallow rooted and produces insignificant flowers and fruit.	A fine textured tree with many of the tolerances as C. equisetifolia. This species has proven to be a good street tree and provides useful functions in park and median landscapes. It becomes drought tolerant with age, but always prefers periodic deep watering. Plate 109

105 Cassia artemisioides

106 Cassia artemisioides

108 Casuarina equisetifolia

107 Cassia wislizeni
109 Casuarina stricta

Ceanothus. Wild Lilac
North America

One of the most popular groups of western natives that provide us with ground covers, shrubs and small trees for various coastal and inland landscape situations. Some 60 native species exist in North America, with a large majority occurring along the Pacific Coast. Approximately 40 species are native to California, with many selected varieties also developed. In nature, as well as in garden situations most species hybridize freely and continue to create variations in plant characteristics when new seedlings germinate.

The Wild Lilacs present a complex set of considerations and opportunities for landscape use. Because of their popularity, a lot of study and propagation development has been carried out which gives us some guidelines as to their use.

Considerations: Many Wild Lilacs prefer coastal slopes and protected foothill situations where reduced summer heat and sun exposure exist. As an underlying growing condition, Ceanothus greatly prefer coarse, well draining soils. In addition, while many wildland species are attractive and popular for domestic landscapes, they tend not to tolerate summer water as they are very prone to root rot and soil fungus diseases. Over the years, many horticultural and selected seedling forms have been developed which show greater adaptability to nursery propagation techniques and garden conditions. Some of these selected forms will tolerate heavier soils, including clays, if special attention to watering is provided. There continue to be new introductions of varieties which make it difficult to keep abreast of the best plant choices.

Most species are fast growing, particularly when planted from small container sizes, and develop into good flowering accent specimens of all sizes and forms. As a plant group, Ceanothus tend to be short-lived, anywhere from 8-15 years. It is also observed that for the first 3-5 years these plants seem to thrive on summer water, but this practice often leads to overgrowth, disease and earlier deaths. Supplemental water should be carefully controlled soon after the plants are established.

Opportunities: A wide range of choices exist among the Wild Lilacs which can suit a variety of domestic and natural landscape needs. Flower colors include white, pale blue, deep blue, purple and rose. Once established, most plants require little care and are relatively pest free. Most species respond well to pruning, not shearing, which should be done after the blooming cycle. Their fast growth rate makes them well suited for quick effects and soil coverage. These plants also provide an important role in soil development through the fixing of nitrogen with their root systems.

Recommendations: First consideration should be given to selecting Ceanothus species which are best suited to either coastal or inland conditions. Areas with well draining soils is the next requirement to look for. From this point, it is necessary to determine the extent of the garden or natural site conditions which the plants will be placed in. Many selected varieties and hybrids tend to offer better performance, as well as tolerance of domestic garden conditions. All plants seem to work well in areas removed from heavy watering and fertilizing. Avoid overhead spray and frequent surface watering in the summer. Plants often work best in perimeter areas, on slopes and as background masses, with a natural leaf litter ground cover within their drip line. However there are many opportunities to introduce species as accent and specimen plants. Due to their fast growth rate, it is usually advisable to do limited pruning and shaping during their first 2-3 years. Further removal of branches as plants mature often reveals interesting branching habits. Propagation by cuttings and planting of small container sizes, usually achieves the best plant growth and adaptation to difficult site conditions. Wherever possible, locate Ceanothus on slopes and banks when clay type soil conditions are encountered.

While a lot of considerations are in order for the use of Wild Lilacs, it can be said that there are many reliable species and very satisfying results can be achieved with them. The following chart summarizes a number of successful species for varying landscape uses. Probably the best way to make a selection is to review this chart with local nurseries for plants which do best in specific locations.

110 *Ceanothus arboreus*

Name	Character	Remarks
C. arboreus Feltleaf Ceanothus	The largest species of Ceanothus, which grows to 25 ft. as a shrub or small tree. Leaves are large, 2-3 in., dark green above, white below, and papery in feel. Pale blue to white flowers occur in large clusters Mar.-May.	Found only on the coastal islands off California, this species has long been used in landscapes and shows very good garden tolerance. Prefers coastal influence, but will do well inland in valleys and foothills if planted on well draining soils and with partial shade. Good for background screens, slopes, patio specimen. C. a. 'Owlswood Blue' is similar, but with larger clusters of richer blue flowers. Plates 110, 111
C. crassifolius Hoary-Leaf Ceanothus	Stiff, mounding shrub, 5-12 ft. high, having small leathery foliage. Individual leaves are toothed, dark green above, white below. Numerous clusters of white flowers occur in early spring and make this species a strong accent in the native landscape.	Hoary-Leaf Ceanothus is found throughout the Chaparral plant community of southern California. Its primary value is for soil stabilization, nitrogen fixing and wildlife habitats in natural areas. Shows fair garden tolerance, but is not highly attractive and is best placed in background areas. Plate 112

112 *Ceanothus crassifolius*

111 *Ceanothus arboreus* 'Owlswood Blue'
113 *Ceanothus cyaneus*

114 *Ceanothus gloriosus*
115 *Ceanothus gloriosus*

Ceanothus. (Cont.)

Name	Character	Remarks
C. cyaneus San Diego Ceanothus	A popular and long time cultivated species which is native to the warm coastal foothills of San Diego County. Grows into a dense rounded shrub, 12 ft. high and as wide, with glossy, light green leaves and long, bright blue flower spikes which are very showy.	Works best in coastal or inland foothills and will not tolerate summer water. Plant on slopes and let survive under natural conditions. It is a very desirable plant for its light geen foliage and flowers, but can be short-lived. Plate 113
C. gloriosus Point Reyes Ceanothus	A low ground cover form of Ceanothus occurring naturally on coastal bluffs from Point Reyes northward. Rounded, 1½ in. leaves with toothed margins are leathery, dark green above, with heavy veins below. Striking blue to purple flowers, Mar.-Apr.	A species suited to coastal gardens, with some summer water and either sun or shade. It hugs the ground, 6-24 in. high and spreads as a dense mat to 4 ft. wide. Tolerant of cold, but not extreme drought. This species and its several related varieties are best planted north of Santa Barbara. One of the more promising varieties, C.g. 'Point Reyes', is a very low plant with rich green foliage and deep blue flowers. Plates 114, 115
C. g. porrectus	Very similar to C. gloriosus, but with small ½ in. leaves. Matures at a height of 18 in., spreads close to 8 ft.	Very good flower display and widely adapted to coastal regions and garden conditions. Needs shade and protection from heat in inland areas. Plates 116, 117
C. g. exaltatus 'Emily Brown'	A taller form which develops into a mounding shrub, 2-3 ft. high and 4-5 ft. wide. Foliage is very small, with toothed edges. Flowers are dark blue and occur in greater numbers than C. gloriosus.	One of the more popular cultivars of the Point Reyes Ceanothus group which offers good drought tolerance and visual appearance. Best used in areas of coastal influence from Santa Barbara to San Francisco.
C. griseus Carmel Ceanothus	Native to the coastal zones from Santa Barbara to Mendocino County. A species with many natural variations in habit, leaf size and flowers. Generally a semi-upright shrub reaching 6-8 ft. high, with deep blue flowers in dense clusters, Mar.-May.	An aggressive grower doing well on slopes and disturbed areas in northern coastal environments. Will tolerate inland conditions in partial shade, along with infrequent water on well draining soils.
C. g. horizontalis Carmel Creeper	A mounding ground cover, 2-3 ft. high, 5-12 ft. wide, densely covered with rich and glossy dark green leaves.	With its profuse medium blue flowers and good garden tolerance, Carmel Creeper has become a favorite large scale ground cover on banks and in mass plantings. Availability from nurseries is good. Prefers locations with coastal influence, will survive in inland areas if planted in partial shade and given periodic watering. Plates 118, 119
C. g. h. 'Santa Ana'	A large, spreading shrub, 3-6 ft. high, 10-15 ft. across with small dark green leaves. Very rich blue flowers occur on long stems from Apr.-June.	This form shows higher tolerance of inland exposure conditions and periodic summer water, particularly in southern California. Excellent for slope and mass plantings with lots of room. Plate 122
C. g. h. 'Yankee Point'	A variety of Carmel Creeper with large leaves, medium to dark blue flowers and very fast growth. Long horizontal stems can be stiffly angular and extend to 8 ft. along the ground.	While best suited to coastal areas, it can adapt to sheltered inland conditions with no summer water. Good as a large area ground cover and bank plant with very neat appearance. Plates 123, 124
C. g. 'Louis Edmunds'	An upright form, 6-12 ft. high, with arching branch character. Large green leaves like C. grisseus and profuse medium blue flowers make it well suited as a background plant or flowering accent during the early spring.	Good garden tolerance, with ability to adapt to inland areas in partial shade and limited water. A good choice for mass and screen planting in parks. Plates 120, 121
C. impressus Santa Barbara Ceanothus	A large spreading mound, 6-10 ft. high, 10-12 ft. wide, with small dark green deeply veined leaves on twisting reddish branches. Deep blue flowers occur in dense clusters Mar.-May, followed by rapid foliage growth.	This species is best planted in large spaces for screen or slope plantings. It responds well to pruning to expose interesting branch structure and will tolerate full inland conditions on well draining soils with no summer water. Plates 125, 126
C. i. 'Puget Blue'	A medium sized shrub, 6-10 ft. high, with small dark green, deeply veined leaves. This variety develops many upright branches and spreads 6-8 ft.	Striking dark blue flowers cover this plant in early spring, making it very showy and useful as a background specimen or slope plant. Sensitive to inland heat and summer water, it prefers loose soils and coastal conditions. Plates 127, 128

116 Ceanothus gloriosus porrectus

117 Ceanothus gloriosus porrectus

118 Ceanothus griseus horizontalis
120 Ceanothus griseus 'Louis Edmunds'

119 Ceanothus griseus horizontalis
121 Ceanothus griseus 'Louis Edmunds'

122 *Ceanothus griseus* 'Santa Ana'

123 *Ceanothus griseus horizontalis* 'Yankee Point'
125 *Ceanothus impressus*

124 *Ceanothus griseus horizontalis* 'Yankee Point'

126 *Ceanothus impressus*

127 *Ceanothus impressus* 'Puget Blue'

128 *Ceanothus impressus* 'Puget Blue'

130 *Ceanothus maritimus*

129 *Ceanothus maritimus*

131 *Ceanothus purpureus*

132 *Ceanothus purpureus*

73

Ceanothus. (Cont.)

Name	Character	Remarks
C. maritimus Maritime Ceanothus	From the coastal bluffs of San Luis Obispo County. This species has small dark green leaves above and whitish below. It develops into a dense mat, 2-3 ft. high, 6-10 ft. across; is covered with clusters of medium blue flowers in early spring.	Best suited to coastal conditions, it does well in rock gardens and as a fine textured ground cover in small spaces. Plates 129, 130
C. purpureus Hollyleaf Ceanothus	A native to the foothills of Napa County, this species is a stiffly branched shrub, 2-4 ft. high, spreading to 5 ft. Leaves are small, dark glossy green with holly-like edges. Deep blue to purple flowers cover the plant in late winter to early spring.	This species tolerates inland conditions well, particularly in northern California. It provides uses as a small scale slope plant, rock garden specimen or filler shrub. Plates 131, 132
C. rigidus 'Snowball'	Rounded shrub, 3-5 ft. in size with many stiff branches that are covered with small leathery dark green leaves. A consistent bloomer producing many white flowers in ball-like clusters which can cover the plant Mar.-Apr.	Good in coastal, intermediate and inland areas on loose soils and with no summer water. Good as a border or slope plant, where it can spread to 10 ft. Plates 133, 134

Ceanothus – Additional horticultural cultivars

Name	Character	Remarks
C. 'Blue Cushion'	A dense, mounding shrub, 3-5 ft. high and 4-6 ft. wide, with small light to medium green foliage. Medium blue flowers cover the plant May-June.	A good border plant with neat growing habits and fair tolerance of summer water. A relatively unknown variety which performs well in coastal zones and in semi-shaded inland areas. Plate 137
C. 'Concha'	A spectacular flowering variety of Ceanothus with small, narrow leaves and arching branches. Reaches 6-10 ft. high and produces many deep blue flowers for an extended period of time, Mar.-May.	Shows good acceptance of coastal and inland conditions, including clay type soils and summer water. A very successful variety having many garden applications. Plates 135, 136
C. 'Frosty Blue'	A large mounding shrub, to 16 ft. high and as wide. Upright branches are densely covered with small glossy green leaves, profuse clusters of bright blue flowers occur May-June.	A good background and screen plant with vigorous growth and good tolerance of garden conditions. Can be shaped into a small tree. Accepts coastal or inland conditions, wants some shade in hot areas. Plates 138, 139
C. 'Joyce Coulter'	A spreading shrub, 3-5 ft. high and 6-8 ft. across, with bright green linear leaves. Clusters of medium blue flowers occur on long stems from Apr.-May.	An excellent performer under garden conditions, including heavy soils. In large areas and banks it becomes a high ground cover. Accepts both coastal and inland conditions with protection from extreme heat. Plates 140, 141
C. 'Julia Phelps'	A medium spreading shrub, to 6 ft. high and 6-10 ft. across. Very small wrinkled foliage occurs on arching branches. A spectacular display of deep blue flowers occurs Apr.-May.	A widely used plant that shows good tolerance of heat and drought. Will not accept too much water or poor drainage. Is best used on slopes, in background plantings away from spray irrigation, and in areas with natural leaf litter. Plates 142, 143
C. 'Mountain Haze'	A moderately sized shrub, 6-8 ft. high and as wide, with small oval leaves that are medium green in color. Light to medium blue flowers occur in clusters for a pleasant display of color in early spring.	Tolerates inland conditions in partial shade, periodic watering, and accepts a wider variation in soil conditions than most Ceanothus. This species has been available for many years and has proven to be a consistent performer, but is not as dramatic as newer introductions. Plates 144, 145
C. 'Ray Hartman'	A large shrub to small tree, with large dark glossy green leaves and profuse displays of medium blue flowers. Naturally develops into a mounding shrub, 8-16 ft. high, 12-15 ft. across. It is a hybrid from C. griseus and C. arboreus.	This is a widely used and very dependable plant for large spaces in both natural and domestic landscapes. With its vigorous growth and rich flowers, it is often a replacement to C. arboreus. Plates 146, 147
C. 'Sierra Blue'	A fast growing shrub, 8-12 ft. high and 10-15 ft. across, with medium green leaves. Deep blue flower plumes cover the plant Apr.-May.	A good slope plant which is tolerant of full coastal and inland exposures and clay soil conditions. Eventually becomes quite large and should be given generous room. Plates 148, 149

133 *Ceanothus rigidus* 'Snowball'

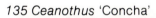
135 *Ceanothus* 'Concha'

134 *Ceanothus rigidus* 'Snowball'

136 *Ceanothus* 'Concha'
137 *Ceanothus* 'Blue Cushion'

138 Ceanothus 'Frosty Blue'

139 Ceanothus 'Frosty Blue'

140 Ceanothus 'Joyce Coulter'
142 Ceanothus 'Julia Phelps'

141 Ceanothus 'Joyce Coulter'
143 Ceanothus 'Julia Phelps'

144 *Ceanothus* 'Mountain Haze'

145 *Ceanothus* 'Mountain Haze'

147 *Ceanothus* 'Ray Hartman'

146 *Ceanothus* 'Ray Hartman'

148 *Ceanothus* 'Sierra Blue'

149 *Ceanothus* 'Sierra Blue'

Cedrus. Cedar

Asia, Africa

Large evergreen conifers, considered mainly for their distinctive character and rich foliage. At least three species and several varieties are in landscape use which offer a range of forms and foliage colors. These plants need generous room for their broad branching habits. They prefer heavy, well draining soils, natural leaf litter, or dry ground cover within their dripline, and periodic deep watering. They perform well under conditions of heat, sun and wind in many plant environments, from coastal plains to interior valleys. All cedars become relatively drought tolerant with age, particularly if planted where their deep root system can get quickly established. Well suited for plantation groupings in regional parks, as well as for large parkways and greenbelts. Individual plants also perform nicely as specimen trees for large buildings.

Name	Character	Remarks
C. atlantica Atlas Cedar	Large evergreen tree from northern Africa, which grows 30-50 ft. high, and develops into a broadly pyramidal form. Branching is open and upright in formal appearance, with light blue-green needle-like leaves. Several varieties of this species exist which offer yellowish to grey-blue foliage, as well as drooping branching habits. *C. a.* 'Glauca' is very popular for its rich grey-blue needles.	Atlas Cedar prefers a well draining soil with infrequent deep watering. It has also been successfully grown on clay type soils and accepts either heat or cold without problem. Young plants tend to develop striking forms and are appreciated for their sculptural qualities. Considered to be a slow growing species, which establishes a deep tap root. Plate 150
C. deodara Deodar Cedar	A fast growing evergreen tree, 40-80 ft. high, 30-50 ft. spread, with an overall pyramidal form. Branches droop pleasantly and are densely covered with soft medium green needle-like leaves. Horticultural varieties of this species offer plants which range from prostrate forms to ones having new foliage which are golden yellow.	Deodar Cedar is a popular tree from Asia, which is best suited to inland and interior valley areas which have deep soils. Drought endurance is good as it develops a tap root for deep soil moisture. As with other Cedrus species, it prefers sun, heat and periodic water. Works well for median plantings, as large specimens and in parks where generous room is available. Plate 151

Centaurea cineraria. Dusty Miller

(C. candidissima) Europe

A mounding, perennial plant, 12-18 in. high, with large chalky white leaves that are heavily lobed. Yellow or purple flowers occur in single thistle-like heads, to 1 inch dia., throughout the summer.
This is the most widely used species of Centaurea for domestic gardens throughout California. It performs well in all warm environments, with a preference for full sun and limited summer water. A common border, ground cover and accent plant valued for its striking foliage. The flowers are showy, but should be removed as they die. Plate 152

Ceratonia siliqua. Carob Tree

Europe, Eastern Mediterranean

A large evergreen shrub or tree with heavy branches and dark green foliage. It naturally develops into a mounding shrub, 15-20 ft. high. With early pruning, it can be shaped into a handsome full dome tree, 25-40 ft. high, 20-35 ft. wide. Flowers of male plants produce strong, disagreeable odor in Oct., female plants produce 3-10 in. long bean pods, and can be a litter problem. These pods are edible and are rich in protein.
Carob Trees are well suited to dry inland, interior and desert plant environments. They develop a deep root system and tolerate full sun, wind, dust, smog and aridity. Prefer periodic deep watering and will not tolerate heavy, wet soils, as they become susceptible to root crown rot. Resistant to oak root fungus. Perform well for shade and specimen plantings, with no turf or spray irrigation within the dripline. A good choice for regional parks. Shrub forms provide excellent mass plantings on gentle slopes and along roadsides. Plate 153

Cercidum. Palo Verde

Southwestern U.S.A., Northern Mexico

Deciduous trees coming from arid and stressful regions of the west. Two species are most commonly found in landscape use, which are both very well adapted to high and low desert landscapes, to hot inland and interior valleys. Most species develop into many branched trees with a broad spreading canopy. The leaves are divided and are dropped under drought and cold stress. Deep watering in the summer will produce fast growth and a lusher appearance.
Cercidium floridum (C. torreyanum), Blue Palo Verde Tree, grows 15-25 feet and has distinctive green bark. Its leaves are finely divided and have a blue-green cast. Small yellow flowers cover the tree during early spring. This is the most popular species which has often been used along dry roadsides and as a garden accent specimen. Plate 154
Cercidium microphyllum (Parkinsonia microphyllum), Littleleaf Palo Verde, is a many branched shrub or small tree, 8-12 feet high. Leaves and bark are pale green, with showy yellow flowers coming in late spring to summer. This is a lesser known species of Palo Verde, which offers good use in rock gardens, on slopes and will develop specimen character with age.

150 *Cedrus atlantica* 'Glauca'

151 *Cedrus deodara*
153 *Ceratonia siliqua*

152 *Centaurea cineraria*
154 *Cercidium floridum*

Cercis occidentalis.
Western Redbud

California, Arizona, Texas, Utah

Deciduous shrub to small tree, 6-16 ft. high, developing many branches low to the base. Heart shaped leaves emerge light green and form an interesting alternating pattern on the branches. Pea shaped flowers occur in large clusters, Mar.-Apr., most commonly magenta, but also white. Thin seed pods develop shortly after flowering, 2-3 in. long, and persist until the next season.
Western Redbud is a widely distributed native throughout much of the Chaparral and Foothill Woodland plant communities of central to northern California, with some occurrences in Kern and San Diego counties. It has proven to be highly adaptable and tolerant of garden conditons throughout much of the state. Prefers deep, well draining soils, but shows good growth in clays. Accepts ample or limited summer water and is oak root fungus resistant. Pruning when young can form this species into a small dome tree, to 18 ft. high. It is a well rounded plant offering foliage, branch and striking flowering characteristics to work with. A wide range of uses are possible, ranging from screen and slope plantings to garden accents and patio trees. Plates 155, 157, 158a, 158b

155 Cercis occidentalis

Cercocarpus betuloides.
Mountain Mahogany

California

Upright evergreen shrub reaching 6-12 ft. high, rarely a small dome tree 15-20 ft. tall. Simple, small, light to dark green leaves have distinctive veins and occur on stiff, whitish branches. Inconspicuous flowers are followed by seed, which have an interesting twisted, tail-like feather attached.
Mountain Mahogany is well adapted and widely distributed among the rocky chaparral foothills throughout California, where its extensive root system enables it to withstand high drought stress. It is another native that should enjoy greater landscape use, particularly on naturalized slopes and for erosion control. It is a simple plant, with an appearance that does not make it a spectacular garden specimen, yet it is clean and tolerant of difficult conditions, including adobe soils. It can be grown from containers or untreated seed where 90% germination success has been achieved. In natural areas, it is an important browse plant for deer. *C. ledifolius,* Curlleaf Mountain Mahogany is a related species growing at higher elevations, with more tolerance for cold. *C. munitifolius,* San Diego Mountain Mahogany, is found in lower California and has adapted to less rainfall. Seeds and cuttings of these species should be used for projects within their natural range. Plates 159, 160

Chamelaucium uncinatum.
Geraldton Waxflower
(*C. ciliatum*)

Australia

Fast growing upright shrub, 5-7 ft. high, with light green, narrow leaves. Profuse displays of light pink flowers occur Jan.-May, which are long lasting on the plant and in cut arrangements. Older plants tend to sprawl and can be staked or thinned to reveal twisted trunks.
Adapts well to coastal, inland and interior valleys, and foothills, but must be given well draining soils. Prefers full sun and likes infrequent deep summer water in hot inland areas. A very good flowering accent, specimen and background plant that easily mixes with natives that dislike frequent moisture. Plates 156, 161

156 Chamelaucium uncinatum

157 Cercis occidentalis

158a Cercis occidentalis (magenta flower)
158b Cercis occidentalis (white flower)

159 Cercocarpus betuloides
160 Cercocarpus betuloides

161 Chamelaucium uncinatum

Cistus . Rockrose
Europe, Mediterranean Region

Small to medium sized evergreen shrubs, consisting of some 16 species, with many improved hybrids for use in dry landscapes. Leaves are typically wrinkled, with a dull finish. Flowers are very showy and most often come with magenta or white petals and yellow centers. Extensive flowering occurs April to July.

Rockroses are highly regarded for their tolerance of heat, sun and drought. This group of plants has been frequently used in coastal and inland landscapes from southern California, to the San Francisco Bay area, and into the foothills of the Sierra Nevadas. Many species show good acceptance of wind, salt spray and poor soils. Some will also naturalize in difficult areas and provide good erosion control. The lower growing varieties offer fair fire resistance when mixed with other low growing, low foliage volume plants.

These plants are easily established from seed or container and do not want much summer water. New plants should be irrigated deeply and infrequently for the first season. By the second year, most plants can survive without water in warm landscapes. Light tip pruning will create denser plants for domestic gardens. Listed below are many of the popular species in common use. Other varieties have been developed and are available from local sources.

162 *Cistus corbariensis*

Name	Character	Remarks
C. corbariensis (C. hybridus) White Rockrose	Mounding shrub, 2-5 ft. high and as wide, with grey-green foliage. Perhaps the heaviest flowering variety, with 1½ in. dia. white flowers with yellow centers. This species is a natural hybrid from C. salviifolius and C. populifolius.	A frequently used plant for coastal and inland gardens. Performs well under harsh conditions and in natural areas. Provides intensive displays of flowers from spring to summer. Plate 162
C. crispus	Low spreading shrub, 1-3 ft. high, with very aromatic, grey-green leaves that have three main veins. Flowers are rose to purple, with yellow centers, 2 in. across, and very similar in appearance to C. villosus.	A good slope and rock garden plant that easily establishes from seed. Its low profile and spreading habit make it suitable for slopes, rock gardens and naturalizing.
C. ladanifer (C. landaniferus maculatus) Crimson-Spot Rockrose	Dense shrub, 3-6 ft. high and as wide. Fragrant leaves are narrow, very sticky, to 4 in. long, and dark green. Large white flowers to 3 in. in dia. have yellow centers and distinctive purple spots at the base of the petals.	One of the nicest flowering species with the same wide tolerances and uses as other Rockroses. It performs very well in domestic gardens along dry borders and mixed with natives. Plate 163
C. laurifolius Laurel-Leaved Rockrose	Upright, open plant, 6-10 ft. tall, developing a sprawling form. Narrow foliage is dark, grey-green and sticky above. Flowers are all white, with yellow centers and grow 2-3 in. across.	A species which can be pruned into interesting forms for small area specimen and accent uses. Not to be used in high fire hazard areas due to its larger foliage volume and height.
C. purpureus Orchid Rockrose	Dense mounding shrub to 4 ft. high, 4-6 ft. spread. Narrow leaves are wrinkled, dark green above, covered with grey hair below. Large, papery flowers reach 3 in. across, are maroon-purple with a single red spot at the base of each petal.	Very good performer under salt spray and sandy soil conditions, in addition to tolerating heat and aridity. Flowers are quite ornamental and work well in mixed plantings. Plate 164, 165
C. salviifolius (C. villosus 'Protratus') Sageleaf Rockrose	A broad spreading shrub, 1-2 ft. high and to 6 ft. wide, with small, wrinkled, grey-green leaves. Flowers are white with orange centers and have yellow spots at the base of the petals; similar to C. corbariensis.	Good inland slope and naturalizing plant, offering soil protection and moderate fire resistance. A successful ground cover in difficult areas and for planting with natives. Plate 167
C. villosus (C. incanus)	Dense mounding, to upright plant, 3-6 ft. tall. Leaves are oval, with one mid-vein, dull green and covered with fine hairs. Flowers are purple-rose to 2½ in. across.	A variety very adaptable to dry areas where it will naturalize to a limited extent. Useful in coastal and inland regions, on slopes, in mixed plantings and for flowering accents. Easily established from seed and needs no summer water after the first season. Plate 166

163 Cistus ladanifer

164 Cistus purpureus

165 Cistus purpureus

166 Cistus villosus

167 Cistus salviifolius

168 *Comarostaphylis diversifolia*

169 *Comarostaphylis diversifolia*

170, 171 *Convolvulus cneorum* (Above, below)

172 *Coprosma kirkii*

173 *Comarostaphylis diversifolia*

174 *Coprosma kirkii*

Comarostaphylis diversifolia.
Summer Holly

California Coastal Chaparral

Dense evergreen shrub or small tree, 6-15 ft. high, with shredded, grey-brown bark and a swollen trunk base at the soil line. Leaves are simple, with spiny edges, 3-4 in. long, leathery and dark shiny green above. Showy white urn shaped flowers occur in clusters Apr.-May, followed by distinctive red berries having a wrinkled texture.

Summer Holly inhabits the coastal foothills from Santa Barbara County southward into Mexico and on the coastal islands. Prefers well draining soils and deep moisture. It is a fairly adaptable plant, that can be used beyond its natural range into the San Francisco Bay region. This is a relatively unknown native plant which offers striking foliage, flower and fruit characteristics, with tolerances for most garden conditions. It is very similar in appearance to *Heteromeles arbutifolia*, Toyon, but with a slower growth rate. With age and size it makes a handsome, multi-trunk specimen and small scale accent plant. Other uses include background, screen and slope plantings. It can be grown from containers, or treated seed, with a 70% germination rate possible. Some 25 other species occur in Mexico which have received little study for landscape use. Plates 168, 169, 173

Convolvulus cneorum.
Bush Morning Glory

Southern Europe

Evergreen sprawling shrub, 2-4 ft. high, spreading 4-6 ft. across. Distinctive silvery-grey foliage is covered with many pink tinted trumpet-shaped flowers with yellow throats from Apr.-Sept.

Established from containers, Bush Morning Glory is an excellent foliage and flower plant for light, dry soils in many locations from coastal valleys to inland and interior regions. Prefers full sun and once established, it shows good drought tolerance and dislikes frequent spraying. Heavy pruning will keep plants more vigorous and neater. A very good accent plant for dry borders, rock gardens, slopes and natural areas. Plates 170, 171

Coprosma kirkii.
New Zealand

A spreading ground cover to low shrub, 1-3 ft. high, forming a dense mat, 2-5 ft. wide. Small leaves are glossy medium green. Flowers and fruit are not significant. Several varieties are also available which offer variegated foliage, smaller leaves, and more prostrate growth.

A good ground cover for mild drought conditions in areas with coastal influence. This species tolerates a wide range of soil conditions, including clay, but should have partial shade and deep watering in inland and interior areas. Removal of upreaching branches keeps this plant low and dense. Overall, this is a handsome ground cover which is well suited to small and medium areas and as a substitute for Prostrate Coyote Bush. It can also be used as an individual plant in rock gardens, and massed for erosion control on banks. Tolerates wind and salt spray and is best used within coastal and inland gardens from southern to northern California. Plates 172, 174

Cotoneaster.

Europe, Asia

A diverse group of evergreen and deciduous shrubs, including some 50 species, which require little attention and provide a large variety of general landscape uses. Plant forms range from ground covers to large shrubs and small trees. Most species develop an arching branching habit, produce small light pink to white flowers, and clusters of red fleshy berries. They prefer full sun and room to develop. Dry soils tend to increase berry production. Almost all plants show some acceptance of dry conditions, but regular deep watering in hot inland areas is usually necessary. A few species are considered drought tolerant, but only after being well established.

Cotoneasters are appreciated for their tolerance of poor soils, need for little care, and many uses. Groundcover varieties do well in rock gardens, for erosion control, and cascading effects. Larger shrubs provide good screen, background, mass and roadside planting. Due to their branching habits, it is desirable to selectively prune to shape as opposed to shearing. Of the many species and varieties available, the following plant types have shown a greater tolerance of dry soil conditions.

175 Cotoneaster lacteus

Name	Character	Remarks
C. buxifolius (C. glaucophyllus) Bright Bead Cotoneaster	An arching shrub, 4-6 ft. high, with oval, grey-green leaves that are covered with many small hairs. White flowers are tinged with pink. Showy dull red berries occur late fall and early winter.	A good slope, low screen and accent plant suited for gardens along the coast, to low desert regions. Prefers well draining soils and deep water in hot areas. Accepts heat, wind and aridity. Plates 177, 178
C. congestus (C. microphylla glacialis)	A slow growing ground cover, to 3 ft. high, spreading 4-6 ft., with arching branches that grow downward. Leaves are small, dark green above and whitish below. Small pink-white flowers are followed by bright red berries.	Good tolerance of all plant environments, ranging from coastal edge to inland, interior and low desert landscapes. A successful small scale rock garden and border plant that will cascade over walls.
C. lacteus (C. parneyi) Red Clusterberry	An arching mound shrub, 6-10 ft. high. Leaves are leathery, dark dull green above, whitish below and grow to 2½ in. long. Conspicuous white flowers occur May-June. Large clusters of showy red berries mature in late fall to winter.	A general purpose plant with tolerance of warm, dry areas throughout the state. Serves well as a background, screen, roadside and slope plant and as a sculptural accent with age. Periodic deep watering is needed in hot locations. Plates 175, 179, 180

Cupressocyparis leylandii. Leyland Cypress

Horticultural Cultivar

Evergreen tree with an upright pyramidal form, 20-30 ft. tall, 8-12 ft. spread. Dark green, scalelike leaves, are flatly arranged on reddish, upright stems. Fast growing, with ample water; becoming drought tolerant with age.

This species is a hybrid between Chamaecyparis nootkatensis, Nootka Cypress and Cupressus macrocarpa, Monterey Cypress. It is a very versatile tree which tolerates heat, cold, smog, wind and limited water. Accepts many soils, including clays and grows in all plant environments from the coast to deserts. It is most frequently used for tall screens and colonnades and as a substitute for Cupressus sempervirens, Italian Cypress. Other uses include individual accent, park and mass plantings. Plates 176, 181, 182

176 Cupressocyparis leylandii

177 *Cotoneaster buxifolius*

178 *Cotoneaster buxifolius*

179 *Cotoneaster lacteus*
181 *Cupressocyparis leylandii*

180 *Cotoneaster lacteus*
182 *Cupressocyparis leylandii*

Cupressus. Cypress

Asia, Europe, Southwest U.S.A., Mexico

A small group of evergreen trees and shrubs, including some 14 species and numerous varieties. Six species naturally occur in California, with at least four of these being found in landscape use. These plants are characterized by tiny scale-type leaves, insignificant flowers and hard brown cones. Their foliage is soft and fine textured, range in colors from bright to dark green and blue-green. Most species develop very regular forms and are often appreciated for colonnades and formal plantings.

Most cypress, when established, show good drought tolerance, as well as acceptance of heat, smog, wind and thin soils. They prefer loose and well draining conditions without a lot of moisture or fertilizer. Infrequent deep watering when young will enable deeper root development and resistance to strong winds. Several of the native species, particularly C. macrocarpa, are highly susceptible to a Cypress canker fungus which quickly kills them. Any plants which contracts this fungus cannot be saved and should be entirely removed to protect healthy plants. Cypress trees are frequently found in symmetrical plantings, along entry drives, and in estate landscapes. Their widespread use is often criticized when they are aligned in long rows and as sentry elements. This situation can often be improved if these plants are arranged in more casual groupings and when placed next to larger buildings which better fit their scale.

Name	Character	Remarks
C. forbesii Tecate Cypress	A moderate sized tree, growing 15-20 ft. tall, fully branched, to 12 ft. wide. Rich green foliage contrasts nicely with glossy red-brown bark.	Native to the Santa Ana Mountains of southern California where it grows on steep canyon slopes in the Chaparral plant community. Highly tolerant of heat, drought, smog and sparse soils. With ample water it will grow very fast, but can become too tall to withstand winds. Often used for slope stabilization and naturalizing road scars in southern foothills, as well as in regional park plantings. Plate 183
C. glabra (C. arizonica) Smooth Arizona Cypress	Large shrub to upright tree, 40 ft. tall and to 20 ft. wide. Foliage varies from blue-green to grey-cast. Bark is cherry red on older stems and trunk.	Arizona Cypress is a successful screen and specimen tree in desert and warm interior environments. When young, this plant is quite uniform, becomes more relaxed with age. Two improved selections are also available, C. g. 'Gareei' and C. g. 'Pyramidalis', which offer variations in foliage color and form. Plate 184
C. goveniana Gowen Cypress	A shrubby tree slowly reaching 40-50 ft. Leaves vary from light to dark green and occur on flat branches.	Gowen Cypress naturally occurs around Mendocino and the Monterey Peninsula, away from the immediate coastal edge. It is very tolerant of many soils, including heavy, and likes inland heat and sun. Not widely known, but is used for screen and individual plantings in areas where it is available.
C. macrocarpa Monterey Cypress	A fast growing tree, with wide spreading branches, 25-40 ft. high and as wide. A species noted for its dark green foliage and picturesque forms.	Monterey Cypress is a popular native tree for coastal landscapes throughout both northern and southern California. With supplemental water, it produces amazing growth, but it is a plant that easily falls victim to Cypress canker fungus. Afflicted trees are distinguished by their yellow and brown foliage and should be removed as quickly as possible. This species has often been used for windbreaks and in park and roadside plantings. Needs generous room where it develops handsome shapes. Not as drought tolerant as other species. Plate 186
C. sempervirens Italian Cypress	A plant coming from southern Europe and western Asia, which naturally has an open, horizontal branching habit and dull green leaves.	This parent species is not commonly used, as improved selections offer better form and foliage characteristics. One very popular cultivar is C. s. 'Stricta', which has a very narrow and columnar form to 60 ft. high. A lower growing selection, C. s. 'Glauca', Blue Italian Cypress, reaches 40 ft. or more and has blue-green foliage. Other cultivars are available depending upon sources. These plants are typically associated with colonnade, accent and sentry plantings, along drives and in gardens of all sizes. They show good tolerance of heat, wind, smog and drought, with a preference for lean, loose soils. Plate 185

183 Cupressus forbesii
185 Cupressus sempervirens

184 Cupressus glabra

186 Cupressus macrocarpa

Cytisus, Genista, Spartium, Ulex.
Brooms

Europe, Asia, Canary Islands

A group of evergreen and deciduous shrubs, including some 80 species and numerous varieties. These plant groups are related and are often confused with each other. They are known for their distinctive green stems and clusters of pea shaped flowers. Many opportunities exist for landscape use, but careful decisions should be made between aggressive and non-aggressive varieties.

The more domestic types of broom which have garden use, include many horticultural selections, that have improved foliage and flower qualities. These non-aggressive plants prefer well draining soils and summer water, in order to achieve their best performance. They like full sun, tolerate coastal and inland conditions, including heat, wind and smog. They can be effectively used as border, ground cover, bank and screen plants. Flower colors range from yellow, cream, pink to red, and cover the plants during early spring. Listed below are several of the varieties currently available.

Cytisus battandieri..........................Atlas Broom
Cytisus kewensis............................Kew Broom
Cytisus praecox.........................Warminster Broom
Cytisus purgans.........................Provence Broom
Cytisus scoparius varieties..............Scotch Broom
Genista athnensis....................Mt. Aetna Broom
Genista lydia................................
Genista monosperma.................Bridal Veil Broom
Genista pilosa..............................
Genista sagittalis.........................

The more drought tolerant varieties of broom are plants causing necessary concern. They have proven to be highly aggressive and well adapted to coastal and inland landscapes throughout California. Several of these species were introduced as early as the 1860's, and were appreciated for their bright yellow flowers and rapid growth. Their popularity continued into recent years, as they have been established on large slopes and disturbed areas, to control erosion and revegetate road scars. However, they produce large quanities of viable seed, and have escaped into natural plant communities.

These aggressive species of broom show wide tolerance of many soils, temperature and moisture conditions. They can effectively compete with most plants of the Coastal Sage and Chaparral plant communities. They are adapted to wildland fires, as established plants regrow from basal roots, while additional seedling populations emerge in the newly cleared areas. Presently, there are citizen groups, State and Federal Park Districts, and the California State Department of Agriculture involved in eliminating these escaped species. The most offensive varieties include:

Cytisus monospessulanus...............French Broom
Cytisus racemosus.......................Easter Broom
Cytisus scoparius........................Scotch Broom
Spartium junceum......................Spanish Broom
Ulex europaeus..................................Gorse

This second list of brooms should be used with great caution. They do provide rapid growth and striking displays of yellow flowers, but are best situated in urban areas where they can be controlled. An additional discussion of these plant groups is provided to further assist in their proper use.

Cytisus: Includes some two dozen species, which are distinguished from Genista species because they lack spines on their branches. Leaves occur singly or are divided into 3 leaflets and are alternate on the stems. Heavy displays of flowers, ranging from white to yellow, are often fragrant and occur in terminal clusters. Most species are easily grown, with several types having naturalized in the coastal bluffs and foothills of northern California in great abundance. Aggressive species should be kept from natural landscapes, but offer bright foliage and flowering accent character in confined urban locations. Several of the newer varieties and species, which do not readily escape, provide uses in many garden situations with limited water. Plates 187, 188

Genista: A large group of plants, including over 60 species. Most plants are densely branched and covered with spines. White to yellow flowers are fragrant and very showy during mid-spring to early summer. Not as aggressive and quick to naturalize as Cytisus species. Many species are well suited to garden use, where they tolerate poor soils and limited summer water. Successful plants in dry landscapes include: *G. germanica; G. hispanica,* Spanish Broom; *G. lydia;* and *G. monosperma,* Bridal Veil Broom. Additional species and varieties are available which provide plants that are good for ground covers, to larger screen sized shrubs. Good for flowering accents, barriers and bank plantings.

Spartium: Consists of one species, *Spartium junceum,* Spanish Broom. A tall, upright shrub to 12 ft. with dark green, usually leafless stems. Bright yellow flowers occur May through September. A shrub very tolerant of adverse conditions in dry foothill areas, including poor soils, heat, drought, smog and aridity. Used largely for revegetating slopes, this species has quickly naturalized in many areas of southern California. It crownsprouts after fires and reseeds extensively to overwhelm local areas of native vegetation. In domestic projects this plant can be kept in good condition with pruning and some summer water. Plates 189, 190

Ulex: Includes about 20 species, from western Europe and north Africa. These are densely branched shrubs with stiff leaves and numerous spines on their branches. Bright yellow flowers occur Feb.-July. One species in particular, Ulex europaeus, Gorse, has become a widespread pest in California. While it has naturalized to a limited extent in southern California, it has established beyond control throughout the northern coastal regions of the state. While these plants produce an abundance of showy flowers in the spring, they are usually not considered very ornamental in appearance, and are seldom found in the landscape industry.

188 Cytisus racemosus

187 Cytisus racemosus

189 Spartium junceum

190 Spartium junceum

Dalea spinosa. Smoke Tree

Southern California, Arizona, Mexico

Finely branched tree, 10-25 ft. high, 10-15 ft. wide. Simple leaves occur for short periods on ashy-grey branchlets. Fragrant dark blue flowers are conspicuous Apr.-June. This tree has a very soft, fine textured appearance, but both stems and branchlets are stiff and sharp.

Smoke Tree is native to desert washes of the Southwest and Baja California, where its common name is derived from its intricate grey branching character. A good accent plant for desert regions, as well as in hot interior landscapes. Plates 191, 192

191 Dalea spinosa

192 Dalea spinosa

Dendromecon. Bush Poppy

California Coastal Islands, Mainland Chaparral

Large evergreen shrubs, including only two species, which are both native to California. These plants offer rich grey-green foliage and produce intensive displays of sulphur yellow flowers from early spring into summer. They demand very careful propagation and planting conditions, which have made them relatively hard to acquire and establish. Loose, well draining soils, full sun and no summer water are basic requirements. They perform well along the coast and inland foothills, in warm locations, and provide very good ornamental and naturalizing qualities.

Name	Character	Remarks
D. harfordii Island Bush Poppy	Large mounding shrub to small tree, 6-20 ft. high, 10-15 ft. wide. Large rounded leaves, 1-3 in. long, have a pointed apex, are rich grey-green. Intense yellow flowers, 1-2 in. dia., cover the plant from March to July.	A species coming from Santa Cruz and Santa Rosa islands that is one of the most spectacular flowering native shrubs and one of the most difficult to propagate and establish. Best suited to coastal foothill locations, but will tolerate inland valley conditions in partial shade. Requires good drainage and needs no supplemental water after established. Plants grow slowly and can be easily shaped and sized after the blooming cycle. A good foliage and flower accent plant for background and slope areas. It is not tolerant of heavy, moist soils. Plates 193, 194
D. rigida Bush Poppy	Medium sized shrub, 3-8 ft. high and as wide. Long pointed, yellow to grey-green leaves, occur on upright stems. Numerous sulphur yellow flowers to 1 in. dia., occur early spring to summer.	A member of the Chaparral plant community throughout California on dry, well draining slopes. This species has little tolerance of summer water or heavy soils. It is well suited for slope stabilization and naturalizing. It is also hard to propagate in nurseries, yet the seed will readily germinate after wildfires and extensive colonies of this plant can be formed. Plates 195, 196

194 Dendromecon harfordii

193 Dendromecon harfordii

196 Dendromecon rigida

195 Dendromecon rigida

Dodonaea viscosa. Hopseed Bush

Arizona, South America

Dense evergreen shrub to small dome tree, 12-16 ft. high. Narrow light green leaves to 4 in. long, occur on upright stems. Flowers are inconspicuous. Clusters of winged seed pods are light pink and noticeable.

Hopseed Bush is a highly adaptable plant to all areas, ranging from the coastal edge to low deserts. It tolerates many harsh conditions, including heat, aridity, heavy and dry soils, alkalinity, salt spray and wind. *D. v.* 'Purpurea' is a popular variety with the same tolerances, but offers bronze to purple-green foliage. Both species are widely used as screens, small patio accent trees, and slope plants. They tolerate drought, as well as frequent moisture, and are very fast growing for quick effects. Some plants tend to be short-lived and others will have large branches die back after a number of years. Plate 198

Echium fastuosum. Pride of Madeira

Canary Islands

A mounding shrub, 4-8 ft. high, with large grey to green leaves on heavy wooded branches. Long spikes of purple-blue flowers extend above the plant from May-June.

A dramatic accent plant, well suited for dry landscape situations along the coastal edge and adjacent valleys. Plants also show good acceptance of inland conditions with regular water and protection from extreme heat. Tolerates marine clay, sterile and rocky soils. Fast growing and short-lived, from 5-7 years. Removal of dead flower spikes can keep plants bushy, or selective pruning can reveal interesting branch structures for sculptural effects. A good plant for slopes, mass and naturalizing along the immediate coast, where it sometimes reseeds on a limited basis. Plates 199, 200

Elaeagnus.

Asia, Europe, North America

A small group of deciduous and evergreen shrubs and trees, including some 24 species. These are tough plants which accept difficult conditions, from salt spray, heat, and sun, to limited moisture. Some species perform well in desert environments, and in clay type or alkaline soils. They require little care, prefer loose soils and good drainage.

Both evergreen and deciduous species are used as screens, windbreaks, slope and background plantings, and other functional uses. They provide interesting foliage character, usually grey-green leaves, and sometimes edible berries. They achieve moderate drought tolerance with age, which makes them useful in roadside plantings and in regional parks.

197 Elaeagnus pungens

Name	Character	Remarks
E. angustifolia Russian Olive	Deciduous shrub to small tree, 15-20 ft. high, with long angular branching habit and rough dark brown bark. Leaves grow to 2 in. long and are very silvery. Flowers are noticed for their strong fragrance in June-Aug., and are followed by small olive-like fruit.	A very tolerant species, well suited to inland, interior valley and low desert areas throughout California. Prefers summer heat and winter cold, tolerates heavy or light soils, wind, and little or no summer water. Russian Olive often develops into an awkward plant, unless pruned or shaped. Can become a striking foliage tree or controlled into a large hedge or screen. Frequently used in remote areas and in regional parks where it receives little attention or care. Plate 201a and b
E. pungens Silverberry Thorny Elaeagnus	Large evergreen shrub, 6-12 ft. high and as wide. Branches are stiff and often have short spines. Leaves are blotchy grey-green, with white or yellow markings and have wavy edges. Inconspicuous flowers occur Oct.-Nov., very fragrant. Small, reddish fruit have a silver cast, mature in May.	A species native to China that is well adapted to coastal, inland, interior and low desert plant environments. It has a basic need for well draining soils and tolerates salt spray, inland heat and smog. Used primarily as a large screen, barrier, slope or background plant where it is appreciated for its foliage contrast with darker green plants. Many varieties of this species are available which offer different foliage colorations. Plates 197, 202

198 *Dodonaea viscosa*

199, 200 *Echium fastuosum* (Above, below)

201a,b *Elaeagnus angustifolia* (Above, below)

202 *Elaeagnus pungens*

Encelia.

Southwestern U.S.A., Mexico, South America

Evergreen shrubs, including about 14 species, that occur in many areas throughout the Southwest, Mexico and South America. These plants are commonly planted by seed in dry landscapes, on slopes and for naturalizing, from the coast to interior deserts. They are appreciated for their bright yellow daisy-like flowers, which occur for many months through spring and summer. Presently, three species are popular in landscape use.

E. californica, California Encelia, is a many branched shrub, 2-4 ft. high, spreading 3-6 ft. wide. Showy displays of yellow ray-flowers cover the plant May-June. This species is found throughout the coastal bluffs and foothills from Santa Barbara County to Mexico. It is a popular slope and naturalizing plant that tolerates clay soils, sun and wind. Performs best in coastal areas, prefers periodic summer water for lusher appearance in hot inland locations. Plates 203, 206

E. farinosa, Desert Encelia, develops into broad rounded shrub 2-4 ft. high and as wide. It has distinctive grey foliage, stiff branching and produces numerous yellow ray-flowers from April-June. This is a plant naturally found on the edges of the Mojave Desert, to inland foothills in Riverside and San Diego counties. It is frequently used in seed mixes for naturalizing and covering dry slopes. It also offers good uses in rock gardens and desert landscapes. Mainly adapted to warm, inland areas, but tolerates coastal conditions well. Accepts poor, shallow, or clay soils, and limited summer water. Due to its easy establishment through seeding, this species is often being introduced far beyond its natural range. Plates 204, 207

E. frutescens actonii, Bush Encelia, is a broad spreading shrub, 3 ft. high, spreading 8 ft. across. Large yellow ray-flowers grow 2 in. dia. This plant also comes from the California deserts and shows good success in seed planting for slope and naturalizing treatments. Accepts full, sun, drought, heat and wind. Grows well in loose soils and in warm environments from the coast to low deserts.

203 Encelia californica

204 Encelia farinosa

Eriobotrya japonica. Loquat

China

A large shrub to small tree, 15-25 ft. high, with very dense foliage. Leaves are large, to 12 in. long, dark green above, rusty below, with coarsely toothed edges. Inconspicuous white flowers are lightly fragrant, from Nov.-Jan. Showy and edible fruit from orange to yellow, occur in clusters in early spring.

A versatile plant that is well adapted to warm inland and interior valley areas. Prefers a deep, heavy, well draining soil and some limestone conditions. It can be left to develop into a massive shrub, or shaped into a round headed tree. Plants achieve a fair degree of drought tolerance as they age, but regular, deep watering is needed for good fruit. Selected varieties should be used when superior fruit qualities are desired. Plates 205, 208
Another species, *E. deflexa,* Bronze Loquat, is well adapted to heat and aridity, but prefers deep watering to survive in hot environments. Landscape uses for both species include screening, tub, espalier, garden and patio specimens. Plates 209, 110

205 Eriobotrya japonica

206 Encelia californica

207 Encelia farinosa

208 Eriobotrya japonica

209, 210 Eriobotrya deflexa (Above, below)

Eriogonum. Buckwheat
Western U.S.A.

This group of annual and perennial shrubs is native to many areas of the west, including the coastal islands. Almost 100 species and varieties alone occur in California, having adapted to extremely different ecological conditions, ranging from dry deserts to alpine meadows. Many of the buckwheats are highly regarded for their ability to endure drought, and offer a wide range of forms and foliage colors from tans to greys. Their late summer blooming cycle is also a distinct advantage in dry landscapes, providing flowers that vary from sulphur yellow to red.

Buckwheats prefer a loose, well draining soil, with full sun for best performance. They will successfully establish at a slower rate on clay type soil that has controlled irrigation and drainage. Most species are easily established from seed and will germinate within 7-10 days. Seeds require no treatment, should be sown in loosened soil, and during the late fall or early winter, to coincide with seasonal rains. Buckwheats are well established by the second summer after planting and usually prefer to survive without supplemental water. Overhead spray irrigation during the summer can encourage severe downy mildew problems.

Some varieties of buckwheat provide excellent accent character and small scale mass plantings in dry garden situations. Either seed or container plants can be used. The more ornamental species should be considered short lived, 3-6 years, with a tendency to become open and leggy with age. Since most species develop foliage growth at the ends of their branches on new wood, it is usually not possible to prune them. Some species are among the best plants to use for large slope plantings and naturalizing, where they offer good soil protection and will reseed over the years. Under full sun and drought conditions, these plants become quite flammable, but will only support low intensity fires due to their limited foliage mass.

Name	Character	Remarks
E. arborescens Santa Cruz Island Buckwheat	A mounding shrub, 3-4 ft. tall by 4-5 ft. dia. Narrow, grey-green leaves occur in whorls on ends of branches. White to pale pink flowers come in Jul.-Aug., and turn rust and brown as they dry.	A plant well suited for coastal edges and gardens where it tolerates sandy soils and salt spray. Can be used as a garden accent plant in partial shade and on well draining soils. An interesting rock garden and naturalizing specimen. Plate 211
E. cinereum Ashyleaf Buckwheat	Loose branching shrub, 3-6 ft. high, 2-4 ft. wide. Grey-green foliage and branches, white to pink flower balls cover the plant July-Sept.	Native to coastal canyons and bluffs from central to southern California. This species provides good use on slopes and in mass plantings in both coastal and inland areas. It can be planted in seed mixes for naturalizing, or used in small groups in rock gardens. Accepts clay soils and coastal winds. Prefers a little summer water when in hot locations. Plate 212
E. crocatum Saffron Buckwheat	A low, compact species to 18 in. high, spreading to 2 ft., with distinctive grey leaves and bright yellow flowers. Native to Ventura County.	Saffron Buckwheat is an excellent small scale ground cover in rock gardens, for banks and in accent plantings. Requires well draining or rocky soils, full exposures in coastal areas, partial shade in inland locations. A much appreciated buckwheat due to its yellow flowers and tight growth habit. Plate 213
E. fasciculatum Common Buckwheat	Common Buckwheat is a dominant species of the Coastal Sage plant community. It is an excellent drought enduring shrub, 1-4 ft. high, which provides an intensive display of white to pink flowers throughout the summer months. These flowers turn to dark red and brown by fall and give a rich, mottled look to large areas of the natural landscape.	This species offers little domestic use in home gardens, but is one of the most successful plants to be used for slope revegetation throughout many areas of California. Best planted from untreated seed in late fall, germination rates of 40-50% can be achieved. Plate 214
E. giganteum St. Catherine's Lace	The largest of the buckwheats, reaching over 5 ft. in height, with grey branches and leaves. White flowers occur in large, flat clusters, June - Aug., turn to tans and brown and persist well into fall.	St. Catherine's Lace develops long tap roots in coarse, well draining soils. It occurs naturally on the coastal islands, where it prefers full sun and no summer water. It develops into a striking accent plant in both ornamental and park gardens, with interesting branch structure and flowers, which can easily be used in dry arrangements. A good slope plant. Will naturalize on coastal bluffs, needs protection from extreme sun in inland areas. Plate 215

211 *Eriogonum arborescens*

212 *Eriogonum cinereum*

213 *Eriogonum crocatum*

214 *Eriogonum fasciculatum*

215 *Eriogonum giganteum*

216 *Eriogonum latifolium rubescens*

Eriogonum. (Cont.)

Name	Character	Remarks
E. latifolium rubescens (E. grande rubescens) (E. rubescens) Red Buckwheat	A low growing, many branched shrub, to 12 in. high, spreading 1-3 ft. Grey-green leaves and branches contrast well with rose-pink flower clusters. Flowers occur on interesting stalks from July-Oct., turn rust-brown with age.	This species is quite attractive for domestic gardens in coastal areas, as both foliage and flowers provide interest. Good for borders, small banks and planters. Sensitive to summer water on poorly draining soils. Plate 216
E. parvifolium Seacliff Buckwheat	A low growing and spreading shrub, 1-4 ft. high, 3-5 ft. wide. Triangular leaves are dark green above, white below, with edges curling under. Clusters of pink to white flowers extend above the plant, May-Sept.	A widespread coastal species found from Monterey to San Diego County, only on sandy soils and bluffs. This is another good species in seed mixes for naturalizing and slope stabilization in coastal zones. Also provides interest in domestic gardens, in small spaces and on banks.

Eriophyllum confertiflorum. Golden Yarrow

California Chaparral

A short-lived, perennial shrub, 1-3 ft. high, with whitish stems. Small grey-green leaves are divided into 5-7 lobes. Small, yellow flowers occur in clusters of 6-8 from May-July and are attractively showy.
Golden Yarrow is widely distributed throughout the coastal foothills, from Mendocino to San Diego counties, inland to the Sierra Nevada, and on the coastal islands. It is a species well suited for natural slopes and erosion control, as it is tolerant of many soils and needs no summer water. It is best planted from untreated seed in fall, with a germination rate of 15-20% possible. Performs well as a flowering accent and should be mixed with other native species such as Common Buckweat, California Poppy, and California Encelia.
E. nevinii, Catalina Silver Lace, is a slightly taller species, with similar showy yellow flowers and handsome foliage. It is suitable for natural or domestic cultivation throughout the warmer coastal regions of the state.
E. staechadifolium, Lizard Tail, grows 1-5 ft., with larger grey-green leaves and clusters of yellow ray-flowers in late spring. This species occurs naturally along the sandy beaches and bluffs from Santa Barbara County into Oregon. Plate 217

Escallonia.

South America

Evergreen shrubs, offering fast growth and rich glossy green foliage. Several species and numerous varieties are available, which provide rose to white flowers and grow to sizes ranging from 4 to 25 feet. Most plants offer a wide range of uses in domestic landscapes as hedges, background and slope elements, and in mixed plantings. Others are successful in large spaces, such as parks and roadsides, where they receive little attention.
These plants are best suited to coastal conditions, with many accepting salt spray, wind and poor soils. They perform best with regular water, but will become moderately drought tolerant with age. When planted in warm inland environments they need partial shade and extra water.
E. bifida (E. montevidensis), White Escallonia, grows into a large shrubby plant 15-25 ft. high. It is useful as a screen and background plant and is covered with clusters of white flowers in spring and summer. A long-lived species for parks, open spaces and windbreaks. Plate 222
E. exoniensis is a very ornamental species which has several varieties to choose from. These plants are smaller growing, from 5 to 10 feet, and produce showy rose-white flowers. Uses include border and mixed plantings, hedges and screens.
E. laevis (E. organensis), Pink Escallonia, has long been a favorite species for general landscape use. It grows 10-15 ft., has light pink flowers, and is best suited to mild areas with regular moisture. All of the Escallonia species can be shaped by tip pruning and enhanced by removal of the dead flower heads. Plates 218, 219

Eschscholzia californica. California Poppy

California, Oregon

Short-lived perennial shrub, 6-15 in. high, with grey to green divided foliage on basal branches. Showy pale, to deep yellow, or orange flowers occur early spring through summer.
This widely distributed plant most frequently occurs in valley grassland areas throughout California. Prefers a heavy, well draining soil and regular winter moisture to enable new seedlings to mature. It is an important species for naturalizing and for color accent in domestic landscapes. In many gardens it is treated as an annual and can be encouraged to bloom longer if the dead flowers are removed. Well suited for seed mixes for fields, on fill slopes, or loose soils, where it will reseed itself from year to year if competition from grasses and other shrubs is not too intensive. In areas of high drought stress these plants will die annually and regrow from seed with the next winter rains. Many variations and localized forms exist. Seed should be collected from areas near the project site to improve plant survival and performance under natural conditions. Germination from untreated seed varies between 50-60%. Plates 220, 221

217 *Eriophyllum confertiflorum*

218, 219 *Escallonia laevis* (Above, below)

220 *Eschscholzia californica*

221 *Eschscholzia californica*
222 *Escallonia bifida*

Eucalyptus.
Australia

A large group of trees and shrubs, including over 500 species from many regions in Australia. More than 100 species have been experimented with in California, with some 30 species now in common landscape use. Much of the success for Eucalyptus adapting to our landscape conditions is due to their aggressive root systems. They are best planted from seed or small containers and given infrequent deep watering. Many species naturally have shallow roots and can often become a problem around drain lines or in areas with surface watering. Most prefer full sun exposure and accept heat, aridity and smog. Good tolerance is shown for varying soil conditions, including sterile, heavy, alkaline, wet or dry.

Sensitivity to cold is the biggest limiting factor in the choice of a particular species, as many plants are quite tender. In addition, several species tend to be brittle wooded and can be damaged in strong winds. Other considerations when using Eucalyptus pertain to their tendency to rob soils and to generate high amounts of litter. Their extensive roots often deplete soils of moisture and nutrients, while their foliage, bark, flowers and seed pods require almost year-round cleanup. Their foliage often contains high amounts of oil which prevents the leaves from decomposing quickly and will eventually sterilize the soil for many understory plants.

From a design standpoint, Eucalyptus offer a very large selection of plants to use. Distinctive forms, foliage, bark, and flower characteristics can be found for almost any project. Flowers range in size and include colors of red, pink, cream to white. Bark is either persistent from year to year, or deciduous and is shedded yearly. Seed capsules are long lasting and in some cases good for dry flower arrangements. The growth rate for most species is very rapid with good soils and moisture. Tip pruning or shaping plants when young can improve their appearance. Staking, which allows good trunk flexibility, encourages better caliper on weaker species.

There is still a lot of opportunity to explore new species of Eucalyptus. A limited group has achieved much popularity, but many other lesser known varieties can be found in experimental gardens and arboretums, and can be grown from seed. The plants listed in the table below represent a range of species suitable for use in warm, dry landscape areas.

Name	Character	Remarks
E. calophylla	Dense, full headed tree, 35-50 ft. high with handsome, wide leaves, 4-7 in. long. Deeply fissured red-brown bark is persistent. Large showy flowers, usually white, occur throughout the year. Varieties are available offering light pink to rose colored flowers.	An excellent foliage, flower and form tree for large streets, parks and specimen planting. Sensitive to cold below 28° F. Tolerates heat, smog and wind. Plates 223, 224
E. camaldulensis (E. rostrata) Red Gum, Red River Gum	A large tree, 60-140 ft. high, with many branched crown and drooping branches. Long, medium green, lance shaped leaves, small inconspicuous white flowers and tiny seed pods. Mottled white and brown bark is deciduous and peels off in long strips.	A widely planted species throughout California, with very good tolerance of heat, drought, cold, desert conditions, wind and alkaline soil. Strong silhouette character and scale for parkways, skylines and open space. Best planted in areas with natural leaf litter understory. Plates 226, 227
E. cinerea	Medium tree, 20-40 ft. high, 25-35 ft. wide, which develops a twisting, irregular branch structure. Distinctive ashy, grey-green foliage and rough, red-brown bark provide good contrasting qualities. Flowers are inconspicuous.	A form and foliage tree which develops interesting character. Hardy to 20° F. Shows good heat, wind, and drought tolerance. Use as background or park specimen. Needs time to fill out. Plate 225
E. cladocalyx (E. corynocalyx) Sugar Gum	A slender tree, 60-80 ft. high, with distinctive puffy clusters of oval shaped leaves. Creamy white flowers occur May-Aug. Bark is tan and deciduous, revealing patches of white on the trunk.	A spectacular skyline tree with its picturesque silhouette character. Does very well on coastal bluffs, where it tolerates poor soils, heat, wind and drought. Hardy to 20° F. Plates 228, 229
E. erythrocorys Red-Cap Gum	Large shrub to small tree, 15-30 ft. high, with irregular branching habit. Bright green leaves, lance shaped, 4-7 in. long, contrast nicely with red caps of flower capsules.	A small scale accent plant that is noted for its bright red flower pods and clusters of pale yellow flowers. Tends to sprawl, needs pruning to develop tree form. Hardy to 25° F., moderately drought tolerant with age. Plate 230
E. globulus 'Compacta' Dwarf Blue Gum	A dense, multibranched shrub-like tree, 25-50 ft. high. Foliage is blue-grey-green and persists on branches low to the ground. Creamy white flowers are conspicuous followed by large 1 in. seed capsules.	Dwarf Blue Gum tolerates difficult conditions in many regions, but has a preference for deep soils and coastal influence. Primarily a utility tree for windbreaks and screens where it can be sheared to any desired height. Quite messy and a soil robber. Plate 231
E. lehmannii Bushy Yate	Large broad shrub to small dome tree, 15-25 ft. high. Leaves, medium green to 2 in. long. Yellow-green flowers occur in large clusters, followed by fused seed capsules which persist for several years.	Well suited for coastal edges with tolerance of sea spray, alkaline soils, humidity, drought and cold to 24° F. A good medium scale plant, often used as a screen or street tree with the lower branches removed. Relatively uniform and neat in appearance for a Eucalyptus species. Plate 232

Eucalyptus. (Cont.)

Name	Character	Remarks
E. leucoxylon White Ironbark	An open and slender tree, 30-60 ft. high, with drooping branches. Long, grey-green leaves, 4-7 in. are curved and sickle-like. Conspicuous cream colored flowers occur periodically during both winter and spring. Bark is deciduous, revealing smooth white trunk with some spots. Variety E. l. 'Rosea' has many clusters of pink-red flowers.	Prefers deep soils and tolerates conditions in coastal or inland zones, including smog, moderate drought, alkalinity, and temperatures to 18° F. A general purpose tree suited for difficult areas in parks, on moderate slopes, and in background plantings. Plate 233
E. macrocarpa Desert Malee	Sprawling shrub, with stiff erratic branching habit, 6-12 ft. high and as wide. Pointed, blue-grey-green leaves are attached close to stems. Large, showy 3-4 in. flowers come in colors ranging from pink, scarlet to white and occur in early spring.	An unusual plant for dry, well draining slopes and no irrigation. Best used in remote garden areas as a seasonal accent and specimen plant. Foliage and seed capsules are quite ornamental. Very similar in appearance to E. rhodantha. Plate 234
E. niphophila Snow Gum	Small tree, with twisting trunk and branches, 15-20 ft. high. Light blue-green lance shaped leaves, 2-4 in., occur on red stems. Inconspicuous yellow-white flowers and tiny seed capsules occur in small clusters.	Very cold tolerant. Accepts wind and drought in all areas of California. Some selective pruning can make this a good specimen plant, otherwise suited for slope and group plantings where it tends to have a distinctive silvery foliage appearance.
E. polyanthemos Silver Dollar Gum	A large tree, 30-80 ft. high, with distinctive bark and blue-grey foliage. Leaves are both round and lance shaped, persistent bark is rough textured, grey to brown. Round clusters of creamy white flowers occur Jan.-Mar., followed by small seed capsules.	A striking tree mainly noted for its foliage. Works well throughout California and tolerates heat, aridity, moderate drought and cold to 24° F. Prefers loose, well draining soils, not heavy and wet conditions. This species is used for many purposes, including accent specimen, mass, park tree and for cut foliage. Plate 237
E. pulverulenta Silver Mountain Gum	Irregular shaped tree, 15-35 ft. high, with sprawling and arching branch structure. Distinctive silver to grey foliage set closely on stems. Conspicuous cream to white flowers occur intermittently fall to spring. Persistant brown bark has ribbony character.	An unusual tree needing selective pruning to control form. More of a garden and background tree for unusual variety. It can be shaped into a specimen with unique character and striking form. Tolerates many conditions, including temperatures to 18° F., moist or dry soils. Plate 235
E. rhodantha	Sprawling shrub, similar to E. macrocarpa, with angular horizontal branches and an overall height of 4-8 ft. Leaves are grey-green and merge onto stems. Large red flowers reach 3 in. across, occur in clusters intermittently spring and fall.	This species performs best on well draining soils without too much water. Cold tolerant to 10° F. A garden curiosity which can be used on banks, as well as be espaliered, or planted in large tubs. Plate 236
E. rudis Desert Gum	Single or multi-trunked tree, 30-50 ft. high, with ends of branches drooping. Leaves are medium green, to 6 in. long. Rough grey-brown bark is persistent on lower trunks. Conspicuous clusters of creamy white flowers occur in early spring.	A sturdy tree for all regions in California, which tolerates heat, aridity, alkaline or saline soils, wind, desert or coastline exposures. Prefers monthly deep watering, well draining soils and survives cold to 16° F. A good medium-sized tree for streets, mass plantings, accents and general landscape use. Plate 238
E. sideroxylon Red Ironbark Pink Ironbark	An upright and open headed tree, 30-50 ft. high. Deep, red-brown to almost black bark, is furrowed and persistent. Thin blue-green leaves, 3-6 in. long, hang downward on branches. Flowers are showy and range from white to pink. Variety E. s. 'Rosea' offers richer pink flowers and is the most popular selection of this species.	A frequently used tree due to its rich foliage, bark and flowering characteristics. Grows well throughout California and prefers coastal influence and well draining soils. Good resistance to frost and temperatures to 20° F. Tolerates wind, desert atmosphere, sterile and alkali soils, sea coast conditions and smog. Very successful in all landscape situations near buildings, in lawns, parks, and street tree plantings. Plates 239, 240
E. torquata Coral Gum	A narrow upright tree, 15-20 ft. high, with persistent rough, red-brown bark. Light grey-green leaves are 3-4 in. long. Showy red flowers and seed capsules occur in winter and summer.	An ornamental Eucalyptus with good foliage and flower qualities. Needs some staking and shaping to develop a strong specimen. Tolerates moderate drought, but is sensitive to temperatures below 30° F. Suitable for small garden spaces, patios, and background areas. Plates 241, 242
E. viminalis Manna Gum Ribbon Gum	A large spreading tree, 80-150 ft. high, with drooping branches. Narrow, medium green leaves are 4-6 in. long. Deciduous bark peels off in long vertical strips to reveal a white trunk. Insignificant white flowers and seed capsules occur all year.	Manna Gum becomes a massive specimen over time and is best suited for large spaces. It prefers deep valley soil conditions, with good tolerance of heat and cold to 15° F. Likes deep watering, produces volumes of litter. Plate 243

223 Eucalyptus calophylla

226 Eucalyptus camaldulensis

224 Eucalyptus calophylla

225 Eucalyptus cinerea

227 Eucalyptus camaldulensis

228 *Eucalyptus cladocalyx*

229 *Eucalyptus cladocalyx*

230 *Eucalyptus erythrocorys*
232 *Eucalyptus lehmannii*

231 *Eucalyptus globulus* 'Compacta'
233 *Eucalyptus leucoxylon*

234 *Eucalyptus macrocarpa*

235 *Eucalyptus pulverulenta*
237 *Eucalyptus polyanthemos*

236 *Eucalyptus rhodantha*

238 *Eucalyptus rudis*

239 *Eucalyptus sideroxylon* 'Rosea'

240 *Eucalyptus sideroxylon* 'Rosea'
243 *Eucalyptus viminalis*

241, 242 *Eucalyptus torquata* (Above, below)

Feijoa sellowiana. Pineapple Guava
South America

A many branched shrub to small canopy tree, 10-20 ft. high and 10-15 ft. wide. Leaves are medium dull green above, whitish below. Clusters of showy red and white flowers occur May-June. Edible green fruit matures in early summer.

A versatile plant which performs best in areas having coastal influence, or in partial shade in warmer inland locations. Soils can vary from heavy to clay types to rocky, with some alkalinity present. Sensitive to prolonged frost and cold below 20° F. Periodic deep watering and valley heat produces large leaves and fast growth. Responds well to pruning and can be shaped into a multi-trunk tree, shrub or hedge. Good as a patio specimen, background screen or espalier plant. Several garden varieties are available for improved fruit characteristics. Plates 245, 246

Fremontodendron. Flannel Bush
California Chaparral

Evergreen shrubs, or small trees, offering spectacular displays of yellow flowers and demanding careful growing conditions. Several species occur throughout the chaparral foothills of California, which offer variations in flowers, foliage and overall plant form. Leaves are usually leathery, covered with fuzzy hairs and are divided into shallow lobes. Forms range from dense spreading shrubs to large plants, with many stiff and upright branches. Flowers range from orange-yellow to pale yellow in color and in size from 1-3 in. across. Most species are adapted to the dry slopes of coastal, inland and interior mountains, where they have very good drainage and receive no summer water.

These are dramatic plants best suited for background and slope plantings, away from summer irrigation, as most species are susceptible to soil fungus diseases. Careful handling when planting is advised and all species should be located on well draining sites with loose soils. Selected varieties are the most popular and available for landscape use. They perform well as fast growing accent, screen and naturalizing plants.

244 Fremontodendron californicum

Name	Character	Remarks
F. californicum Common Flannel Bush	Widely distributed species within 2500-6000 ft. elevation range throughout the coastal and inland mountains, mixed with Chaparral, Yellow Pine Forest and Pinon Juniper plant communities. Plants develop into open and spreading shrubs 10-18 ft. high. Leaves are small, to 1 in. dia. Clear yellow flowers to 1½ in. are nearly flat and cover the plant in early spring.	Easily hybridizes and develops many natural seedling variations, including F. 'California Glory' which is a more profusely flowering plant than its parents. Other available hybrids include F. 'Pacific Sunset' and F. 'San Gabriel', which have similar characteristics, but show more tolerance to garden conditions. Plates 244, 247-250
F. c. ssp. decumbrens	A prostrate form of Fremontia found in El Dorado County. It reaches 3-4 ft. high with a spread of 6-10 ft., and produces red-orange flowers to 1½ in.	Generally not available, but should receive wider attention for use on dry, well draining banks and for regional parks within its native range. Currently being grown in various botanic gardens to discover growth habits and tolerances.
F. c. ssp. napense Napa Fremontia	Medium shrub to small tree, 6-15 ft. high, 1½ in. dia. lemon yellow flowers occur May-June. Leaves vary in size, ½-1½ in., dark green above, either entire or having lobes. A native of the western Sierra Nevada and towards the coast in Napa and Lake counties.	This species is suited to the same uses as other Fremontias, with availability being restricted to areas of its natural distribution.
F. mexicanum Southern Flannel Bush	This species occurs in dry canyons of the Chaparral and Southern Oak Woodland of San Diego County. It has been more popular than F. californicum, with its larger leaves and red-tinged yellow flowers. Flowers reach 3 in. across and are partly hidden by larger 2-3 in. dia. foliage. Develops into an upright shrub, 10-20 ft. high, with typical stiff branching.	This species has been recognized as being one of the best California native plants. While newer seedling variations are being introduced, F. mexicanum is still one of the most frequently used and appreciated of the Flannel Bush group.

245 *Feijoa sellowiana*

246 *Feijoa sellowiana*

247 *Fremontodendron* 'San Gabriel'
249 *Fremontodendron californicum*

248 *Fremontodendron* 'San Gabriel'

250 *Fremontodendron* 'California Glory'

Garrya. Silktassel

Western U.S.A., Mexico, West Indies

A group of shrubs and small trees containing some 15 species, with 6 of these occurring naturally within the Pacific Coast states. They typically have thick, leathery leaves which are curved and showy, creamy-white flower tassels. Species found in California have adapted to the Chaparral plant community in the coastal foothills and interior Sierra Nevada mountain range. They prefer well draining sites, and need no summer moisture. Most species offer good landscape use, with at least three native species and one hybrid currently being grown. Flowering of these plants improves in areas with cold winters and occurs most heavily on male plants.

Name	Character	Remarks
G. elliptica Coast Silktassel	Medium shrub, 6-10 ft. high, or small tree, to 18 ft. Leaves are distinctly warped, leathery, dark green above, covered with woolly hairs beneath. Showy white flower catkins grow 3-8 in. and cover the plant from Dec.-Mar., creating a weeping effect.	Coast Silktassel is a hardy native that adapts to full exposures in the coastal ranges from Ventura County to Oregon. It can easily be used in inland areas where it prefers partial shade and deep watering in hot locations. This species is a good choice for slope, screen and naturalizing plantings in parks and along roads. An improved hybrid, G. e. 'James Roof', produces flower tassels that range 8-12 in. long. These plants show good garden tolerance and provide an unusual flowering accent in the winter. Plate 251
G. fremontii Fremont Silktassel	An upright shrub, 5-10 ft. high, with large glossy leaves, 2½ in. long by 1½ in. wide. Undersides of leaves are pale green. Showy, yellow-white flower tassels grow 3-8 in. long, occur Jan.-Apr. Small blue to black berries, mature in early summer.	Fremont Silktassel is a very adaptable species to coastal, inland and interior foothill regions. Prefers a well draining soil and tolerates full sun, heat, aridity, drought and cold. It has been more popular than G. elliptica, due to its glossy leaves and equally showy display of flowers. An excellent slope, screen and background plant in domestic gardens. As with other species, it prefers some cold weather to stimulate maximum flower production.
G. veatchii Veatch Silktassel	An upright shrub, 4-7 ft. high, with narrow, dark green leaves to 4 in. long. Creamy-white flower catkins grow 2-4 in. during Feb. and March.	Veatch Silktassel inhabits the chaparral slopes of the coastal and inland foothills from San Diego to Santa Barbara counties. It shows good adaptability to coastal conditions, north to the San Francisco Bay region, as well as tolerates inland garden areas. It is suited to the same uses as other species, but is less showy in its display of flowers and has been most frequently used throughout southern California. Plates 252, 253

Gazania.

South Africa

A popular group of perennial ground covers, which have many uses in our landscapes, due to their quick growth and intensive displays of flowers. Flowers can be mixed or have single colors, ranging from yellow to orange, red, lavender, and cream, and will cover these plants in early spring through summer and intermittently all year.
Gazanias enjoy warm, sunny environments and tolerate a wide variety of soil conditions. Once established, they require only moderate levels of water, even in the hottest areas. Both clumping and trailing varieties exist, which work well along borders, in medians, for accent and in ground cover areas. The clumping varieties also provide good use in seed mixes for slope plantings. Seeds readily germinate and provide moderate slope stabilization while longer lived plants start to mature. These plants can also be divided every 3-5 years to stimulate renewed growth. *G. rigens leucolaena*, Trailing Gazania, develops long spreading stems and is particularly well suited to slopes, large ground cover areas and for cascading over walls. It has silvery-grey foliage, bright yellow flowers, and is usually planted from rooted cuttings. This species, along with several of its improved varieties, works well as a transition plant into natural areas and can act as a firebreak if it receives periodic summer moisture. Plates 254, 255

Geijera parviflora. Australian Willow

Australia

Graceful evergreen tree, to 25 ft. tall and 15-20 ft. wide. Long thin leaves, 3-6 in., are pale green and hang from branches. Develops an open character with fine texture and weeping effect. Clusters of pale yellow flowers are noticeable in early spring and fall.
Australian Willow is another good example of a plant having a deep root system which enables it to withstand drought as it ages. However, it will always respond with denser foliage and faster growth with additional summer water. Best suited for mild coastal zones and adjacent inland locations. It tolerates a variety of soils, from sandy to marine clay and prefers full sun. A good choice for many landscape areas and as an alternative to Eucalyptus. Other uses include patio tree, mass groupings, dry stream areas and on slopes. Plate 256

251 Garrya elliptica 'James Roof'

252, 253 Garrya veatchii (Above, below)

254 Gazania rigens leucolaena
255 Gazania species

256 Geijera parviflora

Grevillea.
Australia

Evergreen shrubs and trees, quite varied in character and drought tolerance. Foliage is often needle-like and fine textured in appearance. Flowers are quite showy, range in colors from red, pink, cream to orange. Several species and varieties are available which offer ground cover, shrub and tree forms. They are valued for their foliage and flower character in many landscape situations.

These plants endure dry areas quite well, where they accept neglect and poor soils. Avoid frequent spraying. Give plants in hot locations periodic deep water in the summer. Most plants prefer well draining conditions, and tolerate heat and smog. Often used on banks, along roadsides and in border plantings.

257 Grevillea lanigera

Name	Character	Remarks
G. 'Aromas'	Large shrub, with arching branches and medium green needle-like foliage. Plants reach 5-8 ft. high, 6-10 ft. wide, and produce showy red flowers from late winter to early spring.	A very good slope and screen plant for coastal, inland and interior areas. Tolerates drought, as well as accepts ample summer water. Plate 258
G. banksii (G. banksii forsteri) Crimson Coneflower	Large shrub to small tree, to 15 ft. high, with 4-10 in. long leaves, that are dull dark green and divided into many deep lobes. Large clusters of upright flowers are dark crimson red, occur in spring and are very showy.	A temperamental plant requiring good drainage and limited water. Suitable as a single specimen or massed on slopes and as windbreaks. Plate 259
G. lanigera Woolly Grevillea	Spreading and mounding shrub, 3-5 ft. high, 5-10 ft. across. Linear foliage is dark green above, greyish below. Showy flowers are red and pale yellow, occur late spring to early summer.	Very good sun and drought tolerance makes this plant suited to banks, natural areas and as a large area ground cover. Tolerates full coastal exposures and likes some protection from extreme heat in inland and interior areas. Plate 257
G. 'Noellii'	Spreading shrub, 3-5 ft. high, 4-6 ft. wide with light to medium green needle-like foliage. Showy flowers are pink and white, occur in small clusters.	A widely used variety for banks, medians, screens and large scale ground cover areas. Tolerates many conditions, including poor soils and prefers periodic watering in warm locations during the summer. Plates 260, 261
G. robusta Silk Oak	Large, narrow tree, 50-80 ft. high, 15-30 ft. spread. Produces fast growth and brittle wood. Distinctive, divided leaves are dark green above, silvery below, which shimmer in the wind. Large clusters of very showy, gold to orange flowers occur Apr.-June.	A tree often selected for quick effects in parks, medians and mass plantings. Generates lots of litter and has shallow, invasive roots. Grows best in light, dry soils, with natural leaf litter understory. Tolerates heat, aridity, mild temperatures and full sun. Heavy pruning when young can strengthen plants and make them suitable for street trees and areas with lots of room. Plates 264, 265
G. rosmarinifolia Rosemary Grevillea	Mounding shrub, 3-6 ft. high and as wide. Narrow leaves are dark green above, silky white below. Crimson and cream colored flowers occur primarily Jan.-Mar.	This species works well as a clipped or natural hedge, background and slope plant. Very good tolerance for drought, full sun and heat.
G. thelemanniana Hummingbird Bush	Rounded shrub, 4-8 ft. high, with 2 in. long leaves that are finely divided. Crimson flowers with yellow tips, occur intermittently all year.	A plant used as a flowering accent, for borders and in mass plantings. Tolerates heat, full sun, drought and salt spray, and works well in either coastal or inland environments. Plates 262, 263

258 Grevillea 'Aromas'

259 Grevillea banksii

260 Grevillea 'Noellii'
262 Grevillea thelemanniana

261 Grevillea 'Noellii'

263 Grevillea thelemanniana

264 Grevillea robusta

266 Hakea suaveolens

269 Hakea laurina

265 Grevillea robusta

270 Helianthemum nummularium

Hakea.
Australia

Evergreen shrubs and trees which provide many functional landscape uses. These are tenacious plants, which tolerate full coastal and inland conditions, including salt spray, heat, cold, wind, saline and poor soils. They are quite drought resistant and need good drainage when planted in heavy soils.

Two species of Hakea are most commonly used in dry landscapes. Their flowers are noticeable, but not highly ornamental. Their foliage differs dramatically, one species having needle-like character, the other producing long, lance shaped leaves. These plants are often used as screens, on banks and along roadsides.

267 Hakea suaveolens

Name	Character	Remarks
H. laurina Sea Urchin Hakea	Large shrub to small tree. Simple leaves are pointed, grey-green, 3-6 in. long, with parallel veins. Showy bright red flowers are similar to Bottlebrush, occur Jan.-Mar.	A good background accent, screen shrub, or patio tree if staked and pruned when young. Tolerates saline soils, heat, aridity and drought in coastal and inland areas from both southern to northern California. As a shrub, it develops into a large mound 10-15 ft. high. When used as a tree it can reach 30 ft. tall. Survives in clay type soils with good drainage. Performs well along the coastal edge with periodic salt spray and wind. Plate 269
H. suaveolens Sweet Hakea	Upright shrub or small tree, 10-18 ft. high. Medium green leaves are stiff, pointed and needle-like, giving a light texture, but prickly quality. White flowers occur Nov.-Feb. and are noted for their fragrance.	Sweet Hakea is a tough plant for barrier and screen uses. It can also be shaped into a small dome tree. Tolerates dry soils, smog, sun, drought and salt spray. Prefers light, well draining soils, and will grow in sand at the coast. Often used with conifers due to similar appearance. Plates 266, 267

Helianthemum. Sunrose
Europe, Mediterranean Region, California

Low growing evergreen ground covers and small shrubs, including over 100 species and varieties. The most commonly used selections are hybrids of *H. nummularium*, which come with flower colors ranging from red, orange, yellow, peach to white. These plants range 4-8 in. high, spread 2-3 ft., and flower primarily from Apr.-June.

Sunroses are highly adaptable to all plant environments, and perform very well in full sun, on light soils and in neglected spaces. They do not like frequent watering or disturbance to their roots. Denser growth and fall blooming is stimulated by shearing in late spring. Most varieties are excellent for rock gardens, banks and transitions into natural areas, where they should be considered short-lived. A native species, *H. scoparium* var. *vulgare*, Coast Rock-Rose is a good plant to include in seed mixes for slope and naturalization plantings along the coast. This species produces extensive amounts of yellow flowers in early spring, and adds to the visual richness of mixed plantings. Plates 268, 270

268 Helianthemum nummularium

Heteromeles arbutifolia. Toyon
(Photinia arbutifolia) California

A dense evergreen shrub, 8-15 ft. high and as wide, or a multi-trunk dome tree, 15-25 ft. Large leathery leaves, 1-4 in. long, have distinctive toothed edges. Clusters of small white flowers are conspicuous, occur Jul.-Sept. Large groups of very showy red berries mature Dec.-Feb., and are useful in cut arrangements, as well as for wildlife.
Toyon is one of the most popular and widely used California natives. It inhabits the chaparral foothills throughout the state and shows very good tolerance for many conditions, including heat, smog, wind, light or heavy soils. These plants will develop deep root systems and become highly drought tolerant, but are receptive to summer water in harsh locations. They easily respond to pruning to form everything from hedges to sculptural tree forms. They are often used on slopes, along roadsides, in mass and background plantings. In domestic gardens they mix well with ornamentals and provide seasonal color during the winter. Best planted from small containers and given periodic deep watering. Plates 272, 273

Hypericum. St. Johnswort

Ground covers and shrubs, with distinctive yellow to gold flowers and handsome foliage character. This is a large group of plants, including about 200 species which come from temperate and tropical regions of the world. Four species are native to California, but are seldom used in domestic landscapes.

Several ornamental varieties of Hypericum have been introduced from Europe and Asia which offer very good ornamental character and landscape use. However, one introduction, *H. perforatum,* Klamath Weed, has escaped and become a widely distributed pest throughout much of northern California. The species which are available for commercial planting will accept many soils and limited drought, but most prefer rich soils and ample moisture. They tolerate full sun and heat along the coast, and grow best in partial shade with regular moisture in hot inland and interior environments. Pruning or shearing of these plants in the late winter will remove old stems and encourage tighter and lusher foliage. Two species discussed below show reasonable tolerance in dry landscape areas after they are established.

271 Hypericum calycinum

Name	Character	Remarks
H. beanii (H. patulum henryi)	A rounded mounding shrub, 3-5 ft. high, with large simple leaves to 2½ in. long. Bright yellow flowers can reach 2 in. across and cover the plant from July-Oct.	A good species for borders, mass plantings and flowering accent. It has neat foliage appearance and can be kept small and tight with tip pruning during the dormant winter months. Tolerates acid, heavy, or light soils and is moderately drought tolerant throughout coastal environments. Plates 274, 275
H. calycinum Aaron's Beard Creeping St. Johnswort	Ground cover, to 12 in. high, which spreads over large areas by underground stems. Large bright yellow flowers to 3 in. across, occur late spring through summer.	A tough and handsome ground cover with rich foliage and flower qualities. Tolerates coastal sun and drought, prefers regular water in inland and interior valleys. Performs well on slopes, in medians and in ground cover plantings. This species can become thin and even lose most of its foliage in cold climates. Mowing in the winter every 2-3 years will remove dead stems, improve flower and foliage character. Plate 271

Isomeris arborea. Bladder Pod

California, Mexico

A dense evergreen mounding shrub, 3-6 ft. high and as wide. Pale grey-green leaves are divided into 3 leaflets. Noticeable pale yellow flowers occur Feb.-May. Conspicuous inflated seed pods emerge green, turn tan and persist through summer.
Bladder Pod is a common shrub throughout the Coastal Sage and Grassland plant communities, from San Diego to Los Angeles counties and to the edges of the Mojave and Colorado deserts. It is a hardy plant, accepting marine clays to rocky soils, with a preference for good drainage. Easily planted from untreated seed with a germination rate of 70% possible. While it can be used in desert and rock gardens for a variety plant, it is most often used on slopes and in natural areas where it provides soil stability and moderate fire resistance. It does not need supplemental summer water, but will shed some leaves under high drought stress. This is a relatively unknown native which should receive more attention in landscape projects. Plates 276, 277

272 Heteromeles arbutifolia

273 Heteromeles arbutifolia

274 Hypericum beanii

275 Hypericum beanii
277 Isomeris arborea

276 Isomeris arborea

Jasminum humile. Italian Jasmine

Italy

A large evergreen shrub or woody vine, 10 ft. high, 8-12 ft. wide. Light green leaves are divided into 3-7 leaflets, occur on long arching stems. Clusters of bright yellow, trumpet shaped flowers, are fragrant and are produced summer through fall.

Italian Jasmine is often used on large slopes and along roadsides from coastal to interior valley environments. It shows good tolerance of heat, smog and dust. Under high drought stress, it will die back and shed leaves, but quickly fills out when moisture is provided. In domestic gardens, this species can be clipped into a hedge, or trained onto a trellis. It accepts most soils and looks best with regular water in hot locations. Plate 278 (below)

Juglans californica.
Southern California Black Walnut

A large mounding shrub, to 18 ft. high, or multi-trunk tree, 20-35 ft. high, 20-35 ft. spread. Long, dark green leaves are pinnately divided into 9-19 leaflets and are deciduous. Insignificant flowers occur Mar.-Apr., small edible walnut fruit matures at the end of summer.

Southern California Black Walnut inhabits dry slopes and inland valley areas from San Bernadino to San Luis Obispo counties. It relies upon its extensive root system in deeper soil areas to have adequate moisture during the summer months. This plant is best suited to inland and interior valley areas, and tolerates sun, heat, smog, drought and alkaline soils. A very good plant for parks, slopes and naturalizing, where enough time can be allowed for it to develop some size. Unfortunately, this species is being heavily removed throughout southern California for housing and urban expansion. Older plants can be shaped into broad tree forms. New plants can be established from fresh seed in late fall, or from small containers in early spring. Plates 279, 280

Another species, *J. hindsii,* California Black Walnut, is a larger tree. It grows 30-60 ft. high, 20-50 ft. spread. It shows drought tolerance in its natural range, as well as accepts alkaline soils. It is appreciated for its rich foliage character, often used as a root stock for English Walnut.

Juniperus. Juniper

Europe, U.S.A.

A varied group of coniferous shrubs and trees, with many uses in western landscapes. Commonly known for their dense, evergreen needle and scale-like foliage and hard round berries. Foliage colors come in many shades of green, including blue-green, forest-green, light-green and grey-green. Foliage may also be variegated with yellow and white colors. Flowers are usually not significant. Forms range from low and spreading, to twisting, arching and upright shrubs and trees. Most species have a neat and uniform appearance which many people prefer.

Junipers grow well in all plant environments from the coast to interior valleys and foothills, with a preference for full sun, loose soils and infrequent moisture. However, they show excellent tolerance of many difficult soil conditions, including clays, acid and alkaline. To be avoided are areas with wet heavy soils and deep shade. Some species are highly suited for the coastal edge in sand and accept salt spray, while other plants work best in inland areas with heat, smog, dust and wind tolerances.

Junipers can be used in almost any number of ways. This has led to the use of over 100 species and varieties in western landscapes to date. Low growing forms serve well on banks and slopes which border natural areas. They survive on little water after establishment. Many other species can be used in dry landscapes for screens, colonnades, accent specimens, mass and background plantings. They tend to be slow growing and time should be planned for their development into mature sizes. Several specialized references, as well as arboretum growing grounds show and describe the varieties that are available.

Within this plant group only 4 species are native to California. These plants are not found in common use and do not offer much potential in domestic areas. Such species tolerate dry and difficult environments around deserts and high elevations, and are best appreciated in their natural context. Efforts should be made to protect these plants, as they take many years to achieve mature groupings. Can live to very old ages. Plates 281, 282

Koelreuteria paniculata.
Goldenrain Tree

China, Korea, Japan

Small deciduous tree, deeply rooted, with large pinnately divided leaves having 7-15 lobed leaflets. Often develops into a round dome, 15-30 ft. high, 15-20 ft. wide, with twisting branches. Showy bright yellow flowers occur July-Aug. in large loose clusters, and are replaced by showy inflated seed capsules which persist for many months.

Goldenrain Tree is a widely adapted species accepting either coastal, inland, or interior plant environments. Prefers sun and well draining soils, tolerates heat, wind, smog, alkalai soils and drought. Should be protected from prolonged freezing and needs regular water when young. An excellent small scale street, patio, lawn and park tree. Plates 283, 284

Another species, *Koelreuteria bipinnata* (also *K. integrifolia)*, Chinese Flame Tree, is slightly larger, 25-40 ft. high, spreading 25-30 ft. This is a popular tree for lawns, streets and parks, which offers showy clusters of yellow flowers and red fruit bracts. It will eventually grow under conditions of limited moisture when established in coastal environments. When planted in warm inland and valley areas, it prefers regular moisture for best performance.

279 Juglans californica

280 Juglans californica

281 Juniperus californica

282 Juniperus californica

283 Koelreuteria paniculata

284 Koelreuteria paniculata

Lagerstroemia indica.
Crape Myrtle

China

Deciduous shrub to small dome tree, 10-25 ft. high, 10-18 ft. spread. Distinctive smooth, light brown bark is deciduous. Simple leaves to 1½ in., emerge light green in spring and turn yellow, orange and red in fall prior to dropping. Large terminal clusters of flowers occur July-Sept. that provide a very showy effect. Develops a shallow root system when given surface water.

Crape Myrtle is a highly attractive plant best suited to hot inland and interior valley areas. Too much exposure to coastal dampness and fog causes severe problems with mildew. Many varieties are available, including compact, many branched shrubs, to full trees and offer flower colors ranging from white, pink, rose, red, blue, lavender to purple. Most plants develop low branching, but pruning and staking when young produces very consistent tree forms. These plants prefer heat, deep moisture and well draining soils. However, they will accept many other soils, including clays, and have shown very good drought tolerance with infrequent watering. This is one of the best form, foliage and flowering accent plants for small scale spaces as patio specimens, street trees, and in mixed plantings. Both tree and shrub forms look good in mass plantings. Will often sucker from the root base. Care should be taken in selecting and mixing flower colors. Plates 285, 286, 287

285 Lagerstroemia indica

Lantana.

Tropical U.S.A., Mexico

Evergreen to semi-deciduous shrubs providing up to 12 months of flowering. These plants are highly valued for their tolerance of any soil type and dry heat conditions, with limited moisture. They are best suited to inland and interior environments away from fog and are sensitive to cold below 30° F. where they become partly deciduous and can die back.

Plants which are given lots of water and fertilizer produce lush foliage, but provide less flowering. When under high drought stress, many plants will shed some leaves and look sparse until watered. In 3-4 years time, they get leggy and build up thatch which can be controlled by hard pruning in the early spring. Lantanas have a characteristic leaf odor which is objectionable to some people. The flowers are very attractive to bees.

Two species and many hybrid varieties are available which provide different form and flower characteristics. Plants range from spreading ground covers to mounding shrubs. Flower clusters can consist of single colors, or can be mixed and include orange, yellow, pink, white and lavender.

Name	Character	Remarks
L. camara **Common Lantana**	Mounding shrub, 3-6 ft. wide, with coarse foliage and branching character. Several varieties have been developed from this species which offer other flower colors and form to choose from.	Common Lantana works well as an informal hedge, background and slope plant. It is a fast grower which provides quick effects and flowering accent uses. This species has naturalized to a limited extent. Plates 288, 289, 291
L. montevidensis *(L. sellowiana)* **Trailing Lantana**	A vining ground cover, 1-2 ft. high and 3-6 ft. wide. This is a more cold and drought tolerant species which has lavender-purple flowers.	Trailing Lantana is a common bank and ground cover plant for dry roadsides and foothills. It is very tenacious and tolerates full sun, heat, smog, and poor soils. It will become sparse and of low fire resistance in late summer if it does not receive periodic moisture. Plate 290

286 *Lagerstroemia indica*

287 *Lagerstroemia indica*

288 *Lantana camara* 'Gold Mound'
290 *Lantana montevidensis*

289 *Lantana camara*
291 *Lantana camara* 'Festival'

Laurus nobilis.
Sweet Bay, Grecian Laurel

Europe, Mediterranean Region

A medium sized evergreen shrub to tree, 15-35 feet high, 15-20 feet wide. Often develops into a many branched shrub that can be easily sheared into many shapes, as well as be pruned into a dome shaped tree. Oval leaves are pointed, grow 2-4 in. long, are leathery and dark green. Flowers on the female plants are slightly noticeable and are followed by purple-black berries.

Sweet Bay is a traditional container and topiary plant in many garden situations. It is relatively slow growing and can be shaped into artistic and formal forms for use as hedges, colonnades, specimen and character plantings. When pruned into a standard form, it works well as a street tree or small patio shade tree. Its leaves have long been used in cooking as a seasoning. This species needs little water after establishment, tolerates full sun and heat in most environments, and accepts lean, rocky soils. Plate 292

292 Laurus nobilis

Lavandula. Lavender

Europe, Mediterranean Region

Evergreen ground covers and small shrubs which are known for their purple to lavender flowers and aromatic grey-green foliage. These plants are highly valued for cut flowers, border plantings and in the production of perfume. They want full sun, require little water, and tolerate heat, aridity, and smog. Most species prefer well draining soils, but several will accept clay conditions. These plants can be kept neat and compact if the flower stalks are removed as they finish.

Several species and dwarf varieties of lavender are available for landscape use. *L. angustifolia* (also *L. officinalis, L. spica,* or *L. vera*), English Lavender is most common and frequently used. It has smooth, grey leaves and grows into a rounded shrub 2-4 feet in size. Lavender flower heads occur on long spikes from late spring to summer. *L. dentata,* French Lavender, grows into a 1½ to 3 foot mound and has tightly toothed grey-green leaves which are highly aromatic. This species provides a very long blooming season, with numerous light purple flower spikes. *L. stoechas,* Spanish Lavender, is a stiffer form which grows up to 2½ feet high. Small grey leaves to ½ in. contrast nicely with deep purple flowers. Plates 293, 294

Lavatera assurgentiflora. California Tree Mallow

California Coastal Islands

Large evergreen shrub to small tree, 10-15 ft. high, 10-18 ft. wide. Trunk and branches are light grey. Maple-like leaves are light, pale green and to 4 in. across. Showy rose and white flowers, with distinctive veins, occur most heavily from Mar.-July.

Tree Mallow is an excellent large shrub for use in coastal plant environments, where it performs well as a windbreak or informal screen. Likes humidity and tolerates wet sandy soils to clay conditions and salt spray. Considered drought tolerant along the coast, but is often used in inland areas with some protection from extreme heat and with periodic summer water. It grows rapidly from seed or containers and is used for quick effects. Pruning can control the size, density of foliage, and can reveal the strong branch structure. Considered short-lived, to 10 years, but makes a good accent and specimen plant at early ages. Plates 295, 296

Leptodactylon californicum. Prickly Phlox

California Chaparral

Small shrub, 1-3 ft. high and as wide, with stiff needle-like leaves. Showy displays of white-rose-lavender flowers occur Mar.-June.

Prickly Phlox is an interesting plant, well suited for seed mixes and rock gardens in most plant environments. It naturally occurs in the coastal and inland mountains from San Diego to Monterey counties. It accepts full sun and needs little or no summer water. Recommended uses include slope plantings with other natives, garden accent, and naturalizing. Plate 297, 298

293 *Lavandula dentata*

294 *Lavandula dentata*

295 *Lavatera assurgentiflora*

296 *Lavatera assurgentiflora*

297 *Leptodactylon californicum*

298 *Leptodactylon californicum*

Leptospermum laevigatum.
Australian Tea Tree

Australia

Large shrub, to 15 ft. high and as wide, or small tree to 25 ft. Often a many branched plant, with shaggy twisting trunks that grow along the ground. Small oval leaves are olive green. Showy white flowers occur Apr.-June.
A versatile plant, adapting to many environments including coastal edges, inland and interior valleys and foothills. Prefers slightly acid and light soil conditions and needs good drainage for best performance. Tolerates full sun, heat, aridity, wind and salt spray. Can be densely planted for a natural or clipped hedge, or be used on slopes and in background plantings. Selective pruning can shape this species as it matures into many sculptural forms, which reveals interesting trunk and bark features for specimen and espalier uses. Two varieties exist which offer smaller forms. *L. l.* 'Compactum' grows into a mound, 5-8 ft. high, is more open, very similar in foliage and produces a few flowers. *L. l.* 'Reevesii' has denser, rounded leaves and grows into a 3-5 ft. high mounding shrub. Plates 299, 300

299, 300 Leptospermum laevigatum (Above, below)

Leptospermum scoparium.
New Zealand Tea Tree

New Zealand

A spreading shrub, with upright stems, 6-8 ft. high, 10-12 ft. wide. Leaves are small and pointed, dark green. This parent species is of little ornamental interest, as many hybrid varieties have been developed which offer improved flower and form qualities. Flower types are either single or double, include colors from white, pink, to deep red, and occur from late winter to early spring. Most hybrids are upright shrubs, varying in height from 2-15 ft. depending upon the variety. With age, the larger plants can be shaped into sculptural forms that provide spectacular displays of flowers, along with interesting shaggy trunks. Smaller shrubs work well as individual accents, along borders, for background and slope plantings.
This species and its many variations are well suited for sunny environments from the coastal bluffs to inland and interior valley areas. They tend to be more tolerant of cold than *L. laevigatum*. Prefer regular moisture when young, but want drier conditions and withstand drought with age. Grow best in loose, slightly acid, well draining soils. Plates 301-305

301 Leptospermum scoparium 'Helene Strybing'

Leucophyllum frutescens.
Texas Ranger

Southwest U.S.A., Mexico

Dense, upright shrub with moderate growth rate, 5-10 ft. high, 3-5 ft. wide. Smoky grey-green foliage is accented by small displays of showy purple flowers in summer.
Texas Ranger is a very usable plant for foliage and flower accents in rock gardens, on slopes, as a border, or untrimmed hedge. Well adapted to warm environments and wanting full sun. Best suited to inland and interior landscapes and is naturally adapted to desert conditions. Accepts heat, aridity, wind, drought and prefers well draining soils. In domestic gardens infrequent deep watering and tip pruning can keep plants in richer form. *L. f.* 'Compactum' is a smaller form, to 5 ft. high, with the same foliage and purple flower qualities. *L. f. alba* is a white flowering variety. Plates 306, 307

304, 305 **Leptospermum scoparium** 'Snow White' (Above, below)

302 Leptospermum scoparium 'Ruby Glow'
303 Leptospermum scoparium 'Ruby Glow'

306 Leucophyllum frutescens

307 Leucophyllum frutescens

Limonium perezii.
Sea lavender
(Statice perezii)

Short-lived perennial shrub, 1½-2 ft. high, with large basal leaves which grow to 12 in. long. Striking purple and white flowers occur thoughout the summer months in broad rounded clusters.
An excellent species for warm coastal edges and bluffs, with very good tolerance of salt spray. Adapts to well draining soils and has frequently naturalized along the coast from San Diego to Santa Barbara counties. Can be used in seed mixes for slope planting, or in domestic gardens where it provides long lasting flowering qualities. Considered drought tolerant only under strong coastal influence. It can be grown in inland areas in partial shade and with regular moisture. Good as a border plant, in mixed flower gardens, and for cut flowers. Plate 309

Lippia repens. Lippia
(Phyla nodiflora)

A low growing perennial ground cover, 8-15 in. high, spreading by stems which root in moist soils. Small, medium green leaves, to ¾ in. long, have toothed margins. Flower heads are white to lilac, occur on small stems above foliage.
Lippia is a plant notable for its tough character as a low ground cover or turfgrass substitute. It can be left natural to mound and spread on banks and over walls, or be mowed to 2 in. high to accept moderate foot traffic. It grows well in full sun, in environments from the coast to low deserts. It prefers regular moisture, but can survive on less water than most grasses. In cold areas it becomes dormant and pale, but quickly recovers with spring feeding. Plate 308 (Below)

Lithocarpus densiflorus.
Tanbark Oak
California, Oregon

Narrow upright tree, 40-80 ft. high, 25-40 ft. spread. Low branching and bushy when young. Large leaves reach 4 in. long, have toothed margins, and are covered with white, fuzzy hairs when young. Noticeable white flower catkins occur in early spring followed by acorn fruit.
A very dense, large shrub to tall tree, which is naturally found in the Coast Ranges from Ventura County into Oregon. Prefers well draining soils and deep moisture, but becomes quite drought tolerant with age. It is relatively slow growing and is best suited for regional parks and mass plantings within its natural range. However, it can work well as a street tree or specimen in domestic landscapes. A natural leaf litter understory is recommended. Plates 310, 311

Lobularia maritima.
Sweet Alyssum
Europe

Small perennial shrub, 4-6 in. high, with narrow green leaves and many rounded clusters of small white flowers. Flowers are fragrant and cover the plant during spring and summer, intermittent rest of the year. Several hybrid varieties have been developed which offer more compact growth. Flower colors range from white, pink, to purple. Sweet Alyssum and its many varieties are a successful group of plants for both domestic gardens and large scale slope plantings. Adapts to all plant environments, in full sun, from the coastal edge to interior valleys and foothills. Best treated as annual when used for borders, banks, rock gardens and in mixed flower groupings. These plants have become very popular for use in seed mixes to quickly vegetate new slopes. They establish foliage cover and shallow root systems very fast for soil protection. Care should be taken when using these plants as they have naturalized throughout the west and can grow almost anywhere the seeds are carried. Plates 312, 313

Lotus scoparius.
Deerweed
California

Sparse mounding shrub, 1½-4 ft. high, with basal branches and dark green leaves that are divided into three leaflets. Noticeable yellow flowers occur over many months, Feb.-Oct.
A common shrub found throughout dry landscape areas from San Diego to Humboldt counties, inland to the lower Sierra Nevadas, and on the coastal islands. Within this range, Deerweed is highly adaptable and has devloped at least 4 natural varieties. This native is a good plant for both naturalizing and slope planting. Can be planted from treated seed with 50% germination success; less if seeds are not treated. While it offers little domestic use, it is quite suited to difficult areas in full sun and in transition plantings into natural landscapes. It contributes to soil development by fixing nitrogen with its root system and works well in fire hazard areas due to its low foliage volume. Plate 314

309 Limonium perezii

310, 311 Lithocarpus densiflorus (Above, below)

312, 313 Lobularia maritima (Above, below)

314 Lotus scoparius

Lupinus. Lupine

Europe, U.S.A.

A large complex group of plants, with about 100 species occurring throughout the world, but most strongly represented in the western United States. Some 50 species and many varieties are found in California, five of which are distinctively shrubby perennials. Many localized forms and growth habits occur, which make the identification of native plants quite difficult.

Both annual and perennial Lupines have adapted to many plant environments from coastal edges, to deserts, to high interior mountain elevations. All prefer well draining sites and full sun, but are not particular as to soils. These plants also contribute to soil development, as they fix nitrogen with their root systems. Very good germination can be achieved from fresh, untreated seed, that is collected in early spring and summer. Seeds which have been stored should be soaked in hot water to increase the rate of germination. Most annual species will reseed as long as competition from grasses and other shrubs is not too extensive.

Lupines are primarily known for their palmately divided leaves and showy spikes of pea-shaped flowers. Flower colors are primarily blue-purple, but also include yellow, white, lilac, and occur April to June. Many species and improved varieties are now available, with several offering colorful uses in seed mixes for slope and erosion control plantings in dry areas. They also provide good foliage and flower accent qualities in rock gardens, borders and in mixed plantings in domestic yards. Perennial shrub forms, such as the silver Lupine, live for many years, and can be effectively used in mass or individual plantings. The chart below presents several species of Lupine, but many other useful types exist in localized areas and should be considered.

Name	Character	Remarks
L. albifrons Silver Lupine	Medium sized perennial shrub, 2-6 ft. high, developing a mounding form with many branches. Leaves are divided into 7-11 leaflets and are densely covered with fine, silvery hairs. Showy flowers are blue to purple, on 3-12 in. long stalks, from Mar.-July.	This species is a common inhabitant of the Coast Ranges on dry hillsides and in canyon areas from Humboldt to Ventura counties. It also inhabits the full length of the Sierra Nevada foothills, as well as intermittently in southern California. A very handsome foliage and flowering plant in both domestic and natural landscapes. Plant from fresh seed, with 40% germination possible.
L. arboreus Tree Lupine	A dense shrubby plant, 2-8 ft. high. Leaves medium to greyish green, consist of 6-11 leaflets that are often covered with small, silky hairs. Long stems are covered with pea-shaped flowers, which are usually bright yellow, sometimes white or blue.	Tree Lupine is native to coastal beaches and bluffs from Santa Barbara to Del Norte counties. It is a very striking flowering accent that can develop many interesting forms. Good in sandy soils. Tolerates salt spray and summer drought. 30-40% germination is possible from fresh seed. Plates 315, 316
L. chamissonis Dune Lupine	Mounding to upright shrub, 1-4 ft. high, with dense or open character. Leaves are grey-green, divided into 6-9 leaflets, and are covered with fine hairs. Flower clusters reach 4-6 in., are blue to lavender, with yellow centers.	A common species on the sandy coastal bluffs and valleys from San Francisco through Los Angeles County. Another good plant for dry coastal edges, which can be seeded with 30-40% germination success. Wants good drainage and will provide a pleasant show of flowers during May and June. Plates 317, 318
L. nanus Sky Lupine Annual Lupine	Annual species, 6-24 in. high, with medium green leaves that are divided into 5-7 leaflets. Dense clusters of blue-purple flowers, with white tips occur on many spikes Apr.-May.	A plant often found in valley grassland areas which has become popular in seed plantings for slopes and mixed wildflower effects. Germination rates of 60% can be achieved and yearly reseeding frequently occurs, unless grass competition is too high. Often creates a showy carpet of flowers in early spring and survives until soil moisture runs out. Plate 319
L. succulentus	Annual shrub, 1-2 ft. high, with large divided leaves and upright habit. Stems and leaves are covered with hairs. Long spikes of deep purple-blue flowers occur in spring.	Native to heavy soils and grassland areas throughout California. This is a stout plant that is valued for naturalizing, slope and mixed wildflower plantings. Usually planted from seed in fall, it avoids drought by completing its growth cycle by early summer. Plate 320

315 Lupinus arboreus

316 Lupinus arboreus

318 Lupinus chamissonis
320 Lupinus succulentus

317 Lupinus chamissonis
319 Lupinus nanus

Lyonothamnus floribundus. Catalina Ironwood
California Coastal Islands

A handsome evergreen tree, 15-45 ft. tall, with rich green foliage and thin, red bark. Long, narrow leaves can be entire, divided and/or lobed. Showy clusters of creamy white flowers occur May-June. This species is native to Santa Catalina Island, where it grows in areas of full sun, well draining soils, and no summer water. It has seen only limited landscape use in western gardens as another variety, *L.f. asplenifolius,* Fernleaf Ironwood, offers greater domestic value.

Fernleaf Ironwood occurs on San Clemente, Santa Cruz, and Santa Rosa Islands. It provides rich foliage, bark and flower characteristics for use in many natural and domestic landscapes. It grows into an open tree, 30-50 ft. high, has deeply lobed leaves with notched leaflets, and produces showy cream to white flowers in late spring. This variety develops either single or multiple trunks which are covered with shredded red-brown bark. Selective pruning can produce interesting forms and reveal the bark as the plant ages. It is a plant which tolerates full sun and summer conditions in coastal environments, but prefers partial shade and periodic water in warm inland areas. While it can survive in clay conditions, it responds best to coarse, well draining soils, with natural leaf litter within its dripline. An excellent foliage plant for screens, specimen, and mixed plantings in parks, open space and residential gardens. Plates 321, 322

322 Lyonothamnus floribundus asplenifolius

321 Lyonothamnus floribundus asplenifolius

Mahonia.
Western U.S.A.

A diverse group of evergreen shrubs, including some 9 species and several varieties that occur in the Pacific Coast States. These plants offer rich foliage and showy yellow flower clusters, which are appreciated in coastal or inland landscapes. Leaves are typically divided, leathery, have spines, and range in color from dark, glossy green, to pale grey-green. This genus is closely related to Berberis, Barbery, but is distinguished by not having sharp spines on their stems and branches.

Mahonias are very desirable for both ornamental and natural gardens. A number of hybrids and selections have been developed over the years which provide plants tolerant of many growing conditions. They offer several form, foliage and flower combinations. Most are easy to grow and perform best in well draining soils, with periodic moisture. They accept full sun in coastal and partial shade in inland and interior environments. Most species show good resistance to oak root fungus and are frequently planted around oaks due to their limited need for summer water. While these plants can survive in many dry situations, they will be lusher and larger if given regular water until well established.

Mahonias produce numerous clusters of lemon yellow flowers from late winter to early spring. Showy blue berries mature by mid-summer. Selected species and varieties are useful for screens, barriers, accent, slope and ground cover plantings. They tolerate garden conditions very well, and can be controlled and shaped by removing branches near the ground.

Mahonia. (Cont.)

Name	Character	Remarks
M. amplectans	Dense shrub, 4-8 ft. high and as wide. Distinctive, blue-green leaves are divided into 5-7 leaflets and covered with numerous spines. Large clusters of yellow flowers occur from April-May.	A hardy plant from the inland and coastal mountains in Riverside and San Diego counties. It provides good foliage and flower character on slopes, in mixed and screen plantings and should receive wider attention in our landscapes. Very similar to *M. aquifolium* in habit, but with lighter foliage and a higher tolerance of sun, heat and drought in both coastal and inland gardens. Plant in well draining soils and as a background to dark green plants. Plates 323, 324
M. aquifolium Oregon Grape Hollyleaf Mahonia	A handsome shrub, growing 5-8 ft., with many branches and dense foliage. Leathery leaves are glossy green and divided into 5-9 leaflets, with spines on the margins. Bright yellow flower clusters occur in late winter through spring and are followed by many pale blue berries, which are edible.	Oregon Grape grows in the coastal foothill regions from Humboldt County into British Columbia. It has been a popular landscape plant for many years and shows wide adaption to domestic gardens. New foliage growth is tinged with bronze. Both foliage and flowers make this species desirable for accent, background, slope and screen plantings. A compact form is available which grows to 2 feet. Other varieties provide different foliage and flower characteristics. These plants like coastal sun, part shade in warm areas, rich soils, and periodic summer water. Plate 325
M. 'Golden Abundance' Golden Abundance Mahonia	An upright shrub, 5-8 ft. high, with many basal stems and dense foliage. This variety is a hybrid between *M. amplectans*, where it gets its large yellow flower clusters, and *M. aquifolium*, where it gets its rich, shiny green foliage character.	Golden Abundance Mahonia is proving to be an exceptionally handsome foliage and flowering plant. It adapts well to garden conditions, as well as to heat and limited moisture. Prefers a rich, well draining soil and partial shade in inland areas. Accepts heavier soils with restricted watering. Its long spring blooming period makes it well suited as a flowering accent. Other uses include screen, hedge, slope and mixed plantings. Plate 326
M. higginsae	A stiff upright shrub, 8-12 ft. high. Leaves are grey-green and divided into 1-7 small leaflets, having many spines. Loose clusters of yellow flowers cover the plant in late winter to early spring.	A native of San Diego County, where it inhabits slopes and rocky soils and shows high drought tolerance. Usually not planted as a domestic garden plant, but it is well suited to background and mass plantings in parks and natural areas. Plates 327, 328
M. nevinii Nevin Mahonia	A dense shrub, 3-12 ft. high, with numerous basal branches. Leaves are divided into 3-5 leaflets, are pale blue-green and have stiff spines. Showy yellow flowers occur in early spring.	This species is quite similar to *M. higginsae*, but has received wider attention and use. It is native to dry outwash areas in Los Angeles County, where it survives in full sun, heat and without summer water. It tolerates many soils, as well as smog, drought and is resistant to oak root fungus. A good plant for background, barrier and slope plantings in parks and natural areas. Plates 329, 330
M. pinnata California Holly Grape	A many branched shrub, growing 3-8 ft. high with rich glossy green foliage. Leaves are divided into 5-9 leaflets, are yellow to orange when young and have spines on the margins. Showy clusters of yellow flowers will cover the plant in early spring.	This species comes from the chaparral landscapes throughout California and offers good foliage and flower qualities. Prefers well draining soils, thrives in coastal environments, and accepts ample or limited water in garden situations. An improved hybrid, *M. p.* 'Ken Hartman', offers more consistent growth and rich new foliage color. Another variety, *M. p. insularis*, comes from Santa Cruz and Sant Rosa islands, and is periodically found in domestic landscapes. Plates 331, 332
M. repens Creeping Mahonia	Small spreading shrub, 1-3 ft. high, with leathery, dull green foliage. Leaves divided into 3-7 leaflets, have spines on the margins. Small clusters of yellow flowers come in spring.	Creeping Mahonia comes from the Northwestern states and northern California. It is very useful as a ground cover on banks and under oaks, where it resists oak root fungus. It accepts coastal sun, partial shade in inland areas and needs only limited summer moisture. New growth is red to bronze. Plants spread by means of underground stems. Plate 333

323 Mahonia amplectans

324 Mahonia amplectans

325 Mahonia aquifolium
327 Mahonia higginsae

326 Mahonia 'Golden Abundance'
328 Mahonia higginsae

...nia nevinii

330 Mahonia nevinii

331, 332 Mahonia pinnata insularis (Above, below)

333 Mahonia repens

Melaleuca.
Australia

Large shrubs to small trees, often with twisting branches, shredding bark, and flowers which are similar to Bottlebrush. These are hardy evergreen plants. Some species tolerate full sea coast conditions, others grow well in interior and low desert environments. All perform nicely under conditions of wind, heat, limited moisture, full sun, and poor soils. They tend to grow rapidly, and offer specimen and sculptural uses because of their trunk, bark, flower and foliage characteristics. Also useful for soil stabilization, screening and street trees. Approximately 12 species are currently in landscape use, with others being found in arboretum gardens.

Name	Character	Remarks
M. armillaris Drooping Melaleuca	Fine textured shrub to small tree, 10-25 ft. high and as wide. Many branched, with drooping ends, furrowed bark that peels on older trunks. Light green needle-like leaves. Showy clusters of white flowers on long spikes occur in late spring.	This species is a good coastal plant, tolerating wind, salt spray, and alkaline soils. Prefers good drainage and serves well as a screen, windbreak, and shaped specimen. Very soft, billowy foliage appearance. Plates 334, 335
M. elliptica	Large shrub to small tree, 8-16 ft. high, 10-15 ft. wide, with small rounded leaves to ½ in. Showy red flowers occur in large 2-3 in. long brushes intermittently spring to fall. Develops twisting branch and trunk character.	Tolerant of clay type soils, alkalinity, wind and drought. With age and pruning, makes a soft textured accent and specimen plant. Will also grow well in inland and interior areas and likes periodic deep watering.
M. linariifolia Flaxleaf Paperbark	Small dome tree, to 25 ft., with distinctive tan and white papery bark. Needle-like leaves are light green, with bluish cast, occur on very fine branchlets. Heavy display of showy white flowers cover the tops of the foliage from June-July.	A successful coastal, inland and interior tree, which accepts heat, aridity, clay soils and alkalinity. Young plants need staking and regular moisture. Becomes drought tolerant with age. A good street tree, lawn and park specimen. Plate 336
M. nesophila Pink Melaleuca	Large shrub to small tree, with heavy, twisting branching habit. Pale, olive green leaves are oval to 1 in. long; bark becomes thick and shreds in paper-like appearance. Pink-purple flower balls occur on branch tips from Aug.-Sept. and are quite noticeable.	A species tolerant of many adverse conditions. Grows well at the coastal edge in sandy soils and with sea spray, to interior and low desert areas. Accepts clay soils, alkalinity, heat and is drought resistant. Often allowed to develop into a sculptural shrub with gnarled branches. Plates 337, 338
M. quinquenervia (M. leucadendra) Cajeput Tree	Upright tree, to 40 ft. tall, with narrow blade-like, dull green leaves, to 4 in. long. Very distinctive, thick, papery bark, tan to white. Noticeable creamy white flowers occur summer to fall.	Another adaptable species for coastal, inland interior landscapes. Prefers light soils and regular moisture, but tolerates alkaline or saline conditions, wind, heat and smog. A fine street and lawn tree. Multi-trunk forms are used for accent and specimen plantings. Grows in boggy conditions and sometimes reseeds. Plates 339, 340
M. styphelioides Black Tea Tree	Medium sized tree 15-40 ft., with small, pointed leaves and open branches that droop at the ends. Characteristic thick bark can be darker than most species, sometimes charcoal black. Yellow-white brush type flowers, 1-2 in. long occur in summer.	Black Tea Tree shows the same adaptation to coastal and inland environments as other Melaleucas. Resists oak root fungus, accepts boggy soils, is moderately drought tolerant. Used as a multi-trunk specimen or street tree. Plate 341

334, 335 Melaleuca armillaris (Left, below)

336 Melaleuca linariifolia

337, 338 Melaleuca nesophila (Above, below)

339, 340 Melaleuca quinquenervia (Above, below)

341 Melaleuca styphelioides

Metrosideros excelsus. New Zealand Christmas Tree
(M. tomemtosus) New Zealand

A large evergreen shrub to small tree, reaching 20-30 ft. high, with a dense, bushy habit. Leaves are thick, dark green above, covered with white hairs below. Showy clusters of deep red flowers are dominated by stamen, occur May-July. *M. e.* 'Aurea' has similar foliage character but produces yellow flowers.

A plant for coastal edges and valleys where it tolerates salt spray, wind, sun and drought. Will grow in heavy soils if given good drainage. Does not perform well in areas of aridity, frost and intense heat. Excellent seaside screen and windbreak plant. Successful as a small street tree, in lawns and for background plantings. Plates 343, 344

Mimulus. Monkey Flower
(Diplacus) North and South America, Asia, Australia

A large group of annual and short-lived perennial shrubs, including some 150 species. These plants are known for their narrow, glossy green leaves, and bright, tubular flowers. Flowers occur spring through summer and come in many mixed and pure colors.

Many types of Monkey Flower are native to California, where they occur in both wet and dry locations near the coast, and into the Sierra Nevadas. Species which are adapted to dry landscapes prefer loose, rocky and well draining soils. They provide good use in both domestic gardens and natural landscapes as flowering accents, on slopes and in mixed seed plantings. Seeds sown in the fall will germinate with winter rains. Older plants can be cut back each spring to produce more compact growth and increased displays of flowers.

Several species which are found in landscape use include: *M. aurantiacus (Diplacus aurantiacus)*, Sticky Monkey Flower. This plant grows 3-4 ft., produces large pale orange flowers. *M. longiflorus (Diplacus longiflorus)*, grows 2-3 ft., usually produces cream to pale orange flowers. *M. cardinalis* has bright scarlet-red flowers, grows 1-2 ft. *M. puniceus (Diplacus puniceus)*, grows 1-3 ft., produces dull red to orange-red flowers. These plants frequently hybridize under both natural and garden situations, producing blendings of flower colors. Plates 345, 346

Myoporum.
New Zealand

Evergreen ground covers, shrubs and small trees providing rich, glossy foliage, and serving many functional uses in mild landscape regions. Most species are best suited to coastal environments where they accept full sun, humidity, wind, and dry soils. They grow well in clay soils and accept alkaline conditions. In warm inland areas they like periodic supplemental water, protection from intense sun and winter frost. When given ample water, these plants produce rapid growth and their fleshy leaves contain high amounts of moisture, which makes them fire retardant.

342 Myoporum parvifolium

Name	Character	Remarks
M. debile	Low spreading shrub, 12-15 in. high, 2-4 ft. spread. Branches trail along ground and root in moist soil. Narrow leaves are dark green. Showy pink flowers in spring are followed by rose colored berries.	A successful ground cover plant for small slopes and banks, which produces good foliage character and pleasing flowers. This species shows good drought tolerance in coastal areas, but should be given supplemental moisture in inland locations when fire retardance is wanted.
M. laetum	Large shrub to small dome tree, 25-30 ft. high, 20-25 ft. broad, with dense foliage character. Large, shiny leaves have translucent dots, are lush and almost succulent when plants receive ample water.	An excellent seaside plant which tolerates wind, salt spray, and full sun. Often used for screens, on slopes and can be pruned into a yard tree. Very fast growing when given lots of water, but shows suprising drought tolerance when left to survive on its own. Good in heavy and alkaline soils, is damaged by frost. Plate 348
M. parvifolium (*M. p.* 'Prostratum')	Low growing ground cover, 3-12 in. high, spreading 6-8 ft. Rich green leaves, ½-1 in. long, are accented by small white flowers during the summer.	A handsome ground cover for small banks and garden spaces. Grows best in areas having strong coastal influence where it shows moderate resistance to drought. Tolerates clay soils, some alkalinity, full sun and wind. Spreads quickly when given regular water. Provides moderate fire resistance, but is not suited to large areas as plants can die out in the center. Plate 342, 347

343 Metrosideros excelsus

344 Metrosideros excelsus

345 Mimulus species
347 Myoporum parvifolium

346 Mimulus species

348 Myoporum laetum

349 Nerium oleander

351 Nerium oleander 'Petite Salmon'

353 Nerium oleander 'Mrs. Roeding'

350 Nerium oleander 'Sister Agnes'

352 Nerium oleander 'Rosy Red'

354 Olea europaea

Nerium oleander. Oleander

Europe, Mediterranean Region, Asia

Rounded evergreen shrub, 8-12 ft. high, to small tree to 20 ft. tall. Dense foliage habit consists of long narrow leaves, 4-10 in. long, are dark green and leathery. Showy clusters of single or double flowers occur at the ends of branches and come in colors from yellow, pink, salmon to red. Stems, leaves and flowers are poisonous if eaten.

Several varieties of Oleander are available for landscape use which provide choices of size, flower color, and leaf character. *N. o.* 'Sister Agnes' is a large shrub or small tree reaching 15-20 ft. high, with single white flowers. *N. o.* 'Petite Pink' and 'Petite Salmon' are compact varieties, 3-5 ft. high, offering fine texture. *N. o.* 'Mrs. Roeding' grows 5-7 ft. high, has double pink flowers. *N. o.* 'Rosy Red' reaches 6-10 ft., produces deep pink-red flowers. Many other varieties can be found in addition to these.

Oleanders are hardy plants, well adapted to warm valley and desert plant environments. They tolerate many soils, including poorly drained and saline conditions. Prefer full sun, accept extreme drought, and grow well everywhere except the immediate coastal edge. Are used for screens, windbreaks, and slope plantings. Many miles of Oleander are planted along highways, where they tolerate smog, road dust and neglect. Larger species can be pruned into single or multiple trunk trees for street, patio and accent uses. Dwarf plants work well in narrow medians and show moderate fire resistance in foothill locations. Plates 349, 353

Olea europaea. Olive

Asia Minor

A medium sized evergreen tree, 25-35 ft. high, with a distinctive soft textured foliage appearance. Leaves, 1-2 in. long, are pale olive green above and silvery-white below. Inconspicuous flowers are followed by olives which mature in late fall. With time, these trees develop into a round dome shape and have interesting gnarled trunks. Several varieties of Olive are sold which offer different fruit and form choices. *O. e.* 'Fruitless' and 'Swan Hill' are becoming popular choices for domestic landscapes when the fruit is not wanted. *O. e.* 'Skylark Dwarf' develops into a large shrub, with smaller leaves and tighter foliage.

Olive trees are popular plants for both agricultural and domestic landscape uses. In addition to their edible fruit, their fine texture and subdued foliage color makes them quite useful in many situations. For years, large trees have been transplanted with good success and have become specimen elements in commercial projects. They are also used for street trees, in garden and patio spaces, for screens and background elements. Most species generate lots of leaf and fruit. The fruit can be reduced if the plants are sprayed during the flowering cycle. Are best adapted to warm valley environments in full sun and deep soils. Have proven highly adaptable to coastal zones, desert regions, and thin, rocky soils. Plates 354, 355

Osteospermum. African Daisy

South Africa

Fast growing shrubs and ground covers with evergreen foliage and intensive flower character. These plants are well adapted to full sun, heat, and moderate levels of water in most plant environments from the coastal edge to interior valleys. They prefer well draining soils, and regular moisture when young. Mature plants can be clipped back to maintain compact growth and good foliage condition. *O. barberae (Dimorphotheca barberae),* is a small mounding shrub, 2-4 ft. high, and is considered one of the most drought tolerant species. It produces large flowers, 2-3 in. dia., that are white on top, with lilac tint, blue-purple beneath, and have a deep purple center. Plate 356

O. fruticosum (Dimorphotheca fruticosum), Trailing African Daisy, is a spreading ground cover form that has been very widely used. It grows 12-15 in. high, covers large areas with trailing systems which root when in contact with moist soil. Several varieties are available which provide flower colors from pure white to deep purple. Accepts coastal or inland conditions and smog. It can achieve some drought resistance in cooler areas, becomes sparse and woody if stressed too much in warm inland locations. Periodic mowing will revitalize old plants. This species has been used in fire hazard areas where it shows moderate fire resistance if given regular water.

355 Olea europaea

356 Osteospermum barberae

Parkinsonia aculeata. Jerusalem Thorn, Mexican Palo Verde

Arizona, Mexico, South America

Medium size deciduous tree, 15-25 ft. high, and as wide. Trunk and branches are covered with distinctive yellow-green bark; branches also have many thorns. Long, narrow leaves, to 16 in., have numerous 1/8 in. long leaflets that are bright green in color. Intensive displays of lemon yellow flowers cover these plants in early spring for very showy effect, followed by persistent brown seed pods. Jerusalem Thorn is an excellent choice for desert and other warm landscape regions where it sometimes naturalizes. It prefers full sun, heat, sandy and well draining soils. Accepts alkaline conditions, wind, dust, and aridity. Shows high drought tolerance and yet takes lots of water. Leaves are dropped under drought or cold stress to reveal an intricate branching structure. It is a striking and refreshing foliage and flowering accent plant for use in parks, along highways, and in desert gardens. Other uses include street and patio trees, slope plantings. Plates 357, 358

Pennisetum setaceum. Fountain Grass

(P. ruppelli)   Africa

Clumping perennial grass which develops into a 2-4 ft. high mound. Narrow blade leaves grow to 3 ft. long. Flower plumes reach 4 ft. high on long stems. Flowers are showy, generally white, with some purple tinge. P. s. 'Cupreum' grows a little larger, produces coppery-red foliage and flower plumes. P. s. 'Rubrum' has rose-cast color in the foliage and flower spikes.

Fountain Grass is a popular plant for accent uses in many warm and dry landscape situations. It provides good character in rock gardens, along borders and dry stream beds and in mixed plantings. It is often used in seed mixes for slope and roadside plantings in California. Unfortunately, many plants are reseeding and naturalizing in both coastal and inland environments. These plants are highly tolerant of many soils, accept full sun, wind, smog, aridity, and need little or no summer water. Plate 359

Penstemon. Beard Tongue

North America

A large group of perennial herbs and shrubs with over 200 species found in North America alone. Their strongest occurrence lies in the western United States, with approximately 40 species and many varieties found throughout California. Several of these natives show good performance in the dry landscapes of warm foothill and inland areas away from coastal fog, from San Diego to San Francisco. Are short-lived, will accept limited summer water, but may die earlier if given too much.

Good planting success can be achieved from sowing untreated seed on loose, well draining soils, during summer to late fall. When grown from seed they are relatively slow to start and can be crowded out by more vigorous plants. Penstemons are nicely suited for slope and naturalization plantings, as well as in rock gardens and mixed shrub groups. In addition to the plants listed below, there are numerous introduced and lesser known hybrids available from local sources.

Name	Character	Remarks
P. antirrhinoides Yellow Penstemon	Evergreen shrubby perennial, 2-6 ft. tall, with spreading branches. Small rounded to linear leaves, ½-1 in. long, are medium green. Large clusters of showy tubular flowers occur Mar.-June.	Yellow Penstemon occurs in the Chaparral plant community throughout southern California. It is a very attractive flowering species which thrives in many landscapes well into the San Francisco Bay region. A good slope and transition plant into natural areas which does shed some leaves under high drought stress.
P. centranthifolius Scarlet Bugler	Small perennial shrub, 1-4 ft. high, usually with many slender basal stems. Dull green leaves grow 1-3 in.; scarlet tubular flowers cover the plant Apr.-June.	A good species for slopes and naturalizing which is quite attractive to hummingbirds. It naturally occurs in dry areas of the coastal foothills from San Diego to Lake counties. Bright flowers offer garden uses along borders, on banks, in mixed plantings. Plates 361, 362
P. heterophyllus Foothill Penstemon Blue Penstemon	Evergreen perennial shrub, 1-4 ft. high, with many branches that are woody at the base. Medium green linear leaves, 1-4 in. long, occur on reddish stems. Large tubular flowers are rose to blue and are showy from Apr.-July.	A widespread species found in warm coastal mountains from Los Angeles to Humbolt counties, scattered foothill locations around the San Joaquin Valley and sometimes in San Diego County. Numerous varieties occur within this range, with all plants providing good accent, bank and mixed planting uses in both domestic and natural landscapes. Plate 360
P. spectabilis Showy Penstemon	Rounded, to upright shrub, 2-4 ft. high, with coarse foliage and basal branches. Thick leaves, 1-3 in. long, are roughly serrated. Showy rose, blue or purple flowers occur on long stems Apr.-June.	Showy Penstemon is an inhabitant of dry hills and rocky washes in coastal and inland mountains from Los Angeles to San Diego counties. A plant which is best suited to natural landscapes, with some possibilities in rock gardens.

357 Parkinsonia aculeata

358 Parkinsonia aculeata

359 Pennisetum setaceum

361, 362 Penstemon centranthifolius (Above, below)

360 Penstemon heterophyllus

Photinia.
Asia

Evergreen and deciduous plants, offering lush foliage and large clusters of white flowers. Most species develop into large shrubs and can easily be pruned or shaped into hedges or small dome trees. Several species show good adaptation to California landscapes where they like full sun, deep water, and rich soils. When given ample water they respond with rapid growth; moderate drought tolerance comes with age.

Photinias provide a range of landscape uses from roadside and slope plantings to screens, street trees and patio specimens. Their new foliage is nicely tinted for seasonal accent character and use in cut arrangements. Two species are best suited to warm landscapes which are discussed below.

Name	Character	Remarks
P. fraseri	Broad evergreen shrub, 8-12 ft. high, 10-12 ft. wide. Large glossy green leaves are tinted bright red to bronze when new. Large clusters of white flowers are showy in early spring.	A handsome foliage and flowering accent plant that can be used for screens, hedges, espaliers, and highway plantings. Can be staked and pruned to form small street and patio trees. Accepts full sun and lots of heat; tolerates smog, dust, wind and aridity. This species usually likes regular water to retain lush foliage appearance in warm areas. Becomes moderately drought resistant when planted in deep soils. Plate 363
P. serrulata Chinese Photinia	Large evergreen shrub to small tree, 20-35 ft. high. Leathery leaves, 6-8 in. long, have toothed edges, are bronze cast when young. Showy clusters of white flowers come in early spring, followed by berries that mature bright red by late fall. A smaller variety *P.s.* 'Aculeata', grows 4-6 ft. high, produces shiny green leaves with yellow veins. It is considered a very handsome plant.	Chinese Photinia usually develops into a broad, many branched shrub. It is used for windbreaks, screens, and background plantings in large spaces. Can be pruned into single trunk tree for patio and street tree. Good accent character occurs in spring with fresh bronze growth and many flower clusters. Plate 364

Pinus. Pine
Europe, U.S.A.

Evergreen conifer trees, including some 80 species throughout the northern hemisphere. These plants are quite varied in habit and adaptability and offer many individual choices to work with. Most species prefer loose, well draining soils, which are not too rich, and areas in full sun. They usually have tap root systems, but will develop large lateral roots in areas of shallow soils and surface moisture. Some 50 native and introduced species are in landscape use, with several responding well in areas having long, dry summers. Many of the California native species show high sensitivity to urban air pollution and should be used with caution in urban areas.

Name	Character	Remarks
P. canariensis Canary Island Pine	Narrow columnar tree, 60-80 ft. tall with distinctive branching structure. Dark green needles, in groups of three, grow 9-12 in. long and create a soft textured look. Noticeable cones, 4-8 in. long.	A fast growing and very adaptable species for milder climates. Tolerates extreme urban conditions of dust and smog; grows in coastal, inland, interior and desert environments. Accepts most drought conditions but needs periodic deep water in hot inland and desert landscapes. Prefers loose or sandy soils and is quite pest free. Often used in parks, along streets, in lawns and areas having oak root fungus. A good vertical accent tree for confined spaces. Plate 365
P. coulteri Coulter Pine	Broad open branched tree, 30-60 ft. high. Stiff blue-green needles, 5-10 in. long, occur in groups of three. Very large, heavy cones reach 10-15 in. long and persist for 3-4 years.	A native species found on dry rocky slopes at low to mid-elevations of the inland and coastal mountains from Mexico to central California. Coulter Pine is a well rounded and adaptable plant which tolerates heat, wind, drought and high desert conditions. Not commonly used in urban or domestic landscapes, but is very much suited for regional parks, campgrounds and reforestation. Plate 366
P. halepensis Aleppo Pine	Fast growing tree, 25-50 ft. high, often with spreading and windswept appearance. Small, light green needles come in groups of two. Inconspicuous 2-3 in. long oval cones.	From the Mediterranean region of Europe, this is one of the most versatile and adaptable of the Pine species. Grows everywhere from the coastal edge with salt wind, to low deserts with heat and aridity. Accepts poor and alkalai soils, drought, and wind. Well suited to large spaces in parks, greenbelts, reforestation, erosion control and windbreaks. Plates 367, 368

363 Photinia fraseri

364 Photinia serrulata

365 Pinus canariensis

366 Pinus coulteri
367 Pinus halepensis

368 *Pinus halepensis*

369 *Pinus pinea*

370 *Pinus torreyana*

371 *Pistacia chinensis*

372 *Pistacia chinensis*

Pinus. (Cont.)

Name	Character	Remarks
P. pinea Italian Stone Pine	A large tree, growing 30-60 ft. high. Develops into a round dome when young. Matures into a broad flat topped tree with several heavy branches. Dark green needles 3-7 in. long occur in groups of two.	A species from southern Europe that has found much use along large streets, in parks and as individual specimens. Very uniform when young and stately when old. Adapts to coastal, inland and interior valleys, and high desert conditions. Good for temperate areas where it is protected from cold when young. Becomes tolerant of cold and drought with age. A very bold plant making a strong landscape statement. Plate 369
P. radiata Monterey Pine	Large tree, 70-100 ft. high, developing a pyramidal shape when young. Dense clusters of dark green needles occur in groups of two and three; long narrow cones, to 6 in., persist on branches for 2-3 years.	A fast growing native species which naturally occurs along the coast of central California. It is best suited to coastal landscapes where it becomes drought tolerant, but has been widely planted throughout the state and other regions of the world. Accepts lots of water, but can overgrow and die at early ages. Sensitive to smog. Resistant to oak root fungus. Selective pruning can create interesting specimen character and keep foliage compact. Other uses include park and open space plantings, windrows, and median trees.
P. sabiniana Digger Pine	Fast growing tree to 50 ft. tall, with characteristic split trunk habit. Light grey-green needles, 8-12 in. long, come in groups of three. Cones, 6-10 in. long, persist 3-4 years.	A native species most often found on the dry interior slopes and ridges of the Coast Ranges of California. Good tolerance of drought and very suitable for regional parks, campgrounds and natural areas. In domestic landscapes it becomes more dense and ornamental looking. Prefers well draining soils, tolerates cold.
P. torreyana Torrey Pine	Tall open tree, 20-60 ft. high, with 12 in. long grey-green needles in groups of five. Cones, 4-6 in. long, are rich brown.	A native species found only in a limited coastal area of San Diego County. It has shown adaptability to inland and high desert environments where it needs well draining soils and not too much heat. A good coastal species which accepts salt wind and little care. Not widely planted, but useful for parks, grove plantings and roadsides. Plate 370

Pistacia. Pistache

Europe, Asia

Evergreen and deciduous shrubs to large trees. These are lush appearing plants, with divided leaves. Shrub varieties found in the Mediterranean region of Europe have resinous sap which is used in medicine, dentistry, and in varnishes. Of the two deciduous species common to California landscapes, one is a large, ornamental shade tree and the other produces the edible Pistachio nut. These trees like warm environments and deep soils of inland and interior valley regions. They establish deep root systems, achieve good drought tolerance, and require only infrequent, deep watering.

Name	Character	Remarks
P. chinensis Chinese Pistache	Large deciduous tree, 30-50 ft. high, to 40 ft. wide. Leaves to 12 in. long, are divided into 10-16 pointed leaflets and are reddish when young, turn to bright colors of orange, red, and yellow during the fall before dropping. Female trees produce showy clusters of small red berries which mature to dark blue.	A highly ornamental tree for use in warm, dry landscapes, ranging from inland valleys to low desert regions. Tolerates drought, smog, aridity and slightly alkaline soil conditions. Prefers full sun, heat, and deep soils for optimum root development. These plants need careful staking and pruning when young to achieve a good broad dome shape. Well suited for patio, street tree, park and lawn uses. Plates 371, 372
P. vera Pistachio Nut	Large shrub to broad dome tree, 18-30 ft. high. Leaves are divided into 3-5 leaflets; clusters of edible nuts are enclosed in red-cast husks. Both male and female plants must be grown for fruit; selected varieties offer best crop production.	This species is usually grown as a food crop in valley regions. Young plants need staking and pruning and often develop into many branched trees. Prefers heat, sun, deep soils and infrequent watering. In domestic gardens it can be used in background and small orchard areas, where it becomes quite drought tolerant with age.

Pittosporum.

Australia, New Zealand, Africa, Asia

Evergreen shrubs and trees offering rich foliage and many forms. They are noted for their clean appearance and fragrant, pale yellow flowers. Some 100 species are found throughout the temperate regions of the world, primarily Australia and New Zealand. These plants provide many functional uses in California landscapes, with about 8-10 species and several varieties being found in most nurseries.

Most Pittosporums show wide tolerance of many climate conditions, survive in heavy soils, and develop moderate resistance to drought after they mature. These plants will grow larger, with lusher foliage if given regular moisture, seasonal fertilizer, and when planted in richer soils. Good drainage is necessary. They all grow well under coastal conditions and many will accept full sun to partial shade, in inland environments. Several species perform well in harsh urban areas and accept wind, smog and dust. Pittosporums are easily clipped and shaped for borders, hedges, and screens. The larger growing species are often used along highways, on large slopes, and in mass plantings. With age, these plants can be pruned into sculptural forms for specimen effects in patios and next to buildings. Several of these plants also provide showy flower and fruit characteristics, but litter tends to be a problem around paving.

Dwarf forms and varieties with variegated foliage have been developed, which are quite useful along borders and to contrast with other plants. These plants have been popular for many years and old specimens can be seen in a variety of landscapes.

Name	Character	Remarks
P. crassifolium Karo Tree	Large shrub to small tree, 8-12 ft. high, 6-10 ft. wide. Grey-green leaves are covered with fine hairs and have rounded ends. Small maroon flowers occur May-June, and are fragrant. *P.c.* 'Nana' has similar foliage and flowers, grows into a 3 ft. mound.	A good plant for coastal edges that prefers sandy soils, tolerates salt spray, wind and full sun. Its light foliage makes it well suited for background areas, in mixed plantings and for large spaces. The lower growing form 'Nana' is suited for borders and small mass plantings. Plates 373, 374
P. phillyraeoides Willow Pittosporum	Small upright tree to 18 ft. high, with long narrow leaves that hang from drooping branches. Yellow flowers are both showy and fragrant, occur late winter to early spring, followed by bright yellow-orange berries.	This species has a very fine texture and distinct willow-like appearance. It shows good tolerance of heat, aridity, poor soils and accepts drought when mature. Good for inland, interior and protected desert environments. Often used as a small specimen tree, along dry streams, next to pools, and around patio spaces. Plate 375

373 Pittosporum crassifolium

374 Pittosporum crassifolium

375 *Pittosporum phillyraeoides*

376, 377 *Pittosporum rhombifolium* (Above, below)

378, 379 *Pittosporum tobira* (Above, below)

380 *Pittosporum tobira* 'Variegata'

381 Pittosporum undulatum

382 Pittosporum undulatum

383 Pittosporum viridiflorum
385 Plumbago auriculata

384 Pittosporum viridiflorum

386 Plumbago auriculata

Pittosporum. (Cont.)

Name	Character	Remarks
P. rhombifolium Queensland Pittosporum	Large shrub to small tree, 15-30 ft. high, with glossy green foliage. Leaves are distinctly diamond shaped and toothed on the edges. Small white flowers in summer are followed by showy clusters of orange berries.	A good species for warm inland and interior areas which responds well to heat and infrequent deep watering. Likes fertile soils, with good drainage, and does well in most garden areas. Often used as a large screen or slope plant that can eventually be shaped into a many branched tree. Young plants need good staking and pruning to develop forms for street tree and patio plantings. Accepts smog, dust, and wind. Leaves and berries can create litter problems. Plates 376, 377
P. tobira Tobira Mock Orange	Dense mounding shrub, 8-16 ft. high, 10-15 ft. spread. Rich, dark green leaves grow to 3 in. long, with rounded apex. Pale yellow flowers occur in large clusters and are quite fragrant, smelling like orange blossoms; are followed by inconspicuous green berries. P. t. 'Variegata' has light grey-green leaves and grows into a smaller, 5-8 ft. mound. A compact form, P. t. 'Wheeler's Dwarf', is a dense rounded shrub, 1-3 ft. high, with handsome foliage character.	Tobira Pittosporum is a highly adaptable plant, useful for many landscape situations. Tolerates full coastal exposure as well as conditions in inland and interior plant environments. Resists oak root fungus, accepts some alkalinity and light frost. Serves well for foundation plantings, hedges, in containers and for foliage contrast. With age, can be pruned into a many branched specimen shrub or small tree. Plates 378, 379, 380
P. undulatum Victorian Box	Large mounding shrub to medium sized tree, 35-40 ft. tall, with a pyramidal shape. Large dark green leaves to 5 in. long, have distinctive wavy margins. Small white flowers occur in early spring and are fragrant. Pale orange berries mature by fall.	A species which provides very lush foliage character and many uses in warm landscapes. Tolerates sun, wind, heat, smog and dust. Survives in heavy soils with good drainage. Often used as a large screen, background and slope plant along roadsides where it requires periodic watering and little maintenance. Can be shaped into a handsome patio and lawn tree with single or many branches. Litter from fruit is often a nuisance. Plates 381, 382
P. viridiflorum Cape Pittosporum	Large shrub to small tree, 15-25 ft. high, with a rounded form. Large leaves, 3-4 in., are dark green and have a rounded apex. Noticeable clusters of pale yellow flowers are fragrant. Fruit is pale orange to yellow.	Cape Pittosporum is very similar to P. tobira, but with larger sized leaves and overall height. It is a good foliage plant for use as a street and patio tree, large hedge and screen plant. Needs support and pruning when young to establish round dome tree shapes. Tolerates drought after establishment. Prefers areas having coastal influence, and well draining soils. Plates 383, 384

Plumbago auriculata. Cape Plumbago

(P. capensis)

South Africa

A sprawling, vining shrub, 5-6 ft. high, 8-12 ft. wide. Bright green foliage provides fresh character in dry landscapes. Large rounded clusters of white to pale blue flowers cover these plants for many months, mainly Mar.-Nov. P. a. 'Alba' has similar foliage and offers all white flowers.
Cape Plumbago is a very versatile plant. It can be used to cascade down large slopes and over walls, trained onto fences, and clipped into informal hedges. It tolerates conditions in all environments from the coast to deserts, including heat, sun, aridity, smog, and wind. Can be damaged by heavy frost, but quickly regrows. Becomes highly drought tolerant with age, will remain more lush if given periodic summer water. Older plants can be heavily pruned to revitalize woody parts and keep the foliage more compact. Plates 385, 386, 387

387 Plumbago auriculata

Prunus.
Northern Hemisphere

Evergreen and deciduous trees and shrubs, including some 175 species which occur mainly in the northern hemisphere. 20-30 species are native to North America, with at least 7 species and several varieties found in California from the Coast Ranges to both the high and low desert environments. This group has much horticultural importance and includes popular crop plants such as almonds, apricots, cherries, prunes and peaches. Many ornamental flowering varieties of these fruit bearing species have been developed and are in widespread landscape use. As a rule, these deciduous flowering and fruiting varieties perform best with ample moisture and are not recommended for their drought tolerance. It is the evergreen group of these plants, mainly natives, which provide many useful roles in dry landscapes. These plants are very adaptable to the full range of coastal and inland plant environments in California. They have a basic need for well draining soils and are tolerant of heat, aridity, wind, and limited moisture. At least two native species have long been in landscape use and are well known for their rich shiny foliage and dark berry-like fruit. These plants are best installed from fresh seed or small containers, with efforts made to prevent root coiling, in order to promote stronger, faster growth. Periodic summer water is recommended for the first 1-2 summers to support these plants.

388 Prunus caroliniana

Name	Character	Remarks
P. caroliniana Carolina Laurel Cherry	Many branched shrub to small tree, 20-40 ft. high, 15-30 ft. spread. Bright, shiny, evergreen leaves form an interesting pattern on stems. Noticeable groups of pale white flower clusters occur Apr.-June. Blue-black berries mature in summer and fall which persist until spring. Varieties P. c. 'Bright 'n Tight' and 'Compacta' are more dense and grow to lower heights.	A handsome plant from the Southeastern U.S.A., often used for screens and small lawn and street trees. Very much appreciated for its rich foliage character. Responds nicely to shearing or pruning. This species adapts well to coastal, inland, interior, and low desert environments, where it becomes quite drought tolerant with age. Prefers coastal climates, good drainage and rich soils. Withstands heat, aridity and wind. Should be given regular moisture and protection from cold when young. Plates 388, 389, 390
P. ilicifolia Hollyleaf Cherry Islay	Large evergreen mounding shrub to tree, 15-30 ft. high, with a dense branching habit. Medium to dark green leaves are wavy and have distinctive toothed edges. Showy displays of creamy white flower spikes occur May-June, followed by persistent red-purple fruit.	A wide ranging native species common to the dry slopes and valleys of the Coast Ranges from Napa County to Mexico. Often used for background and screen plantings, where it provides good density and foliage qualities. Can be sheared or pruned into a shade or specimen tree. Tolerant of coastal, inland and interior foothills and valleys with a preference for well draining sites. Shows drought tolerance and offers very good use on slopes in both natural and domestic landscapes. Resistant to oak root fungus. Plates 391, 392
P. lusitanica Portugal Laurel	Large evergreen shrub, 10-18 ft. high, or medium-sized tree, 25-30 ft. Handsome foliage character consists of 5 in. long leaves, which are glossy dark green and with toothed edges. Showy flower spikes have many cream-white flowers. Clusters of bright red or purple berries mature in fall.	Native to Portugal and Spain, where it is planted for its foliage character. Accepts heat and sun, likes deep soils, where it tolerates moderate drought. A good background screen, natural or clipped. Can be trained into a single or multi-trunk park or street tree.
P. lyonii (P. integrifolia) Catalina Cherry	Evergreen shrub to tree, 15-45 ft. high, 20-30 ft. spread. Glossy dark green leaves, 2-5 in. long, are wavy and pointed. Showy, creamy white flower spikes occur Apr.-June. Large black cherry fruits mature late summer.	Native to the chaparral canyons on the Coastal Islands of California. This species has been widely used in coastal and inland environments and will often hybridize with P. ilicifolia to produce plants which bear resemblances to both species (P. ilicifolia integrifolia). This is another plant with high resistances to drought and oak root fungus. Well suited for slopes, screens and naturalizing. Older plants make good shade and street trees, but their fruit creates stains and a litter problem. Plates 393, 394

389, 390 Prunus caroliniana (Upper left, above)

391 Prunus ilicifolia
393 Prunus lyonii

392 Prunus ilicifolia

394 Prunus lyonii

Psidium. Guava
Brazil

Evergreen shrubs to small trees, providing good ornamental character and edible fruit. These plants are best grown in warm and mild coastal valley environments, in deep soils, without frost. With age, they develop moderate drought resistance and interesting branch structure. They are often used as foliage plants on slopes, in planters, and in domestic garden spaces. Mature plants can be pruned to create accent and patio specimens.

Name	Character	Remarks
P. guajava Guava	Large shrub, to small tree, 15-30 ft. Leaves grow to 6 in. long; have salmon cast when young. Large, edible fruit, to 3 in., makes good jelly. Selected varieties are available which offer more consistent fruit quality.	Guava is a plant suited only to mild southern coastal regions, away from frost, in warm sheltered areas. Its ornamental character makes it suited to specimen uses as a many branched shrub or tree. Likes deep loamy soils. Periodic deep water is needed for best fruit production.
P. littorale (P. cattleianum) Lemon Guava Strawberry Guava	Medium size shrub, 8-12 ft. high, with sinuous trunk structure and smooth golden-tan bark. Glossy green leaves, 2-3 in. long, are bronze when new. Flowers are inconspicuous. Two selections are most commonly used for their edible fruit. P. l. littorale, Lemon Guava, has 1½ in. dia. yellow fruit that has a tart aftertaste. P. l. longipes, Strawberry Guava, produces red fruit that is quite sweet.	These plants are more widely adapted than P. guajava, due to their increased tolerance of cold. They prefer warm, sunny locations, in deep, rich soils. In coastal and inland portions of California, they will achieve moderate drought tolerance with age. The trunk, bark and foliage character is ornamental and useful for specimen, accent and container plantings. Plates 396, 397

Punica granatum. Pomegranate
Southern Asia

Large deciduous shrub, to small tree, which offers distinctive ornamental character and large, edible fruit. Plants have rich green foliage; new leaves are bronze-cast, old leaves turn bright yellow in cool areas for seasonal accent. Many varieties have been produced which offer single or double flowers, in colors from orange, cream, red to variegated. Large fruit, to 5 in. dia., is both showy and edible; good for jellies and wine. Larger plants can be pruned into small trees to reveal rough bark and gnarled trunks; dwarf varieties become many branched shrubs. Pomegranite is a popular ornamental and agricultural tree. It is adapted to full sun, heat, and deep soils where it produces the most flowers and fruit. It prefers periodic deep watering and good drainage; has adapted well to rocky and heavy soil conditions. Large trees can be transplanted and are often used for specimen and accent plantings for their foliage, trunk, and flower character. Other uses include background plantings, containers, and small garden trees. These plants are most successful in inland and valley areas, but they will accept coastal and desert conditions as well. Plates 395, 398, 399

395 Punica granatum

Pyracantha. Firethorn
Southern Europe, Western Asia

A diverse group of shrubs, with glossy evergreen foliage and distinctively showy fruit. Many species and varieties are in landscape use, which show excellent tolerance of harsh conditions, including sun, wind, drought, aridity, and poor soils. Selected varieties can be used for ground covers, espaliers, and tubs, to slope, barrier and screen plantings. They dislike wet soils or being subjected to frequent spraying from irrigation systems. Low growing species such as P. 'Red Elf', 'Tiny Tim', and 'Walderi', provide moderate fire resistance if given periodic summer water.

Firethorns offer a wide variety of ornamental character. They produce large clusters of cream to white flowers which are pleasantly fragrant. Numerous berries are produced and range in color from pale orange to bright red; persist from summer through winter. Most varieties have sharp thorns on the branches which are hidden by rich foliage. A range of plant sizes are available, from ground covers to large, 10-15 ft. high shrubs. All can be shaped and sized by tip pruning or shearing.

A number of pests and diseases can afflict these plants, including fireblight, woolly aphids, and red spider mites; periodic checking and maintenance is needed. Plates 400, 401

396 *Psidium littorale*

397 *Psidium littorale*

399 *Punica granatum* (Double flower)

398 *Punica granatum*
400 *Pyracantha species*

401 *Pyracantha 'Santa Ana'*

Quercus. Oak

Evergreen and deciduous trees, including over 300 species throughout temperate and tropical mountain regions of the world. Some 15 species and several varieties are found in California, which have adapted to a wide range of plant environments, from coastal foothills to 10,000 ft. elevations in interior mountains. These natives provide a rich influence in this state in both man-made and natural landscapes. However, many species have been valued for their wood, removed for agriculture, or lost through urban expansion and do not exist in the large numbers of 100 years ago. Emphasis is now placed upon the preservation and replanting of such species in an attempt to maintain their role in California. In addition, several varieties have been introduced to the west which are in common landscape use and have shown good adaptation to many site conditions.

Most types of oaks have a basic need for well draining soils and careful summer watering. They are naturally adapted to long dry seasons as they often develop extensive lateral and tap roots which draw moisture from large areas of soil and from various ground water areas. With the renewed interest and concern for oaks there has been a lot of study done to determine the best planting and management guidelines regarding them. Summarized below are several key recommendations for their treatment.

Established trees have shown the highest sensitivity to disease and construction damage. The area within the foliage dripline must be handled with particular care. Surface watering and frequent moisture on the trunks during the summer months create ideal conditions for Armillaria Root Fungus (Armillaria mellea) to thrive and attack trees. Also, the addition of fill soils against the trunk, or the covering and compaction of soil with pavement within the dripline, prevents normal wetting, drying and breathing of soils from occurring. Lowering the soil level around established trees will often reveal and destroy critical lateral and feeder roots which are necessary for healthy survival. The basic recommendation when working around any oaks is to preserve the natural conditions within their dripline area and to allow leaf litter or shredded wood mulch to protect the soil. For more domestic appearances, it is possible to plant certain understory plant species which require little or no summer water. Such shade and drought tolerant plants include species of Ribes, Arctostaphylos, Ceanothus, and Mahonia.

In other instances, we find that mature trees have depended upon high groundwater tables and natural drainage patterns to sustain them during the summer. Many deaths have resulted from site grading and lowered groundwater levels due to well pumping. In areas where these situations have developed, it is found that established trees can benefit from periodic deep water and light fertilizing through the late spring. Since evergreen oaks are dormant in late summer and fall, they should not be deep watered during this period as they can be stimulated into growth, and be prevented from having a needed rest cycle.

Newly planted native and introduced oaks of all species tend to show better resistance to disease and disturbance related problems. They are best planted from fresh seed or small containers in loose soils, in an effort to achieve uninhibited root development. Monthly summer water at the dripline for the first several years will achieve larger plants and more extensive roots for good drought tolerance. Regardless of the better durability of these newly planted species, it is best to treat them similar to existing trees as they grow older. Prevent soil compaction, summer spray irrigation, fill or wet soils against the trunk, and allow natural leaf litter to cover soil within the dripline.

401 Quercus lobata

Name	Character	Remarks
Q. agrifolia Coast Live Oak	Evergreen tree, developing a broad round dome from 30-60 ft. high, 35-80 ft. wide. Rich, shiny green leaves, 1-3 in. long, are stiff and curved under with sharp spines on the edges. A relatively fast growing species, adding 2-4 ft. per year under good conditions. The greyish brown bark remains smooth when young and develops fissures with age. Acorns are thin and pointed to 1½ in. long.	Native to the Coast Ranges from Mendocino to San Diego counties. It is one of the most common and well known oaks throughout California. Often inhabits low hills and valleys in the Oak Woodland and Oak Grassland plant communites, as well as in semi-moist canyons. A widely adapted species which has been successfully planted throughout the state, from coastal foothills to interior valleys. A very strong foliage and form tree which begins to achieve good character between 20-25 years. Uses include street and park trees, individual specimen and mass plantings. Plates 402, 403
Q. chrysolepis Canyon Live Oak	Evergreen shrub to tree, 30-40 ft. high, developing a very rounded spreading form 30-40 ft. wide. Thick leathery leaves are medium green above, lead-grey beneath. Leaves have many shapes, but are usually wavy, with irregularly toothed margins, or entire with a single pointed tip. Either single or multi-trunked, with distinctive scaly bark. Large acorns are fat, with broad basal cups that are densely covered with golden fuzz.	A widespread tree throughout the Western states, with frequent occurrences in 2000-5000 ft. elevations of coastal and interior mountains of California. It is mainly found in small shrub and tree stands in the Chaparral and Mixed Evergreen Woodland plant communities. Not as widely used as other oak species, but accepts same conditions and offers same uses. Slow growing with good form and height to 20 ft. achieved in 20-30 years. Plates 404, 405

Quercus. (Cont.)

Name	Character	Remarks
Q. douglasii Blue Oak	Deciduous tree, growing upright to 40 ft. and eventually developing a broad crown to 50 ft. wide. Noticeable light grey bark is heavily scaled. Acorns of many shapes grow thick and rounded to narrow and pointed. Distinctive blue-green leaves are quite varied in shape, but are generally oblong, with shallow irregular lobes, with and without spines.	One of the most heat and drought tolerant species, which inhabits many of the dry perimeter foothills surrounding the San Joaquin Valley. It often occurs on shallow and rocky soils in Oak Grassland and Woodland plant communities and is quite slow growing. Under natural conditions, trees with 14 in. diameters can be 170 years old. Faster growth and good character is obtained in moister environments. While individual specimens are periodically found in domestic landscapes, this species is used in regional parks and foothill areas where time can be allowed for growth. Plates 406, 407
Q. dumosa California Scrub Oak	A highly variable shrub to small tree, with rough flaky bark. Foliage and acorns are seldom alike on any two plants, as many local variations and hybrids freely occur. Leaves do tend to be small, to 1 in., are curved or wavy and have very spiny margins.	A common species to the Chaparral plant community throughout California, which often grows in dense thickets on dry exposed slopes. Very little ornamental value is seen, but it is a good erosion control plant for natural landscapes.
Q. engelmannii Mesa Oak Englemann Oak	Evergreen to briefly deciduous tree, 30-50 ft. high, equal spread. Thick leaves are light to deep blue-green and come in many shapes from oblong to rounded, with smooth or spiny margins. Deeply furrowed bark on trunks is grey-brown; heavy acorns in large cups grow 1-1½ in.	A species native to southern California, which once was very frequent to the San Gabriel and Palomar mountains on dry gravelly plains and mesas. Often mixed with Q. agrifolia in Oak Grassland and Woodland plant communities, it has become a heavy victim of urbanization. Roots often reach ground water sources and support relatively fast growth, with plants growing to 15 in. caliper in 40 years. A prized specimen tree where it has been preserved. This species offers good park, shade, street tree and naturalizing uses throughout dry coastal and inland foothill regions. Plates 408, 409
Q. ilex Holly Oak	Evergreen tree, 25-40 ft. high, 20-35 ft. spread. A tree of moderate growth that is upright and pointed when young, rounded with age. Dull green, oval leaves, 1-3 in., are pointed and often have irregularly toothed margins. Greyish bark is smooth on branches and fissured on the trunk; acorns reach 1½ in. long, with the cup covering half the fruit.	An introduced species from the Mediterranean region of Europe. Adapts widely to California, from the coastal edge to interior and low desert environments. Prefers a deep, well draining soil and periodic water, but accepts clay type and poor soils with slower growth. Needs protection from prolonged cold when young, tolerates heat, smog, aridity, drought, salt spray and wind. A popular tree for streets, parks and residences, and is often used in place of other native oaks where summer water is too frequent. Plate 410
Q. lobata Valley Oak California White Oak	Large deciduous tree, 60-75 ft. tall, with broadly spreading canopy, 50-80 ft. Deeply fissured bark is grey-brown; long slender acorns, grow 1-3 in. Large papery leaves are 3-4 in. long, with deeply rounded lobes.	The primary occurence of Valley Oak in California is in the Oak Grassland plant community of the San Joaquin Valley. Largest specimens grow in deep rich soils with their roots reaching groundwater sources. Smaller plants exist on the more rocky and drier foothill areas and often mix with Q. douglasii. A magnificent specimen tree to be preserved where possible, and one that is quite easily disturbed and killed by improper construction and management practices. New plants can develop 20 in. trunk diameters in 20-30 years with normal moisture. A grand park tree which needs time to mature. Plate 401, 411
Q. suber Cork Oak	Evergreen tree, 40-60 ft. tall and as wide. Distinctive greyish corky bark covers the trunk and stems; light green leaves to 3 in. long are lightly toothed and hang in pendulous clusters on older trees.	Cork Oak has been introduced from the Mediterranean region of Europe and shows good adaptation to our warmest and driest locations. It performs well in valley areas and is quite good in low deserts. Tolerates heat, smog, aridity, wind and drought when established. A good specimen tree for foliage and bark character and is often used for park and street trees, as well as along highways. Plates 412, 413

402 Quercus agrifolia

403 Quercus agrifolia

404 Quercus chrysolepis
406 Quercus douglasii

405 Quercus chrysolepis
407 Quercus douglasii

408 Quercus engelmanii

409 Quercus engelmanii

410 Quercus ilex

411 Quercus lobata

412 Quercus suber (Bark)

413 Quercus suber

Rhamnus. Coffeeberry, Buckthorn

Temperate regions, California

Evergreen and deciduous shrubs to small trees, including 100 species from many warm regions of the world. Five species and several varieties are native to California. These plants are appreciated for their durable foliage, and are often used for utilitarian purposes in hot and arid landscapes. Berries can be noticeable on some species and do provide some ornamental value. Not particular as to soils and will accept either clay types or rocky conditions. Native varieties can be established from containers, or fresh seed, with germination rates varying between 30-70%, depending upon the species. Once established, these plants can survive under normal rainfall conditions in most inland and foothill plant environments throughout the state. However, periodic moisture and protection from intense sun in hotter regions is recommended. Frequent hybridization among native species has produced many forms and varieties, which should be selected for their localized adaptations and tolerance of dry environments. This group of plants are used for slope stabilization, naturalizing and screen plantings. Several species which grow to larger sizes, can be pruned into specimen shrubs, or be trained for use as street trees. In dry landscapes and under stressful conditions, they retain rich and handsome foliage character.

414 Rhamnus crocea ilicifolia

Name	Character	Remarks
R. alaternus Italian Buckthorn	Evergreen shrub, with moderately fast growth, 10-20 ft. high and as wide. Dark green leaves to 2 in. long, with toothed edges. Inconspicuous flowers in early spring are followed by blue to black berries. Improved varieties offer plants with more variegated foliage and which grow with more consistent form.	Italian Buckthorn comes from Europe and has proven to be a widely adaptable plant to all landscapes throughout California. It tolerates most soils, heat, aridity, smog, wind, drought or consistent moisture. Easily sheared into a hedge or pruned into a tree for domestic gardens. Performs well on slopes and provides food for birds. Plates 415, 416
R. californica California Coffeeberry	Dense rounded shrub, 8-12 ft. and higher, with pale olive-green leaves. Inconspicuous greenish flowers are followed by noticeable, red to black berries by late summer. Many natural variations occur which produce plants of different sizes, densities and leaf configurations. In addition, two selected forms are available which offer larger, denser and broader leaves. R. c. 'Eve Case' grows 4-8 ft. and is a very neat, compact shrub. R. c. 'Seaview' is a lower growing form, 18-30 in., that is well suited to banks and ground cover areas in coastal zones.	California Coffeeberry is a fairly common shrub to the chaparral foothills, of the coastal ranges and inland mountain foothills, from Oregon to Mexico to parts of Arizona. This species and its two selections are best suited to environments with coastal influence and some summer water for best appearances. However, they can be used in many inland and interior landscapes in partial shade. Very tolerant of soils, including clays and provide good wildlife value. Seeds can be collected from localized forms and planted fresh with 30% germination success. Plates 417, 418
R. crocea Redberry	Evergreen shrub, 3-10 ft. high, with stiffly branched character. Very small leaves, ¼-½ in., have finely toothed margins and are dark, shiny green above, pale below. Insignificant flowers in winter are followed by noticeable small red berries in late summer, which attract birds.	Redberry occurs on dry Chaparral slopes in the Coast Ranges from Sonoma to San Diego counties. It shows good tolerance for dry landscapes in both coastal and inland locations, but looks best with periodic deep moisture. Can be clipped into a hedge or used as a background plant. Good slope stabilization value. Can be planted from fresh seed with 60% germination possible. Plate 419
R. crocea ilicifolia Holly-leaf Redberry Holly-leaf Coffeeberry	A larger leaved variety of Redberry which ranges in height from 5-15 ft. Light to dark green leaves are wavy, have strongly toothed edges, grow ½-1½ in. long. Noticeable red berries ripen in late summer to fall.	This is a more popular and drought tolerant variety which is found throughout California in both the Coast Ranges and Sierra Nevadas. It is more upright and open in form, with lusher foliage appearance. Accepts heat, aridity, smog, wind and many soils. Used for slope stabilization, naturalizing, screen and background planting in coastal, inland and interior foothills. Planted from container, or seed with a germination rate of 70% possible. Plate 414

415 Rhamnus alaternus

416 Rhamnus alaternus

417, 418 Rhamnus californica (Above, below)

419 Rhamnus crocea

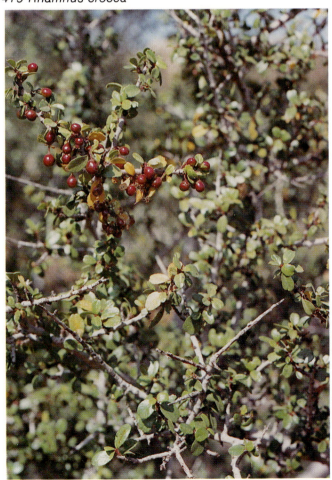

Rhus. Sumac
Subtropical regions, California

A large group of plants, including some 150 evergreen and deciduous species in temperate and sub-tropical regions of the world. Five species and several varieties are native to California, chiefly in warm, dry environments. One native, R. diversiloba (also Toxicadendron diversilobum), Poison Oak, is a notorious plant for causing skin irritation. It also happens to be one of the most widespread shrubs in the state. The other species of Rhus offer good landscape uses under drought conditions and are becoming more recognized for their value in slope stabilization, mass and naturalized plantings. Wherever possible, they develop a deep tap root to survive in dry environments. In addition to the native plants, at least one introduced species accepts drought and heat, particularly in interior and low desert environments. These plants prefer well draining soils and appreciate periodic, deep summer water. Usually installed from containers, but fair germination rates for native species results from planting treated seed.

420 Rhus integrifolia

Name	Character	Remarks
R. integrifolia Lemonade Berry	Evergreen shrub, 4-15 ft. high, spreading 6-15 ft. Thick, leathery leaves are rounded with lightly toothed edges and strong veins on the underside. Noticeable clusters of pink to white flowers occur Feb.-Mar., followed by flat berries ¼-½ in. long which taste like sour lemon.	A native to the coastal bluffs and plains from Santa Barbara to San Diego counties, with periodic occurrences in inland foothill and outwash locations. An excellent plant for slope stabilization and screening in coastal zones, through northern California. Tolerates sea air and persistent wind, which often shapes it into a broadly spreading form. Shows good performance under drought stress within areas of coastal influence, but can be planted in inland areas with periodic deep water. Can easily be shaped into hedges small trees or be espaliered. Germination from treated seed can reach 80%. Plate 420
R. lancea African Sumac	Small evergreen tree, eventually developing into a dome 25 ft. high. Glossy, medium green leaves are divided into 3 long leaflets and hang loosely from branches. Distinctive rough, red-brown bark. Both flowers and small berry-type fruit are inconspicuous. A refreshing foliage plant in hot areas that can be pruned to have one or more trunks.	An introduced species which likes both heat and sun. Very good for interior and desert locations where it accepts wind, aridity, and drought. Grows well in coastal areas, but with a more open habit. A good street or lawn tree and patio specimen which responds well to additional fertilizer and watering. Plates 421, 422
R. laurina (Malosma laurina) Laurel Sumac	Broadly spreading, to semi-upright evergreen shrub, 6-15 ft. high and as wide. Long curved leaves, 2-4 in., have rounded ends and occur on reddish stems. Foliage gives off aromatic odor on hot days and when crushed. Showy white flower plumes occur June-Aug. Small white fruit mature in early winter and are attractive to birds.	Native to the southern California coastal plains and protected inland foothills. It is one of the very few large evergreen shrubs which survives the high drought stress of the Coastal Sage plant community by developing a large root system. It is usually an indicator species of warm, frost-free areas, as it is tender to temperatures below 30° F. However, it is well adapted to both cold and fires, as it readily stump sprouts after it has been damaged. Best suited to coastal and inland foothill areas for slope stabilization and mass plantings. Usually planted from containers, it can be sown from seed soaked in hot water with a 30% germination rate. Plates 423, 424
R. ovata Sugar Bush	Dense evergreen shrub, 5-12 ft. high, with equal spread. Heavy leathery leaves, with distinctive mid-vein and pointed apex, are glossy dark green and occur on heavy branches. Showy clusters of flowers are white and pink tinged, occur Mar.-May.	Perhaps the most popular and versatile of the native Sumac species. Sugar Bush is a high heat and drought accepting plant. Found in warm coastal foothills from Santa Barbara to San Diego counties, to the inland mountains of southern California. More tolerant of cold and adaptable to northern coastal and inland areas on well draining sites. Can be grown in domestic gardens with summer moisture for background, screen and small tree elements. Well suited to slope and mass plantings along roadsides and in parks. Planted from container or treated seed with 30-40% germination rate possible. Plates 425, 426

421 Rhus lancea

422 Rhus lancea

423 Rhus laurina
425 Rhus ovata

424 Rhus laurina
426 Rhus ovata

Ribes. Currant, Gooseberry

California

This group of plants includes 120-150 species of evergreen and deciduous shrubs which are found in many parts of the world. Approximately 28 species and numerous varieties are found in California, with several showing good performance in dry and semi-shaded environments. Plants which are identified as currants do not have spines on their branches. Gooseberries will have sharp spines at distinct nodes, as well as sometimes have bristles over many of their branches.

Several native species are commonly used in dry landscapes where they provide rich flower and foliage character. They are often planted under oaks where they tolerate partial shade and require limited summer water. These plants have a natural rest and dormant period by late fall and should not be watered into lush growth during this time. With high drought stress, they will shed some of their leaves, but will quickly fill out after seasonal rains. Several species and some improved varieties provide various combinations of foliage, flower and form characteristics. Ribes prefer slightly acid soils, leaf mulch and good drainage conditions. They will tolerate clay conditions on sloping ground and show good resistance to smog. In coastal areas they accept full sun. When planted in inland and interior areas they prefer some protection from intense heat and like periodic water.

427 Ribes sanguineum

Name	Character	Remarks
R. aureum Golden Currant	Tall deciduous shrub, 3-8 ft. high, with light green foliage. Leaves are divided into 3-5 lobes; showy tubular flowers are yellow, occur Feb.-June. Plants produce red, orange or black berries which are eaten by wildlife.	Golden Currant inhabits many moist to dry environments throughout California. It offers refreshing light foliage and pleasing flower character in both domestic and natural landscapes. It prefers well draining soils, partial shade in hot locations and periodic moisture. A good background, naturalizing and seasonal accent plant. Plate 430
R. sanguineum Red Flowering Currant	Upright deciduous shrub, 5-10 ft. tall, with large, papery, maple-like leaves. Small flower clusters are pale to bright red and cover the plant in late winter. This species has many natural variations and includes one very popular variety, *R. s. glutinosum*, Pink Flowering Currant. Several other selections and hybrids have been produced which offer different shades of pink to red flowers.	Native to the Coast Ranges from Marin County north to British Columbia. It inhabits semi-moist slopes and canyons and is best adapted to northern coastal areas. However, it grows successfully in southern gardens when given some shade and periodic water. A good flowering accent and background plant. Plate 427 *R. s. glutinosum* is a widely used variety which has larger foliage and produces spectacular 3-6 in. long clusters of light pink flowers. It is naturally found along the coast from San Luis Obispo to Del Norte counties and has proven to be quite heat and drought tolerant. Plates 428, 429
R. speciosum Fuchsia-Flowering Gooseberry	A small deciduous shrub, 3-6 ft. high, with arching branches that are covered with many spines and bristles. Rich, glossy green leaves contrast well with deep red, fuchsia-type flowers from Jan.-April. Foliage is dropped under high drought stress in late summer. Can be evergreen if given supplemental water.	This species is native to semi-moist canyons and slopes of the coastal foothills from San Diego to Monterey counties. It is often an understory plant in the Chaparral and Oak Woodland plant communities. It has shown good adaptation to domestic garden conditions and will tolerate heavy soils if given good drainage. Used as a flowering accent, barrier and understory planting for oaks. Plate 433
R. viburnifolium Evergreen Currant Catalina Perfume Currant	An evergreen, clumping plant, to 3 ft. high, 4-5 ft. wide, with many long basal branches. Rich, dark green leathery leaves provide pleasant fragrance when wet or crushed. Insignificant maroon flowers occur Feb.-Apr. Plants will root along stems when in contact with moist soils.	Evergreen Currant is naturally found in moist canyons on Santa Catalina Island and in a few areas of Mexico. It has become a popular native plant for ground cover use under oak trees and in other areas of shade and dry soils. Sheds leaves under drought stress, but quickly recovers with supplemental water or seasonal rains. Takes full coastal exposures throughout the state and partial shade in many inland enviornments. Tolerates heavy and clay soils on well draining sites. Works on banks for erosion control. Plates 431, 432

428 *Ribes sanguineum glutinosum*

429 *Ribes sanguineum glutinosum*

430 *Ribes aureum*

431, 432 *Ribes viburnifolium* (Above, below)

433 *Ribes speciosum*

Robinia pseudoacacia.
Black Locust

Central and Eastern U.S.A.

Fast growing deciduous tree, 40-70 ft. high, 30-40 ft. wide, with open and sometimes irregular branching habit. This species has furrowed grey-brown bark on the trunk and thorns on smaller branchlets. Long leaves are divided into 7-19 rounded leaflets, emerge light green and turn deep blue-green. Showy, white pea-shaped flowers form grape-like clusters, are quite fragrant, occur May-June.

A very aggressive tree which tolerates the most adverse plant environments including heat, cold, aridity, drought, smog and poor soils. It has naturalized in the northern Sierra Nevadas as well as in wet and dry stream beds throughout much of California. Care should be taken when using this plant because of its readiness to escape. However, it performs well in extremely hot and dry landscapes, including interior desert regions. Sometimes used as a street tree, but often best suited to difficult areas in large parks and greenbelts. Many hybrids have been developed from this species which offer pink, rose to magenta flower colors and are more ornamentally attractive. Plates 434, 436, 437

434 Robinia ambigua 'Idahoensis'

Romneya coulteri. Matilija Poppy

Southern California, Mexico

Spreading perennial shrub, 4-8 ft. tall, with numerous long stems developing from the root base. Thin grey-green leaves are roughly divided. Bold white flowers with yellow centers, reach 6-8 in. across, occur June-July. Leaves and some stems die back in late summer under drought conditions.

A spectacular flowering accent plant for warm coastal and inland regions. Native to coastal washes and hillsides from Santa Barbara to San Diego counties and into Mexico. Plants spread from underground roots and can form dense colonies on slopes and in ravines. In some areas it can become too invasive, as well as be a high fire hazard. Tolerates any soil and moisture conditions, including drought. Wants full sun. Stems are often removed each year to encourage new growth and heavier flowering. Fairly difficult to propagate and establish, but a striking plant for dry gardens, slope stabilization and mass plantings. Grows well in northern coastal and inland environments. Plates 438, 439

Rosmarinus officinalis. Rosemary

Europe, Mediterranean Region

Evergreen, upright to spreading shrub, 3-6 ft. high, 3-8 ft. spread, with dense needle-like foliage. Leaves to 1 in. are dark green above, whitish below, are aromatic and often used for seasoning. Small, violet-blue flowers occur mainly Apr.-May, but intermittently all year in warm locations and provide a noticeable cast of color over the plant.

A widely adapted species for all plant environments, from the coast to low desert regions. Tolerates wind, aridity, smog, poor and dry soils. Prefers full sun and heat. Requires good drainage for best performance. In hot interior and desert areas periodic summer water is needed. Overwatering causes rank and haphazard plant development which can be controlled by tip pruning and removal of overgrown branches. Very attractive to bees.

Several varieties of Rosemary have been developed which provide richer flower color and different growth habits. R. o. 'Prostratus' is one of the most popular low growing forms, to 3 ft. high, which shows similar tolerances as the parent species. It is often used as a ground cover on any size bank or slope, cascades over walls. A fair plant for transitions into natural areas, but definitely needs regular moisture to make it moderately resistant to fires. All plants tend to build up a lot of dead wood, ground cover forms in particular, and should be heavily pruned or replaced every 5-8 years. Plates 435, 440, 441

435 Rosmarinus officinalis

436 Robinia pseudoacacia

437 Robinia pseudoacacia

438 Romneya coulteri

439 Romneya coulteri

440 Rosmarinus officinalis

441 Rosmarinus officinalis 'Prostratus'

Salvia . Sage
Temperate Regions, California

A large group of aromatic herbs and shrubs, including over 500 species, thoughout most warm regions of the world. At least 12 shrub species are native to California, occurring in the dry coastal foothills to interior desert environments. These plants usually have basal branching structures, aromatic foliage, and shallow fibrous root systems. Most species also produce rounded thistle-like flower clusters at distinctive nodes on plant stems, which persist for many months.

Several native species are in landscape use for slope stabilization and naturalizing disturbed areas. Easily established from seed in late fall, they need nothing but the seasonal rains to germinate and survive. Care must be taken not to soak seeds in water prior to planting as they will quickly decompose and should be hand sown. It is also known that these natives often shed some leaves under periods of high drought stress, and become quite flammable during the late summer and fall. They tend to be short-lived, 5-10 years, but new seedlings are always present to replace old plants. Some of the hybrid native varieties offer better aesthetic character and are used as accents in dry gardens. They will accept summer moisture and will develop lusher foliage, but at the expense of being even shorter-lived, as the summer is their dormant period for rest. They all do well in full sun, with heat and aridity, tolerate shallow soils, and perform best on well draining sites. Several species, such as Black Sage, are very valuable bee plants for the production of honey.

A number of introduced species from the Southwest and Mexico, provide good ornamental character, and are used in domestic gardens. These plants accept sun, heat, and drought, as well as clay type soils. They work well along borders, on banks, in rock gardens and mixed plantings.

442 Salvia mellifera munziw

Name	Character	Remarks
S. 'Allen Chickering'	Small perennial shrub, 2-5 ft. high, 2-4 ft. wide. Dull grey-green foliage contrasts nicely with rich blue flower clusters, which occur from spring to early summer.	A natural hybrid between S. clevelandii and S. leucophylla. It provides good ornamental flower character for use in dry garden areas, on banks and for naturalizing.
S. apiana White Sage	Upright shrub, 3-8 ft. high, 3-6 ft. wide, with distinctive grey foliage which is not aromatic. Noticeable light purple flowers occur on long stalks, Apr.-May.	Found on well draining soils, at lower elevations, from Santa Barbara to San Diego counties and inland to the Colorado Desert. A common member of the Coastal Sage plant community which provides best use in slope plantings in natural areas. Can be a specimen plant in dry gardens. Highly drought tolerant. Can be planted from seed with 60-70% germination success. Plate 443
S. clevelandii Cleveland Sage	Rounded shrub, 1-3 ft. high, with strongly veined, grey-green foliage. Showy blue-purple flower clusters are very fragrant, occur May-Aug.	A native to the coastal and inland foothills of San Diego County. More attractive than most other native species and well suited for dry garden effects. Other uses include slope and mixed plantings with other low water accepting plants.
S. columbariae Chia	This annual herb is known for its deep blue flower heads and seeds which are exceptionally rich in protein. It has medium green basal leaves, and produces long flower stalks in early spring.	A highly adaptable plant for dry inland, interior and desert environments. Seeds provide high wildlife and commercial food value. It is used as an accent plant in mixed wildflower gardens. Plate 444

443 Salvia apiana

444 Salvia columbariae

445 Salvia leucantha

446 Salvia leucantha

447 Salvia lemmonii

448 Salvia lemmonii

450 *Salvia leucophylla*

449 *Salvia leucophylla*
451 *Salvia sonomensis*

452 *Salvia sonomensis*
453 *Salvia spathacea*

Salvia. (Cont.)

Name	Character	Remarks
S. greggii Autumn Sage	Small evergreen shrub, growing into a 2-4 ft. mound. Medium green leaves, ½-1 in. long, grow on upright branches. Showy, crimson flowers occur on spikes from summer through fall. Very similar in appearance to S. lemmonii.	An introduced species from Texas and Mexico. This plant accepts both garden and natural conditions, including heavy and alkaline soils, sun and drought. Good for borders, banks and accent uses.
S. leucantha Mexican Bush Sage	A more domestic Sage species with dense, heavily veined, greyish-green foliage. Long purple flower spikes and white flowers occur early spring and fall. Planted from containers, it grows 2-3 ft. high and as wide. Plants tend to build up thatch which can be removed with heavy pruning.	This introduced species tolerates drought, as well as heavy soils, and performs well on exposed banks and in small masses within coastal and inland landscapes. Its lusher appearance makes it more attractive for garden uses and it will accept some summer water. Plates 445, 446
S. leucophylla Purple Sage	A species commonly found in the coastal foothills from San Luis Obispo to Orange counties. Develops into a loosely mounding shrub, 2-6 ft. high, and has narrow, wrinkled, grey-green leaves. Showy purple flower balls occur on long spikes at periodic intervals May-June.	This species is well suited to dry gardens and for slope stabilization within its natural range. Tolerates limited summer water on well draining sites, and has been successfully used in several inland locations. Planting can be achieved by seed with 45-55% germination. Plates 449, 450
S. lemmonii	Spreading shrub, 1-3 ft. high, 3-5 ft. wide. Small, dark green leaves are fragrant. Numerous rose-lavender flowers provide seasonal color in spring and fall.	An introduced plant from Arizona and Mexico. Provides good ornamental character, and tolerates sun and limited moisture. Used for borders, naturalizing, and on banks. Plates 447, 448
S. mellifera Black Sage	An upright plant, 2-5 ft. tall, with very aromatic dark green leaves. Noticeable pale blue flower clusters occur at distinct nodes on long branches Apr.-June. A lower growing form, S.M. 'Prostrata' is available from various native plant nurseries. This plant offers more compact foliage and performs well on banks, with mixed wildflowers and in transitions into natural areas.	One of the most widespread species of the Coastal Sage plant community throughout California. An important bee plant in this state, most frequently used for slope stabilization and recovering disturbed natural areas. Highly adaptable to all dry, exposed landscapes, and usually planted from seed with 30-40% germination success. Plate 442
S. officinalis Garden Sage	Small shrub, 12-24 in. high, with very aromatic foliage. Simple leaves are thick, wrinkled and grey-green. Clusters of 3-6 flowers are rich violet-blue, occur on tall spikes from May-July.	Garden Sage comes from the Mediterranean region of Europe, where it grows on dry banks and stony soils. It offers both landscape and culinary uses. As an herb, it is used in cheese and wine making and for tea. It is a good rock garden, naturalizing, border and bank plant in full sun. It grows in all plant environments, from the coast to inland foothills, and tolerates drought, heat and wind. Can be planted from containers or seed.
S. sonomensis Creeping Sage	A very prostrate plant, 6-12 in. high, spreading 2-3 ft. Dull green foliage tends to clump at ends of branches. Blue-purple flowers occur on leafless stems, May-July.	Creeping Sage is gaining importance as a drought tolerant and fire retardant plant in dry sage and chaparral landscapes. Its very low habit and spreading nature make it well suited for slope stabilization and transitions into natural areas. Fires are diminished by its minimum height and foliage mass. Grown from containers or seed which has been scarified with cold temperatures. Germination rates range up to 25%. Plates 451, 452
S. spathacea Hummingbird Sage	Perennial herb with basal foliage and coarse textured appearance. This species mounds 1-2 ft. high and produces showy clusters of deep red flowers on spikes, which extend above the leaves. Plants grow from seed or spread by underground rhizomes.	Native to many foothill areas from Solano to Orange counties. This plant accepts lots or little water, sun or shade, and heavy soils. Used on banks, for flowering accent and border areas. It is quite tolerant of garden conditions. Plate 453

Sambucus. Elderberry

California, North America

Deciduous shrubs or small trees, containing some 20 species and varieties. Several species are native to California. Two are quite widespread and adapted to warm, dry landscapes. These are large bushy plants which produce many branches, light to medium green foliage, and showy clusters of white to cream flowers.

S. caerulea (S. glauca), Blue Elderberry is very common throughout the Coast Ranges across to the Sierra Nevada foothills, and along the coast into British Columbia. It is a mounding plant, 10-18 ft. high, that can be shaped into a round dome tree. White flowers are followed by clusters of pale blue berries which are used in making wine, jellies, and pies.

S. mexicana is the species most commonly found throughout southern California. It is very similar in appearance to Blue Elderberry, but has paler green leaves. This species is widely adapted to dry landscapes, poor soils, and full sun.

Native elderberries are not as ornamental as many other plants, but they provide very good service in regional parks, on dry slopes, and for naturalizing. Plants can become deciduous by early fall when they experience high drought stress. They are very tenacious and grow in many harsh areas which makes them of value in coastal and foothill landscapes. Plates 456, 457

Santolina.

Europe, Mediterranean Region

Low growing herbs and shrubs, including some eight species, that offer good foliage and flower character. Most species in landscape use are commonly grown as ground cover and border plants, in full sun, and on well draining soils. In coastal areas these plants can survive on their own. When planted in warm inland locations, they need periodic summer water. Their low profile makes them suited to perimeter plantings in high fire hazard areas. Large quantities of round flower heads grow above the foliage, are showy, and should be trimmed off when dead.

Name	Character	Remarks
S. chamaecyparissus **Lavender Cotton**	Ground cover, 12-24 in. high, spreading 3-4 ft. Distinctive grey foliage contrasts well with bright yellow flower heads in spring.	A striking foliage plant that performs well on banks, along borders, and on medium sized slopes. Takes full sun, dry soils, prefers good drainage and periodic summer water in inland and desert environments. Covers soils in a mounding fashion. Older plants can die out in areas, which can be prevented by periodic pruning. Plates 454, 459
S. rosmarinifolius	Small mounding shrub, 12-24 in. high, and as wide. Long, thin leaves are pale green, fine textured. Showy yellow flower heads occur in spring.	A relatively unknown species from southern Europe which offers another choice for ground cover and border uses. Shows good tolerance of sun, heat, and limited moisture. Will develop into a neat mound. Plate 455
S. virens	Small spreading shrub, 12-24 in. high, 18-30 in. spread. Bright green foliage creates lush, fine textured quality. Pale yellow to lime flower heads are showy in spring.	A very rich shrub for ground cover, bank, and border uses. Needs a little more water than other species of Santolina, but accepts full sun, heat, and aridity. Adapted to high fire hazard areas when given summer water. Plates 454, 458

454 Santolina chamaecyparissus (Left) Santolina virens (Right)

455 Santolina rosmarinifolius

456 Sambucus mexicana

457 Sambucus mexicana

458 Santolina virens

459 Santolina chamaecyparissus

Schinus. Pepper Tree
South America

Evergreen and semi-deciduous trees, including some 15 species which come mainly from South America. Several species are in landscape use and provide quite different foliage and form characteristics. Both male and female plants produce flowers, with only the female plants producing fruit. The wood of many plants is brittle and subject to wind damage. Some species develop shallow, aggressive root systems and will produce large amounts of litter. However, these are quite versatile plants and are used in many situations. They can be treated as multi-stemmed shrubs or shaped into trees and can be used in both domestic and natural landscapes. They also serve well as specimen plants, along roadsides and on gentle banks. Pepper Trees grow under a wide range of conditions, including heat, sun and smog, from coastal zones to interior valleys and low desert regions throughout California. They develop good drought tolerance with age and some have even naturalized in canyon areas in southern coastal areas. They are easily planted from containers, with periodic deep watering recommended for best root development. Selective pruning of these plants can reduce problems with weak branches and create many desirable shapes.

460 Schinus molle

Name	Character	Remarks
S. molle California Pepper Tree	Large mounding shrub, to rounded tree, 20-40 ft. high, spreading 20-50 ft. Attractive light green leaves grow 6-12 in. long, are divided into as many as 60 leaflets and hang from the branches in weeping effect. Inconspicuous flowers occur mainly in summer followed by pale red berry-like fruit which persist into winter. Distinctive light brown, scaly bark covers gnarled trunks. Overall soft textured and light green foliage is appreciated in dry landscapes.	This species offers many mixed values and problems. It is very useable for roadside, background and specimen plantings in large areas. It is highly tolerant of difficult areas with poor soils and drainage, wind, dust, and limited water. However, it develops a voracious root system, generates large amounts of litter, and is a fire hazard. Plants should be treated like Oaks, with care being given to the foliage dripline area. Avoid summer water after the first 4-5 years, repair cut or broken limbs and periodically check for heart rot and root rot diseases which often come from excessive summer moisture and age. Best used in regional parks and countrysides where natural leaf litter can collect under the plant. Plates 460, 461, 462
S. polygamous Peruvian Pepper Tree	Evergreen dome tree, 15-25 ft. high, with dark green leaves and thorns at the ends of the stems. Trunks have rough, dark brown bark, insignificant flowers and dull purple fruit which occur in summer.	A once widely planted species which has been overshadowed by S. molle and S. terebinthifolius. It becomes quite dense and can be shaped into screens or rounded tree forms. A very tolerant plant in hot, dry and arid areas, and has naturalized on a limited basis in southern California. It accepts most soils, including clays and alkaline, or wet conditions. Well suited for barrier, background and slope plantings, or can be developed into yard and shade trees. Plates 463, 464
S. terebinthifolius Brazilian Pepper Tree	Evergreen shrub to small dome-shaped tree, 15-30 ft. tall and as wide. Dark green leathery leaves reach 6-8 in. long and are divided into 7 rounded leaflets. Trunks have coarse, grey-brown bark as they age. Noticeable clusters of white flowers occur in summer, followed by showy groups of red berries on female plants, which mature in late summer and remain into winter.	A very popular plant that is used in most areas of California, from coastal regions to interior valley and low desert zones. It does not develop the same problems with roots and produces less litter than S. molle. As a tree form, it is frequently used for lawn, street, courtyard and accent purposes. It is also a very effective shrub plant for roadsides, slopes and mass plantings in dry landscapes. It responds well to pruning and can become a clipped screen, as well as a multi-trunk specimen plant with the same tolerances as other Pepper Tree specimens. Plates 465, 466

461 Schinus molle

462 Schinus molle

464 Schinus polygamous

466 Schinus terebinthifolius

463 Schinus polygamous
465 Schinus terebinthifolius

173

467 Simmondsia chinensis

468 Simmondsia chinensis

469 Tamarix aphylla
470 Tamarix aphylla

471 Tecomaria capensis
472 Tecomaria capensis

174

Simmondsia chinensis. Jojoba, Goat Nut

Southwest U.S.A., Mexico, Baja California

A widely distributed plant throughout the desert regions of the Southwest. Jojoba develops into a large mounding shrub with dense foliage character. Plants grow 6-8 ft. high, spread 8-14 ft., and are covered with thick, pale green leaves. Inconspicuous flowers are followed by nuts on female plants, to 1 in. dia. Nuts are edible and highly valued for their oil content which has many commercial uses.

Jojoba is well adapted to inland foothill and desert regions, where it normally grows in frost free areas. Efforts are being made to grow this plant commercially for the oil in its fruit. Landscape uses include screen, slope and background plantings. It prefers full sun, good drainage, and survives without summer water if not being grown for fruit production. Plates 467, 468

Tamarisk aphylla. Tamarisk, Athel Tree

North Africa, Middle East

A large shrub to tree, 25-50 ft. tall, characterized by rough brown bark and fine textured branching. Long, jointed branchlets appear like leaves, have grey to blue-green cast. Small leaves appear as scales at the joints of branchlets when plants have ample moisture.

Tamarisk is a popular valley and desert tree that has been frequently used for windbreaks, sand stabilization, and large specimen elements. It shows a higher tolerance of alkaline soils beyond other plants, thrives in full sun and heat. Depends upon a deep and invasive root system to find moisture. A good choice for difficult soils, and in large spaces where its abundant litter drop can be absorbed. Periodically used in domestic and park landscapes, but needs shaping and maintenance for good appearance. Plates 469, 470

Tecomaria capensis. Cape Honeysuckle

(Tecoma capensis)

South Africa

Evergreen shrub, with a spreading and vining habit, 8-12 ft. high, 10-15 ft. wide. Rich, glossy green leaves are divided into small wrinkled leaflets. Clusters of long tubular flowers occur late fall through winter, are bright orange to red. *T. c.* 'Aurea' is a variety offering lighter foliage and yellow-orange flowers.

A fast growing plant for coastal to desert regions where it tolerates sun, wind, heat, and salt air. Needs protection from heavy frost in cooler areas. Best planted in deep soils with good drainage, where it becomes moderately drought tolerant with age. This is a lush foliage and flowering accent plant which is often planted along highways, on large slopes, and in many garden areas. It can be trained onto a wall or trellis where it grows 15-18 ft. high. Needs plenty of room, but can be sheared to control size and form hedges. Plates 471, 472, 473

473 Tecomaria capensis 'Aurea'

474 *Thevetia peruviana*

475 *Thevetia peruviana*

477, 478 *Trifolium fragiferum* O'Connor's (Above, below)

476 *Trichostema lanatum*

Thevetia peruviana.
Yellow Oleander

(T. neriifolia) South Africa

Large shrub, 6-10 ft., or small dome tree, 10-18 ft., with bright, glossy green foliage. Leaves are narrow, 3-6 in. long, create billowy texture; showy and fragrant yellow flowers bloom all summer. Large fruits mature in fall and can be a litter problem. Leaves and fruit are very poisonous.

Yellow Oleander is adapted to frost free, warm environments. It grows in desert and valley regions where it thrives in heat, as well as coastal and inland areas in sunny locations. Prefers deep, well draining soils. Young plants need ample water and tend to be shallow rooted. A schedule of deep watering will enable mature plants to achieve moderate drought resistance. Useful for hedges, accent plantings, and small trees. Valued in warm areas for its bright foliage color and showy flowers. Plates 474, 475

Trichostema lanatum.
Woolly Blue Curls

California Coastal Chaparral

A small, evergreen shrub, with an open branching habit. Distinctive blue-purple flowers on long stalks occur from spring into summer, have noticeable stamen and woolly character. Leaves are narrow, 1-2 in. long, dark green on top, covered with white hairs below.

Native to dry slopes and low elevations in the coastal foothills from San Diego to Monterey counties. This is a striking accent plant when in bloom. Often used along borders, in mixed wildflower plantings, and for naturalizing. It needs good drainage, full sun to part shade, and no summer water. It has proven to be difficult to start from seed, however, some seedlings do appear around established plants on their own. Plate 476

Trifolium fragiferum var. O'Connor's.
O'Connor's Legume

Australia

A low growing perennial ground cover, 6-15 in. high, which spreads by numerous horizontal stems. Deep green foliage is clover shaped. Many round, white to pink flower heads, occur from spring through summer.

O' Connor's Legume is becoming a popular slope cover and erosion control plant thoughout coastal and inland areas of southern California. It shows good tolerance of sun, heat, and limited moisture. Accepts heavy or light soils, alkaline or saline conditions, and poor drainage. It is most frequently established by seed, and provides permanent soil coverage by developing roots up to 6 ft. deep. The best performance of this plant is achieved by stressing it with limited water, too much irrigation creates taller growth, to 12-15 in., and invites pests such as snails and nematodes. Periodic mowing revitalizes overgrown areas and maintains a lower growth habit. In Australia, it is often used as a lawn substitute, which suggests the same opportunities for California gardens. It will tolerate frequent mowing, ½-1 in. high, and accept moderate levels of foot traffic. Plates 477, 478

Tristania conferta.
Brisbane Box

Australia

Medium, to large evergreen tree, 40-70 ft. high, that develops into an upright dome. Trunk and branches are covered with attractive red-brown bark that peels each year. Large, glossy leaves, 3-6 in. long, are bright green above, pale green below. White flowers and woody seed capsules are inconspicuous.

Brisbane Box is appreciated for its foliage, form, and bark character. It is similar in appearance to eucalyptus, and often used in place of them. Prefers a rich, loose soil, and ample water when young. Mature trees can achieve moderate drought tolerance when planted in mild coastal environments. Will accept inland conditions, including heat, wind and smog. Often used for street, lawn and park trees, as well as in small domestic garden spaces. Plate 479

479 Tristania conferta

Viguiera. Sunflower

Southwest U.S.A., Mexico

A large group of evergreen herbs and shrubs, including some 150 species, five of which are native to dry landscapes in California. These plants are distinguished by their bright yellow, daisy-like flowers, which grow on long stems above the foliage. Most species show good tolerance of heat, sun, and drought. They are most often planted from seed to stabilize slopes and revegetate disturbed areas.

V. deltoidea var. *parishii*, Desert Sunflower, is a broad, mounding plant, 2-3 ft. high, 5-7 ft. across. It grows throughout the Mojave and Colorado deserts into areas of San Diego County. Yellow flowers contrast nicely with blue-green foliage.

V. laciniata, San Diego Sunflower, is a low growing shrub 18-24 in. high, spreading 4-6 ft. This is a commonly used species which provides bright flower accent character and erosion control uses. Plate 483

V. dentata, is a species from Mexico. It develops into a medium-sized shrub, 3-5 ft. high, 6-8 ft. across. It shows good performance on dry slopes, in full sun, and accepts heat, aridity, and wind. Showy yellow flowers accent the plant from early spring through summer. Plate 482

Xylosma congestum.

(Xylosma senticosum)

China

A large mounding shrub, 8-15 ft. high, or small dome tree, 15-25 ft. tall, with bright green foliage. Leaves are glossy, 2-3 in. long, and have toothed edges. Flowers and fruit are inconspicuous. Another variety, *X. c.* 'Compacta', grows 4-8 ft., and often has spines on its branches.

Xylosma is one of the most popular foliage plants for general landscape use. With its light green color, and ease of growth, it is used for screens, on slopes, in background areas and for roadside plantings. Can be planted in tubs, trained as an espalier, and with age, be shaped into a small tree. It tolerates a wide range of soil conditions, accepts sun, part shade, heat, wind and smog. Normally, it has evergreen foliage, but young plants will drop leaves with heavy frost. Prefers regular moisture and seasonal feeding, becomes drought tolerant with age. Plates 484, 485

Zauschneria.

California Fuchsia

A group of short-lived perennial ground covers or shrubs, including four species that are native to California. These plants are known for their bright red, tubular flowers, and grey-green foliage character. They are planted by seed and used for slope, naturalizing, and mixed wildflower plantings. Their late summer flowering period provides good color accent and value for birds.

Z. californica, California Fuchsia, is a low spreading plant, 1-2 ft. high, 3-5 ft. across. A widely planted species, useful for borders, on banks, and in dry garden areas. Several hybrids of this plant have been produced, which offer white flowers and lower growth. Plates 486, 487

Z. cana, is a small mounding plant, 1-2 ft. high. It provides attractive flower and foliage character for rock gardens and transitions into natural areas. Plates 480, 481

480, 481 Zauschneria cana (below, right)

482 Viguiera dentata

483 Viguiera laciniata

484 Xylosma congestum

485 Xylosma congestum

486 Zauschneria californica

487 Zauschneria californica

Zelkova serrata . Sawleaf Zelkova
Japan

Deciduous tree, 40-60 ft. high, which develops a broad canopy shape. Large, papery leaves, 2-4 in. long, have coarsely toothed edges, and are similar to American Elm. Foliage is attractive in fall when it turns deep red before dropping.
Sawleaf Zelkova shows wide tolerance of climate and soils in plant environments throughout California. It accepts alkalai conditions, wind, heat, and cold. Mature plants survive with little water. Young plants should be irrigated on a deep, infrequent basis. A good form and foliage plant for lawns, parks, street tree and specimen uses. Plate 488

Zizyphus jujuba . Chinese Jujube
China

Medium-sized deciduous tree, 20-30 ft. high, 15-20 ft. wide. Bright green leaves, 2-3 in., with a distinctive midvein, hang from branches, turn showy yellow in fall. Datelike fruit, to 2 in., are green when young, mature red. Fruit is edible fresh or can be dried. Selected varieties are available for improved fruit character.
A rich foliage plant that develops a weeping habit. Grows in many plant environments, from the coast to deserts. It accepts heat, sun, aridity, saline and alkaline soils. Best drought tolerance is achieved when planted in deep soils, along with periodic watering when young. This is a handsome and durable plant that is used for park, open space, and specimen plantings. Plates 489, 490

488 Zelkova serrata

489 Zizyphus jujuba

490 Zizyphus jujuba

INDEX

A
Acacia 35
Achillea 42
Adenostoma sparsifolium 42
Aesculus californica 42
African Daisy 139
Agonis flexuosa 42
Ailanthus altissima 42
Albizia julibrissin 44
Alkaline soils 32
Arbutus menziesii 44
Arbutus unedo 44
Arctostaphylos 46
Artemisia 54
Athel Tree 157
Atriplex 56
Australian Tea Tree 124
Australian Willow 110

B
Baccharis 58
Beard Tongue 140
Beefwood 66
Bird of Paradise Bush 62
Black Locust 164
Black Walnut 118
Bladder Pod 116
Bottlebrush 64
Bougainvillea 60
Brachychiton 60
Buckwheat 98
Buckthorn 158
Bush Morning Glory 85
Bush Poppy 92

C
Caesalpinia gilliesii 62
California Buckeye 42
California Poppy 100
California Tree Mallow 122
Calliandra 62
Callistemon 64
Cape Honeysuckle 175
Cape Plumbago 149
Carob Tree 78
Cassia 66
Casuarina 66
Catalina Ironwood 130
Ceanothus 68
Cedar 78
Cedrus 78
Centaurea cineraria 78
Ceratonia siliqua 78
Cercidium 78
Cercis occidentalis 80
Cercocarpus betuloides 80
Chamelaucium ciliatum 80
Chinese Jujube 180
Cistus 82
Coffeeberry 158
Comarostaphylis diversifolia 85
Convolvulus cneorum 85
Coprosma kirkii 85
Cotoneaster 86
Coyote Brush 58
Crape Myrtle 120

Cupressocyparis leylandii 86
Cupressus 88
Currant 162
Cypress 88
Cypress, Leyland 86
Cytisus 90

D
Dalea spinosa 92
Deerweed 126
Dendromecon 92
Dodonaea viscosa 94
Drought deciduous plants 29
Dusty Miller 78

E
Echium fastuosum 94
Elaeagnus 94
Elderberry 170
Encelia 96
Eriobotrya japonica 96
Eriogonum 98
Eriophyllum confertiflorum 100
Escallonia 100
Eschscholzia californica 100
Eucalyptus 102
Evergreen plants 28

F
Feijoa sellowiana 108
Fine textured soils 33
Firethorn 152
Flannel Brush 108
Fountain Grass 140
Fremontodendron 108

G
Garrya 110
Gazania 110
Geijera parviflora 110
Geraldton Waxflower 80
Genista 90
Goat Nut 175
Golden Yarrow 100
Goldenrain Tree 118
Gooseberry 162
Grecian Laurel 122
Grevillea 112
Guava 152

H
Hakea 115
Helianthemum 115
Heteromeles arbutifolia 116
Hopseed Bush 94
Hypericum 116

I
Invasive plants 31
Isomeris arborea 116
Italian Jasmine 118

J
Jasminum humile 118
Jerusalem Thorn 140
Jojoba 175
Juglans californica 118

INDEX

Juniper 118
Juniperus 118

K
Koelreuteria paniculata 118

L
Lagerstroemia indica 120
Landscaping with California Natives 16
Lantana 120
Laurus nobilis 122
Lavandula 122
Lavatera assurgentiflora 122
Lavender 122
Lavender, Sea 126
Leptodactylon californicum 122
Leptospermum laevigatum 124
Leptospermum scoparium 124
Leucophyllum frutescens 124
Leyland Cypress 86
Limonium perezii 126
Lippia 126
Lippia repens 126
Lithocarpus densiflorus 126
Lobularia maritima 126
Lupine 128
Lupinus 128
Lyonothamnus floribundus 130

M
Madrone 44
Mahogany, Mountain 80
Mahonia 130
Manzanita 46
Matilija Poppy 164
Melaleuca 134
Metrosideros excelsus 136
Metrosideros tomemtosus 136
Mexican Palo Verde 140
Mimulus 136
Moisture seeking plants 30
Monkey Flower 136
Mountain Mahogany 80
Myoporum 136

N
Nerium oleander 139
New Zealand Christmas Tree 136
New Zealand Tea Tree 124

O
Oak 154
Oak root fungus 31
Olea europaea 139
Oleander 139
Olive 139
Osteospermum 139

P
Palo Verde 78
Palo Verde, Mexican 140
Parkinsonia aculeata 140
Pennisetum ruppelli 140
Pennisetum setaceum 140
Penstemon 140
Pepper Tree 172
Photinia 142
Plant selection guide 8

Plant lists 27
Planting guidelines 16
Planting from containers 17
Planting from seed 19
Planting on slopes 22
Planting for fire safety 24
Pine 142
Pineapple Guava 108
Pinus 142
Pistache 145
Pistacia 145
Pittosporum 146
Plumbago auriculata 149
Plumbago capensis 149
Poinciana gilliessi 62
Prickly Phlox 122
Pride of Madeira 94
Prunus 150
Psidium 152
Punica granatum 152

Q
Quercus 154

R
Red Shanks 42
Redbud, Western 80
Regional Plant Environments 2
Rhamnus 158
Rhus 160
Ribes 162
Robinia pseudoacacia 164
Rockrose 82
Romneya coulteri 164
Rosmarinus officinalis 164
Rosemary 164

S
Sagebrush 54
Saline soils 32
Saltbush 56
Salt spray 33
Salvia 166
Sambucus 170
Santolina 170
Sawleaf Zelkova 180
Sea Lavender 126
Schinus 172
Senna 66
She-Oak 66
Silk Tree 44
Silktassel 110
Simmondsia chinensis 175
Smoke Tree 92
Southern California Black Walnut 118
Spartium 90
St. Johnswort 116
Strawberry Tree 44
Sumac 160
Summer Holly 85
Sunrose 115
Sweet Alyssum 126
Sweet Bay 122

T
Tamarix aphylla 175
Tanbark Oak 126

INDEX

Tecomaria capensis 175
Texas Ranger 124
Thevetia peruviana 177
Toyon 116
Tree-of-Heaven 42
Trichostema lanatum 177
Trifolium fragiferum var. O'Connor's 177
Tristania conferta 177

U
Ulex 90

V
Viguiera 178

W
Walnut, Black 118
Western Redbud 80
Wild Lilac 68

X
Xylosma congestum 178

Y
Yarrow 42
Yarrow, Golden 100

Z
Zauschneria 178
Zelkova serrata 180
Zizyphus jujuba 180